Oracle SQL Foundations

A Hands-On Guide to SQL Queries, Aggregations, and Data Management

By

Chandraish Sinha

BooksDistrict
www.booksdistrict.com

Legal Notes

First Edition
ISBN: 978-0-9992449-8-2

Dedication

To all aspiring data professionals

beginning their journey with Oracle SQL

About the Author

Chandraish Sinha is the Founder and President of **Ohio Computer Academy**, an organization dedicated to practical, real-world IT education.

A lifelong advocate for technology training, he leads with the guiding principle: *Inspire, Educate, and Evolve*. With over 25 years of experience in the IT industry, Chandraish specializes in developing practical learning resources and scalable solutions that empower individuals and organizations to make data-driven decisions with confidence.

His expertise spans a wide range of data management, database, business intelligence, and visualization platforms, including Oracle Database, Oracle SQL, Tableau, Power BI, QlikView, Qlik Sense, IBM Cognos, SAP BusinessObjects, and Actuate BIRT. Driven by a passion for data and problem-solving, he continually explores technologies that enable deeper insight and smarter decision-making.

Chandraish is the author of multiple books on dashboarding, data analytics, business intelligence, and technology education tools.

Amazon Author Page:

https://amazon.com/author/chandraishsinha

He also shares practical insights and tutorials through his blogs:

- Ohio Computer Academy Blog (https://ohiocomputeracademy.com/blogs/)
- Learn Tableau Public (https://www.learntableaupublic.com/)
- Learn All BI (https://www.learnallbi.com/)

Connect with him on LinkedIn:

linkedin.com/in/chandraishsinha

Other Books by the Author

1. *IT Career Guide for Beginners*
2. *Tableau for Job Seekers*
3. *Excel Basics to Advanced*
4. *Dashboarding with Tableau*
5. *Mastering Power BI (Second Edition)*
6. *Mastering Power BI (First Edition)*
7. *Tableau Unlimited*
8. *Implementing Tableau Server*
9. *QlikView Essentials*
10. *QlikView Questions and Answers: Guide to QlikView and FAQs*
11. *Tableau 10 for Beginners*
12. *Tableau Dashboards: Step-by-Step Guide to Developing Visualizations in Tableau 9.2*
13. *Tableau Questions and Answers: Guide to Tableau Concepts and FAQs*
14. *How to Be a Successful IT Professional in the USA: A Checklist and Easy Guide to Success*

Acknowledgments

With gratitude to all readers whose continued support and thoughtful feedback inspire the ongoing effort to teach, write, and share knowledge with clarity and purpose.

Special appreciation goes to the students and learners at Ohio Computer Academy, whose curiosity, dedication, and insightful questions have helped shape the practical direction of this book. Each classroom session and discussion added depth, refinement, and real-world perspective to the examples and exercises presented here.

Sincere thanks to the Ohio Computer Academy team for their steadfast support and shared belief in our mission to Inspire, Educate, and Evolve. Their collaboration and commitment make every new learning initiative possible.

Preface

Technology continues to evolve at a remarkable pace, yet at the center of every modern system lies one constant—data. No matter the role in IT—whether building applications, designing dashboards, managing cloud infrastructure, or automating workflows—the ability to understand and work with data remains fundamental.

Throughout years of teaching and working with students and professionals, one pattern has consistently emerged: those who build a strong foundation in databases and SQL progress faster and with greater confidence in their careers. Oracle SQL, in particular, provides a structured and powerful way to interact with data. It is more than just a query language—it represents the core principles behind how enterprise systems store, retrieve, and manage information at scale.

Across specializations such as Business Intelligence, Data Science, Software Development, Cloud Computing, and Automation, SQL plays a central role. Tools like Tableau, Microsoft Power BI, Python-based data platforms, and cloud services such as Amazon Web Services (AWS) rely heavily on SQL concepts for data access and transformation. A strong understanding of SQL makes it significantly easier to learn and work with these technologies.

Oracle SQL Foundations provides a practical starting point for learners entering the world of data. The journey begins with essential concepts—understanding databases, data types, and query structures—and gradually progresses into more advanced topics such as aggregations, subqueries, performance considerations, and data management techniques.

The structure of this book reflects the teaching philosophy practiced in the classroom. Each concept is clearly explained, followed by guided, step-by-step exercises designed for real Oracle environments. Practice questions and solutions at the end of each chapter provide additional reinforcement and encourage active learning.

This book is intended for:

- Students beginning their journey in Information Technology
- Professionals transitioning into data or analytics roles
- Trainers seeking a structured and practical teaching resource
- Anyone who wants a solid foundation before advancing to more specialized data or cloud technologies

All examples and exercises are based on the **BDS Training Dataset**, designed to simulate realistic business scenarios and provide consistent hands-on experience.

The goal is not simply to teach syntax, but to build true understanding. By the end of this book, readers should be able to query, manage, and analyze data with clarity—while understanding the reasoning behind each statement they write.

It is sincerely hoped that this book becomes more than a technical manual. May it serve as a gateway to understanding the language of data and as a foundation for continued growth in the field of technology.

Book Structure

The book is organized into 11 chapters, each building progressively on the concepts introduced earlier. Together, they guide learners from foundational principles to practical, real-world application.

Chapter 1: Getting Started with Oracle SQL

This chapter introduces the fundamentals of relational databases and the role of SQL in managing data. It covers key features of Oracle SQL, provides an overview of the Oracle database architecture, and presents the training dataset used throughout the book for hands-on learning.

Chapter 2: Setting Up the Environment

This chapter explains how to access Oracle using Oracle FreeSQL (online environment) and Oracle Database Express Edition (XE) with SQL Developer for local practice. It demonstrates how to create connections, open worksheets, and execute SQL scripts to establish a fully functional workspace.

Chapter 3: Writing SELECT Queries

This chapter builds a strong foundation in query writing. It covers the structure of the SELECT statement, filtering data with WHERE, sorting results using ORDER BY, and removing duplicates with DISTINCT.

Chapter 4: Working with Conditions and Operators

This chapter focuses on controlling query logic using comparison, logical, and range operators. It demonstrates combining multiple conditions, handling NULL values, and applying pattern matching with LIKE and IN for flexible data retrieval.

Chapter 5: Functions and Expressions

In this chapter, you will explore Oracle's built-in text, numeric, and date functions for calculations and data manipulation. It introduces expressions, conditional logic using CASE and NVL, and techniques for customizing query output.

Chapter 6: Data Aggregation and GROUP BY

This chapter presents methods for summarizing and analyzing data using aggregate functions such as SUM, AVG, COUNT, MIN, and MAX. IT covers grouping data with GROUP BY and filtering aggregated results using HAVING, supported by practical business examples.

Chapter 7: Combining Data with Joins

This chapter demonstrates how related data across multiple tables can be connected using joins. It covers INNER JOIN, OUTER JOIN, LEFT JOIN, RIGHT JOIN, CROSS JOIN, and SELF JOIN operations, showing how to retrieve meaningful combined results that reflect real-world relationships.

Chapter 8: Working with Subqueries

This chapter examines subqueries—queries nested within other queries—for retrieving dependent results. It includes single-row and multiple-row subqueries, correlated subqueries, and their use within WHERE, FROM, and SELECT clauses.

Chapter 9: Mastering Set Operators

This chapter explains how to combine query results using UNION, UNION ALL, INTERSECT, and MINUS. It demonstrates managing duplicates, aligning column structures, and applying set operators for efficient data comparison.

Chapter 10: Views and Materialized Views

Through this chapter, you will learn how views simplify complex queries and how materialized views enhance performance by storing precomputed results. It includes examples demonstrating their creation and practical use.

Chapter 11: Creating and Managing Tables

This chapter covers creating and modifying tables, defining constraints, and performing data manipulation operations such as INSERT, UPDATE, and DELETE. It also introduces table maintenance tasks including truncating, renaming, and altering table structures.

How to Use This Book

This book is designed to help readers learn Oracle SQL through a structured, hands-on approach. Each chapter begins with a clear explanation of key concepts, followed by practical examples and step-by-step exercises.

The examples are based on the BDS Training Dataset, which represents a simplified business environment with tables such as *Orders*, *Customers*, *Category*, *Products*, *SalesPersons*, and *Branches*. Practicing alongside the examples using the provided SQL scripts and datasets will reinforce both understanding and confidence.

At the end of each chapter, practice questions and answers are included to strengthen learning and provide opportunities for review. These exercises can support classroom instruction, self-study, or preparation for certification exams.

For the best learning experience, it is recommended to:

- Complete the chapters in sequence, as each topic builds upon the previous one.
- Experiment with queries beyond the provided examples to deepen understanding.
- Practice using both Oracle FreeSQL (online environment) and Oracle Database XE with Oracle SQL Developer (local environment).

Following this approach will help build not only conceptual clarity but also practical SQL proficiency.

After reviewing this section, proceed to "**Downloading the Code**" to set up the datasets and scripts required for the exercises.

Downloading the Code

All datasets and SQL scripts used in this book are available for download from the BooksDistrict website. These resources allow readers to replicate every example and exercise demonstrated throughout the chapters.

Download Location:

https://booksdistrict.com/resources/oracle-sql-foundations/

Included Files:

- `BDS_Training_Data.xlsx`: Contains the training dataset in Excel format, including `Orders`, `OrderDetails`, `Customers`, `Products`, `SalesPersons`, and `Branches` tables.
- `BDS_Training_Data_Create_Insert_Scripts.sql`: Contains the SQL statements used to create the tables and insert the training data.
- `Chapter11_Create_Alter_Table_Statements.txt`: Includes table creation scripts along with the ALTER TABLE statements demonstrated in *Chapter 11, Creating and Managing Tables*, for modifying existing table structures.

Instructions:

1. Download the data folder to a convenient location on your computer.
2. Extract the **`Data.zip`** file to access the dataset and SQL script files.
3. Detailed instructions for running the scripts are provided in *Chapter 2, Setting Up the Environment.*

All files are provided for educational purposes only and are intended for non-commercial use as part of the *Oracle SQL Foundations* learning materials published by BooksDistrict.

Errata

Every effort has been made to ensure the accuracy of the content and code examples in this book. However, occasional errors may occur during the editing, formatting, or printing.

Readers are encouraged to report any issues, typographical errors, or inaccuracies found in the book or its accompanying scripts.

To report an error or provide feedback:

Email: hello@booksdistrict.com

Subject line: Errata - *Oracle SQL Foundations*

Constructive feedback is sincerely appreciated. All messages are personally reviewed, and corrections will be addressed in future updates where necessary.

Table Of Contents

1. **Getting Started with Oracle SQL** 1
   - Introduction 1
   - Fundamentals of Relational Databases 1
     - Key Characteristics 2
     - Advantages of the Relational Model 4
   - Introduction to SQL 4
     - Case Sensitivity and Syntax Notes 6
   - Key Features of Oracle SQL 6
     - Common SQL Objects 7
   - Oracle Database Architecture 8
   - Introduction to the Training Dataset 10
     - Benefits of Using This Dataset 11
   - Conclusion 11
   - Practice Questions 12
   - Practice Answers 12
2. **Setting Up the Environment 15**
   - Introduction 15
   - Overview of Oracle SQL Environments 16
     - Oracle FreeSQL versus Oracle Database XE 16
   - Using Oracle FreeSQL 18
     - Key Features of Oracle FreeSQL 18
     - Working with Oracle FreeSQL 19
     - Setting Up the Dataset for the Book 20

Running Scripts in Oracle FreeSQL *20*
Verifying the Dataset in Oracle FreeSQL *23*
Installing Oracle Database XE 24
Prerequisites for Installation 24
Installing Oracle Database XE 24
Verifying and Connecting to Oracle XE 29
Setting Up SQL Developer 32
Downloading and Installing SQL Developer 32
Creating a New Connection in SQL Developer 33
Running SQL Scripts 34
Conclusion 37
Practice Questions 37
Practice Answers 38
3. **Writing SELECT Queries 39**
Introduction 39
Understanding Oracle Data Types 40
Quoting and Formatting Rules 40
The DESC Command 41
The SELECT Statement 43
Selecting specific columns 45
Using an Alias 46
The WHERE Clause 48
The ORDER BY Clause 51
The Distinct Clause 53
Conclusion 54
Practice Questions 54

Practice Answers....55
4. **Working with Conditions and Operators....57**
Introduction....57
Using Comparison Operators....58
Using Logical Operators....63
AND Operator....64
OR Operator....65
NOT Operator....66
Perform Pattern Matching....67
Handling NULL Values....70
Filtering Data Using Lists and Ranges....73
IN Operator....73
NOT IN Operator....74
BETWEEN Operator....75
Conclusion....76
Practice Questions....77
Practice Answers....77
5. **Functions and Expressions....79**
Introduction....79
Functions in SQL....79
Purpose of Functions....80
Types of SQL Functions....80
Syntax of Functions....81
Applying Text Functions....81
UPPER() and LOWER() Functions....83
LENGTH() Function....84

SUBSTR() Function 85

INITCAP() Function 86

TRIM() Function 87

LPAD() and RPAD() Functions 88

REPLACE() Function 89

INSTR() Function 91

CONCAT() Function and || Operator 92

Applying Number Functions 93

ABS() and SIGN() Functions 94

CEIL() and FLOOR() Functions 95

ROUND(), TRUNC(), and MOD() Functions 97

POWER(), SQRT(), EXP(), and LN() Functions 99

LOG() Function 101

Working with Dates in Oracle 102

SYSDATE, CURRENT_DATE, and SYSTIMESTAMP Functions....104

LAST_DAY, ADD_MONTHS, and NEXT_DAY Functions 105

ROUND and TRUNC Functions on Dates 107

TO_DATE Function 109

TO_CHAR Function 110

Using EXTRACT and TO_CHAR in Date Analysis 112

Writing Conditional Expressions 114

NVL Function 115

NVL2 Function 116

CASE Expression 118

DECODE Function 120

Conclusion 122

Practice Questions 122
Practice Answers 123
6. **Data Aggregation and GROUP BY 127**
Introduction 127
Introduction to Aggregation 128
Common Aggregation Functions 128
SUM() Function 129
AVG() Function 130
COUNT() Function 131
MIN() and MAX() Functions 132
Using the GROUP BY Clause 133
Filtering Groups with Having 139
Rules for Using Aliases in Clauses 139
Finding Duplicates in a Table 142
Conclusion 145
Practice Questions 145
Practice Answers 146
7. **Combining Data with Joins 147**
Introduction 147
Understanding Joins 148
Need for Joins in SQL 148
Role of Keys in Joins 148
Identifying Join Columns 150
Types of Joins in Oracle SQL 150
INNER JOIN 151
Table Aliases 153

Choosing the First Table in a Multi-Join Query....157
OUTER JOIN....158
LEFT OUTER JOIN....159
RIGHT OUTER JOIN....161
FULL OUTER JOIN....163
CROSS JOIN....166
SELF JOIN....169
Best Practices for Using Joins....171
Conclusion....173
Practice Questions....174
Practice Answers....175
8. **Working with Subqueries....177**
Introduction....177
Understanding Subqueries....178
Introduction to Subqueries....178
Writing Effective Subqueries....179
Advantages of Using Subqueries....179
Single-Row Subqueries....179
Working with Single-Row Subqueries....180
Subqueries in the HAVING Clause....183
Multiple-Row Subqueries....185
Working with Multiple-Row Subqueries....185
Writing Effective Multiple-Row Subqueries....186
Multiple-Column Subqueries....189
Working with Multiple-Column Subqueries....189
When to Use Multiple-Column Subqueries....190

Writing Multiple-Column Subqueries 190

Correlated Subqueries 194

Working of a Correlated Subquery 194

Writing Correlated Subqueries 195

Existence Checks Using EXISTS 197

Best Practices for Using Subqueries 202

Subqueries at a Glance 205

Conclusion 206

Practice Questions 207

Practice Answers 207

9. Mastering Set Operators 209

Introduction 209

Understanding Set Operators 210

Types of Set Operators in Oracle 210

Set Operators versus Joins 211

UNION Operator 212

UNION ALL Operator 215

INTERSECT Operator 217

MINUS Operator 219

Conclusion 222

Practice Questions 223

Practice Answers 223

10. Views and Materialized Views 225

Introduction 225

Introduction to Views 226

Advantages of Views 226

Limitations of Views 227
Creating and Managing Views 227
Dropping a View....................228
Updating Data through Views....................229
Read-Only View 230
Introduction to Materialized Views 232
Creating and Managing Materialized Views....................233
Refreshing a Materialized View 234
Manual Refresh (ON DEMAND)....................*234*
Automatic Refresh (On Commit)....................*234*
Dropping a Materialized View 235
Comparing Views and Materialized Views 237
Conclusion....................239
Practice Questions....................239
Practice Answers 240
11. Creating and Managing Tables 243
Introduction 243
Introduction to DDL and DML Statements....................244
DDL (Data Definition Language) 244
DML (Data Manipulation Language) 244
Table Structure and Data Types 246
Types of Constraints in Oracle....................246
Common Oracle Data Types 247
Creating Tables 248
Defining Constraints....................250
The ALTER TABLE Command....................250

Verifying Constraints Using Data Dictionary Views 253

Understanding Foreign Key Constraint 257

ON DELETE CASCADE 258

Creating Tables Using CTAS 260

Inserting Data into Tables 261

Different Ways to Insert Data 262

Best Practices for Inserting Data 262

Managing Transactions (COMMIT and ROLLBACK) 263

Inserting Values into Selected Columns 268

Inserting Query Results into a Table 269

Updating Data in Tables 271

Deleting Data from Tables 273

Managing Tables 275

Dropping Tables 275

Truncating Tables 277

Renaming Tables 278

Adding New Columns 280

Modifying Columns 282

Dropping Columns 283

Enabling and Disabling Constraints 284

Conclusion 286

Practice Questions 287

Practice Answers 288

INDEX 289

Chapter 1
Getting Started with Oracle SQL

Introduction

Oracle SQL is the foundation for interacting with one of the most widely adopted relational database management systems in the world.

This chapter introduces the essential concepts required to begin working with Oracle SQL. It explains the role of SQL in managing relational data and introduces the training dataset used throughout this book.

This chapter will cover the following topics:

- Fundamentals of Relational Databases
- Introduction to SQL
- Key Features of Oracle SQL
- Oracle Database Architecture
- Introduction to the Training Dataset

Fundamentals of Relational Databases

A relational database is a type of database that organizes data into tables (or relations), where each table consists of rows and columns. This model was introduced by Edgar F. Codd in 1970 and has since become the most widely used approach for storing structured data in modern systems.

Key Characteristics

Relational databases organize data into **tables** made up of rows and columns. Each table represents an entity, such as `Customers` or `Orders`, and relationships between tables are defined using **keys** to maintain data consistency.

The main components of a relational database include:

- **Tables**: Store data for specific entities.
- **Columns**: Define attributes with specific data types such as `VARCHAR2`, `NUMBER`, or `DATE`.
- **Rows (Records)**: Represent individual entries in a table.
- **Primary Keys**: Uniquely identify each record (for example, `CustomerID`, `OrderID`).
- **Foreign Keys**: Link related tables by referencing primary keys (for example, `CustomerID` in `Orders` links to `Customers`).

Relational databases also support relationships between tables to represent how data is connected. Common relationship types include:

- One-to-Many: One customer can have many orders.
- Many-to-One: Each order belongs to one salesperson.
- Many-to-Many: A product may appear in multiple orders.

The following Figure 1.1 illustrates how the `Customers`, `Orders`, and `OrderDetails` tables are connected:

Customers Table

CustomerID	CustomerName	Region
C054	Shannon Jones	Oklahoma
C087	Tammy Young	Hawaii

Orders Table

OrderID	CustomerID	OrderDate
O1001	C087	2023-02-07
O1002	C054	2023-02-25

OrderDetails Table

OrderDetailID	OrderID	ProductID
OD1000	O1001	P0045
OD1001	O1001	P0018

Figure 1.1*: Relationship between Customers, Orders, and OrderDetails tables*

Figure 1.1 demonstrates how data is related across the following three tables:

- The `Customers` table stores customer information, with `CustomerID` serving as the primary key.
- The `Orders` table records each purchase, using `OrderID` as the primary key and `CustomerID` as a foreign key to link each order to a customer.
- The `OrderDetails` table stores line items for each order, with `OrderID` acting as a foreign key to associate products with specific orders.

This structure reflects a typical relational design, where data is distributed across related tables to support scalability, integrity, and efficient querying.

Advantages of the Relational Model

The relational model offers a range of benefits that support both routine operations and long-term scalability in data-driven environments. Key advantages include:

- **Data Integrity**: Use of keys and constraints ensures data accuracy and consistency.
- **Normalization**: Data can be organized to minimize redundancy and dependency.
- **Flexibility**: Easy to query, insert, update, and delete data using SQL.
- **Scalability**: Supports large volumes of data across multiple users and applications.
- **Security**: Access can be controlled at various levels using roles and privileges.

Introduction to SQL

Structured Query Language (SQL) is the standard language used to interact with relational databases. It allows users and applications to define, access, manipulate, and control data stored in a database system. SQL is both powerful and flexible, making it an essential skill in data management and analysis.

SQL statements are broadly categorized into several key types, each serving a specific purpose in database operations:

- **Data Definition Language (DDL)**: DDL statements are used to define and modify the structure of database objects such as tables, views, and indexes. Common DDL commands include:
  - `CREATE`: Creates a new database object (for example, `CREATE TABLE`).
  - `ALTER`: Modifies the structure of an existing database object.
  - `DROP`: Removes a database object.
- **Data Manipulation Language (DML)**: DML statements are used to insert, update, delete, and retrieve data stored in database tables.

Common DML commands include:

- `INSERT`: Adds new rows to a table.
- `UPDATE`: Modifies existing rows.
- `DELETE`: Removes rows from a table.
- `SELECT`: Retrieves data from one or more tables.

- **Data Control Language (DCL)**: DCL statements control access to data and database objects. Common DCL commands include:
  - `GRANT`: Assigns privileges to users or roles.
  - `REVOKE`: Removes previously granted privileges.
- **Transaction Control Language (TCL)**: TCL statements manage database transactions to maintain data integrity. Common TCL commands include:
  - `COMMIT`: Permanently saves changes made during the transaction.
  - `ROLLBACK`: Reverts changes made during the current transaction. *ROLLBACK TO SAVEPOINT* undoes changes made after a specific savepoint.
  - `SAVEPOINT`: Creates a point within a transaction that can be used for partial rollback.

The following table summarizes the four major categories of SQL commands introduced earlier:

Table 1.1: *Quick Reference: Categories of SQL Commands*

Category	Full Form	Purpose	Examples
DDL	Data Definition Language	Defines and manages the structure of database objects.	`CREATE`, `ALTER`, `DROP`
DML	Data Manipulation Language	Manipulates data within tables.	`SELECT`, `INSERT`, `UPDATE`, `DELETE`
DCL	Data Control Language	Manages access rights and permissions.	`GRANT`, `REVOKE`
TCL	Transaction Control Language	Manages transactions and ensures data integrity.	`COMMIT`, `ROLLBACK`, `SAVEPOINT`

DDL statements implicitly commit changes and therefore cannot be rolled back, while DML statements must be explicitly committed to be saved. TCL commands are used to control and manage these transactions.

Case Sensitivity and Syntax Notes

When writing Oracle SQL statements, keep the following syntax rules in mind:

- SQL keywords are not case-sensitive.
- Oracle SQL statements typically end with a semicolon (;).
- String literals must be enclosed in single quotes (`' '`).

TIP: Understanding ANSI SQL
ANSI SQL, also known as standard SQL, is the version of SQL defined by the American National Standards Institute (ANSI) to promote consistency across relational database systems. Most relational databases, including Oracle, implement ANSI SQL standards. Writing queries in ANSI-compliant syntax helps improve portability across platforms like SQL Server, PostgreSQL, and MySQL. Oracle SQL supports ANSI SQL while also providing additional features that are specific to Oracle.

SQL serves as the foundation for all interactions with a relational database. From defining structures and manipulating data to querying and controlling access, SQL enables comprehensive data operations.

Key Features of Oracle SQL

Oracle SQL extends the ANSI SQL standard with additional capabilities for data management, performance, and enterprise scalability. Its main features include:

- **ANSI and Oracle Extensions**: Supports standard SQL along with Oracle-specific features like `DUAL`, `SYSDATE`, `ROWNUM`, and `CONNECT BY`.
- **Comprehensive Data Types**: Includes `VARCHAR2`, `NUMBER`, `DATE`, `CLOB`, `BLOB`, `XMLTYPE`, and support for user-defined types.
- **Advanced Querying**: Provides analytical functions (`RANK`, `LAG`, `LEAD`), hierarchical queries, set operators, subqueries, and the `MERGE` statement.
- **Transaction Control**: Commands such as `COMMIT`, `ROLLBACK`, and `SAVEPOINT` help maintain consistency during multi-step operations.

- **Data Integrity**: Enforces business rules using constraints like `PRIMARY KEY`, `FOREIGN KEY`, `NOT NULL`, `UNIQUE`, and `CHECK`.
- **Performance Optimization**: Supports B-tree and bitmap indexes, materialized views, and a cost-based query optimizer.
- **Security**: Offers granular access control through `GRANT`, `REVOKE`, roles, and row-level security.
- **PL/SQL Integration**: Combines SQL with procedural logic for stored programs, loops, and exception handling.

Together, these features support the development, management, and optimization of enterprise-scale relational databases using Oracle SQL.

Common SQL Objects

Oracle databases consist of various objects that store and manage data. Understanding these objects provides context for how SQL interacts with the database.

The following table summarizes the most commonly used SQL objects in Oracle:

***Table 1.2**: Common SQL Objects*

Object Type	**Description**
Table	It stores data in rows and columns. It is the fundamental storage unit in a relational database.
View	A virtual table created from one or more tables using a query; used for security and simplification.
Index	Improves data retrieval speed by maintaining a separate data structure for quick lookups.
Sequence	Generates unique numeric values, often used for primary keys.
Synonym	Provides an alternative name for a database object.
Schema	A logical collection of objects owned by a user.
Constraint	Defines rules to maintain data integrity (for example, PRIMARY KEY, FOREIGN KEY).

These objects form the core components of any Oracle database. Understanding their purpose lays the foundation for learning how Oracle organizes, stores, and manages data.

Oracle Database Architecture

Oracle Database is designed to manage large volumes of data efficiently. Its architecture consists of logical structures, physical files, memory areas, and background processes that work together to store and retrieve data reliably.

The architecture can be broadly divided into the following components:

- **Logical Structure**: These are database-level components used to organize and manage data. These include:
  - Tablespaces: Logical storage units that group related data.
  - Schemas: Collections of database objects, such as tables, views, and indexes owned by a user.
  - Segments, Extents, and Blocks: Lower-level storage units that manage space allocation within tablespaces.
- **Physical Structure**: Represents the actual files stored on disk. These include:
  - Data Files: Store the actual database data.
  - Control Files: Maintain metadata about the database structure and file locations.
  - Redo Log Files: Record all changes made to the database for recovery purposes.
- **Memory Architecture**: Oracle uses the two primary memory areas to process database operations. These include:
  - SGA (System Global Area): Shared memory used for caching data and SQL-related components.
  - PGA (Program Global Area): Memory allocated for session-specific operations such as sorting and calculations.

- **Background Processes**: These include processes to handle tasks such as writing data, recovery, and system maintenance. Common background processes include:
  - DBWR (Database Writer): Writes modified data blocks to disk.
  - LGWR (Log Writer): Writes redo information to the redo log files.
  - SMON (System Monitor): Performs instance recovery and cleanup operations.
  - PMON (Process Monitor): Cleans up failed user processes.
  - CKPT (Checkpoint Process): Coordinates checkpoints and updates file headers.
- **Instance and Database**:
  - An Oracle **instance** consists of memory structures and background processes that manage database operations.
  - An Oracle **database** refers to the physical set of files that store the data.

The following Figure1.2 illustrates the Oracle Database Architecture:

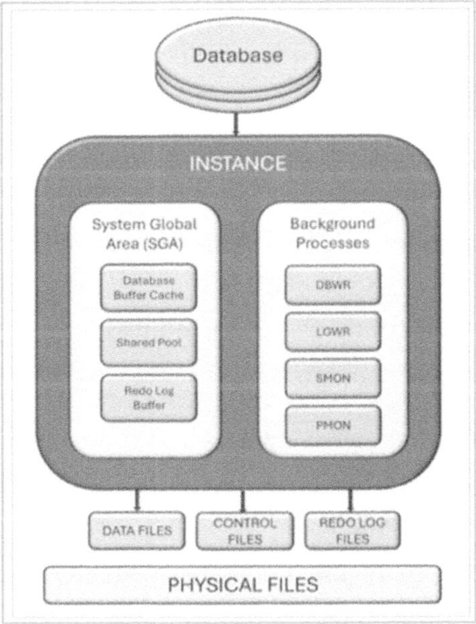

***Figure 1.2**: Overview of Oracle Database Architecture*

An Oracle database consists of physical files that store data, whereas an Oracle instance includes memory structures and background processes responsible for managing access to that data. A single database may be managed by multiple instances, as in Oracle Real Application Clusters (RAC) environments.

Introduction to the Training Dataset

To support hands-on learning and practical application of Oracle SQL concepts, this book uses a sample dataset titled **`BDS_Training_Data`** throughout the chapters.

This dataset is designed to simulate real-world business operations in a retail environment. It contains multiple related tables representing common business entities such as `Orders`, `OrderDetails`, `Customers`, `Products`, `Category`, `SalesPersons`, and `Branches`. The dataset follows a relational model and includes realistic data types, values, and relationships, making it suitable for practicing SQL queries and understanding database design principles.

A companion file named **`BDS_Training_Data.xlsx`** is provided with this book. It contains all the tables used in the examples and exercises, allowing the dataset structure to be explored before working with it in Oracle SQL.

Table 1.3*: Tables included in the BDS_Training_Data Dataset*

Table Name	**Description**
`Orders`	Contains order-level information such as order ID, customer ID, order date, shipping mode.
`OrderDetails`	Stores individual line items for each order, including quantity, unit price, discount, and profit.
`Customers`	Stores customer details including name, region, and market segment.
`Products`	Lists products with associated cost, unit price, and category.
`Category`	Defines product categories and sub-categories.
`SalesPersons`	Stores employee information including position, location, salary, and reporting structure.
`Branches`	Represents regional branches with city and branch names.

Benefits of Using This Dataset

The dataset is structured to include features such as:

- Primary and Foreign Keys: To demonstrate joins and enforce data integrity.
- Multiple Relationships: One-to-many, many-to-one, and many-to-many examples across tables.
- Numeric and Textual Data: Suitable for aggregation, filtering, and grouping operations.
- Time-based Fields: Fields such as `OrderDate` and `ShipDate` are useful for date functions and time-based analysis.
- Realistic Business Context: Appropriate for building practical queries and small projects.

This dataset will be used consistently throughout the book to demonstrate SQL syntax, query construction, data transformation, and reporting logic using Oracle SQL. As new concepts are introduced, examples from **`BDS_Training_Data`** reinforce learning through practical application.

Conclusion

This chapter introduced the foundational concepts of Oracle SQL and explained how it is used to store, retrieve, and manage data within a relational database. The structure and purpose of the BDS_Training_Data dataset were also presented, providing a practical foundation for learning throughout the book.

With these basics established, the next chapter, **Setting Up the Environment**, focuses on creating a working setup using Oracle FreeSQL and Oracle Database Express Edition (XE) to begin executing SQL queries hands-on.

Practice Questions

Complete the following questions to reinforce concepts covered in this chapter:

1. What is the primary purpose of Oracle SQL, and how does it interact with relational databases?
2. What are the main components of Oracle Database architecture?
3. What is ANSI SQL and why is it important?
4. What are the main categories of SQL commands?
5. How do primary keys and foreign keys help define relationships between tables in a relational database?

Practice Answers

The answers to the preceding questions are as follows:

Answer 1

Oracle SQL is Oracle's implementation of Structured Query Language (SQL), used to define, manipulate, and query data in relational databases. It allows structured data to be organized into tables and enables operations such as retrieving, inserting, updating, and deleting data stored in tables.

Answer 2

Oracle Database architecture consists of:

- Logical Structures (tablespaces, schemas, segments)
- Physical Structures (datafiles, control files, redo logs)
- Memory Structures (SGA, PGA)
- Background Processes (DBWR, LGWR, SMON, PMON)
- The Oracle Instance and the Database

Answer 3

ANSI SQL is the standardized version of SQL defined by the American National Standards Institute. It provides a consistent, portable foundation for SQL syntax that is supported across different relational database systems, including Oracle.

Answer 4

The main categories of SQL commands are:

- **DDL** (Data Definition Language): CREATE, ALTER, DROP
- **DML** (Data Manipulation Language): SELECT, INSERT, UPDATE, DELETE
- **DCL** (Data Control Language): GRANT, REVOKE
- **TCL** (Transaction Control Language): COMMIT, ROLLBACK, SAVEPOINT

Answer 5

A primary key uniquely identifies each record in a table, ensuring that duplicate rows do not exist. Foreign keys reference primary keys in related tables, establishing relationships between tables and enforcing referential integrity within the database.

Chapter 2
Setting Up the Environment

Introduction

Before writing and executing SQL statements, it is essential to have a properly configured Oracle SQL environment. A stable setup ensures that database objects, scripts, and exercises can be created, tested, and reused efficiently throughout the learning process.

This chapter provides a step-by-step guide to setting up both *Oracle FreeSQL (formerly Oracle Live SQL)*—a browser-based environment suitable for quick practice, and *Oracle Database Express Edition (XE)*—a locally installed database that supports the persistent storage of database objects. The chapter also introduces *SQL Developer*, Oracle's graphical interface for database development and management.

This chapter will cover the following topics:

- Overview of Oracle SQL Environments
- Using Oracle FreeSQL
- Installing Oracle Database XE
- Setting Up SQL Developer
- Running SQL Scripts

Overview of Oracle SQL Environments

Oracle provides multiple environments to work with SQL, each designed for specific purposes such as learning, development, testing, and production. Understanding these environments helps in selecting the most suitable platform for executing SQL statements and managing database objects.

In this book, the following two primary environments are used:

- **Oracle FreeSQL (formerly Oracle Live SQL)**: A cloud-based environment that runs entirely in a web browser—ideal for quick learning and practice without requiring local installation.
- **Oracle Database Express Edition** (XE): A locally installed database that supports persistent storage of tables, views, and other database objects, making it ideal for comprehensive exercises.

Additionally, **Oracle SQL Developer**, a graphical client tool for connecting to and managing Oracle databases such as *Oracle XE,* is used. SQL Developer provides an intuitive workspace for writing SQL queries, executing scripts, and exploring database objects in the local environment.

Oracle FreeSQL versus Oracle Database XE

Both Oracle FreeSQL (formerly Oracle Live SQL) and Oracle Database Express Edition (XE) can be used to practice and execute SQL commands. While they offer similar functionality, they differ in setup, persistence, and administrative capabilities.

Table 2.1 highlights the key differences between the two environments:

Table 2.1*: Oracle FreeSQL versus Oracle Database XE*

Feature	**Oracle FreeSQL**	**Oracle Database XE**
Type	Cloud-based browser environment	Locally installed database
Installation	No installation required	Must be installed on a computer
Access	Requires an active internet connection	Works offline after setup
Persistence	Temporary workspace; object retention is not guaranteed	Data persists between sessions
Admin Privileges	Limited privileges (no system access)	Full admin control
Performance	Depends on internet/Oracle's server load	Faster local performance
Security/Privacy	Data is stored in Oracle-managed cloud environment	Data stored locally
Ideal For	Learning, practice, and demos	Projects, extended development work
SQL Developer Integration	Not supported	Fully supported

Before You Begin

This book can be practiced using either Oracle FreeSQL or Oracle Database Express Edition (XE).

Choose the environment based on convenience:

- **Oracle FreeSQL**: Requires no installation and runs entirely in a web browser.
- **Oracle XE**: Requires local installation and supports persistent storage of database objects. Oracle SQL Developer is used as the graphical interface when working with Oracle XE.

Once the choice is made, all examples in this book can be executed in that chosen environment.

Using Oracle FreeSQL

Oracle FreeSQL is a web-based platform hosted by Oracle that allows users to execute SQL and PL/SQL statements directly from a browser. It requires no installation and is suitable for quick demonstrations, short exercises, and learning fundamental SQL concepts.

Once configured, this environment can be used throughout the book for examples and exercises based on the training Dataset.

Key Features of Oracle FreeSQL

Oracle FreeSQL includes several features that make it a practical and convenient environment for learning and practicing SQL:

- **No Installation Required**: Runs entirely in a web browser with no setup or configuration.
- **Write and Execute SQL and PLSQL**: Supports `SELECT`, `INSERT`, `UPDATE`, DDL, and PL/SQL blocks in a real Oracle database environment.
- **Script Library**: Provides access to sample scripts and tutorials covering Oracle SQL and PL/SQL topics.
- **Personal Workspace**: Allows scripts to be saved under an Oracle account for reuse across sessions.
- **Schema Browser**: Displays tables, columns, and data types for quick schema exploration.
- **Oracle-specific Features**: Supports Oracle-exclusive syntax, data types, and functions, enabling practice with true Oracle SQL.

While Oracle FreeSQL is well-suited for learning and experimentation, it has a limitation:

- Restrictive Administrative Access: Administrative commands such as CREATE USER and system-level privilege management are not supported.

These features define Oracle FreeSQL as a practical, browser-based tool for learning and experimenting with SQL in a real Oracle environment.

Working with Oracle FreeSQL

Follow these steps to set up the environment and begin running queries:

1. Visit the website:

   Go to https://freesql.com/

2. The landing page (refer to Figure 2.1) opens the FreeSQL Worksheet automatically. This worksheet is the primary interface for writing and executing SQL statements.

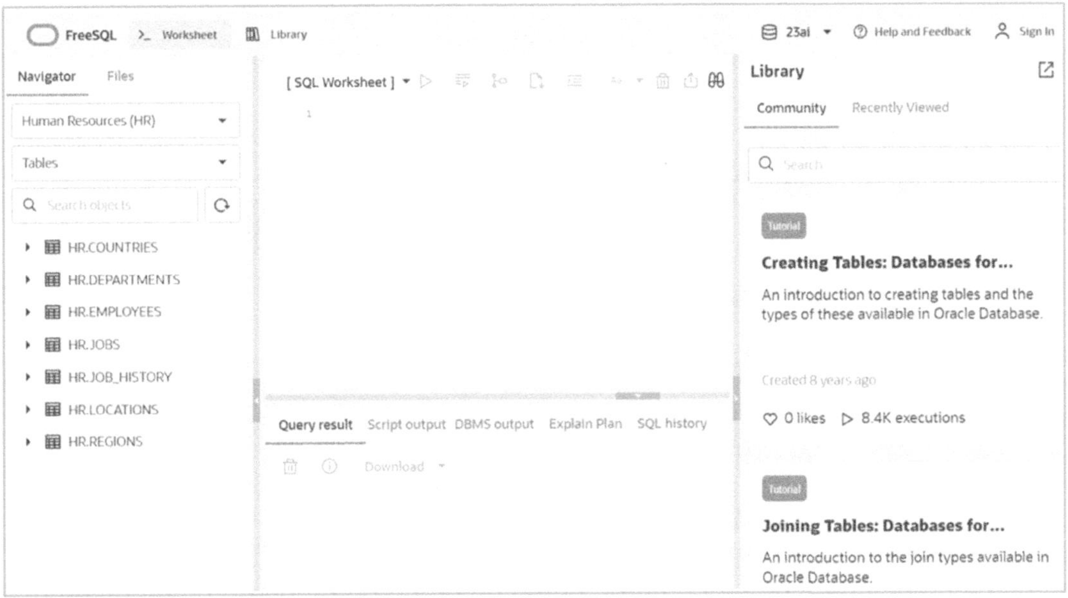

***Figure 2.1**: Oracle FreeSQL Worksheet Interface*

3. Sign in or create an Oracle account: Click **Sign In** at the top-right corner. This opens the Oracle account sign-in page:

   a. If you already have an Oracle account, enter your credentials and sign in.

   b. If not, click **Create Account** and follow the prompts to register. The Oracle account sign-in option is shown in Figure 2.2:

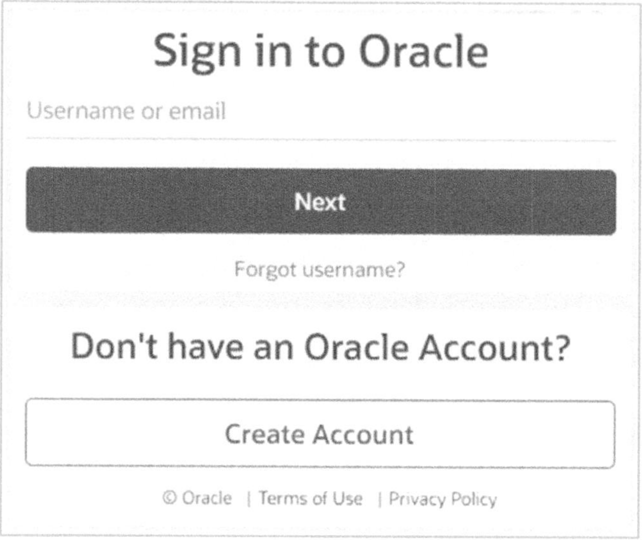

***Figure 2.2**: Sign in to the Oracle Account*

After signing in, scripts can be executed, work can be saved, and the script library becomes accessible.

Setting Up the Dataset for the Book

To initialize the sample training database used throughout this book, create and populate the tables using the provided SQL scripts.

The script file `BDS_Training_Data_Create_Insert_Scripts.sql` is available in the **Data** folder included with the book.

Instructions for accessing this folder are provided in the *Downloading the Code* section at the beginning of the book.

Running Scripts in Oracle FreeSQL

The steps to run the scripts in the Oracle FreeSQL environment are as follows:

1. Visit: https://freesql.com and sign in using the Oracle account created earlier.
2. After signing in, the landing page with SQL Worksheet opens up automatically.

3. On the right, under **Library**, select the **My Content** tab. It will display two options: **Create tutorial or script** and **Upload script**, as shown in Figure 2.3:

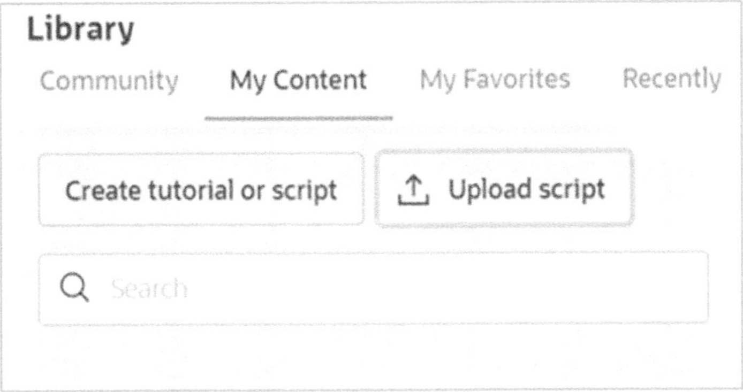

***Figure 2.3**: My Content Tab under Library*

4. Select **Upload script** to upload the script.
5. In the **Upload script** dialog, use **Select File** to browse to the downloaded script file `BDS_Training_Data_Create_Insert_Scripts.sql`. Additionally, assign a name, review the minimum database version, and optionally add a description, as shown in Figure 2.4:

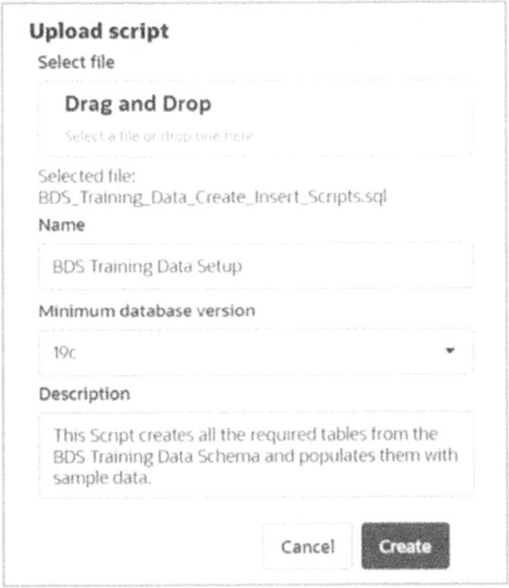

***Figure 2.4**: Upload script dialog showing the required fields*

6. Click **Create** to upload the script, after which it can be executed.

7. On the next screen, the script contents are displayed along with the total number of SQL statements contained in the script. Click **Run Script** to execute the script, as shown in Figure 2.5:

***Figure 2.5**: Dataset setup script ready for execution*

8. After execution completes, the results panel displays the execution status of the script. A summary message confirms the number of SQL statements executed and indicates whether the script ran successfully or encountered errors. This script runs 246 statements successfully and creates 14 objects. This 14 objects include 7 tables and 7 primary/foreign key constraints.

9. Select the **Worksheet** option from the top left to navigate to the SQL Worksheet.

10. To verify the created tables, select **My Schema** from the left panel and select **Tables**. All tables created by the script will appear as shown in Figure 2.6:

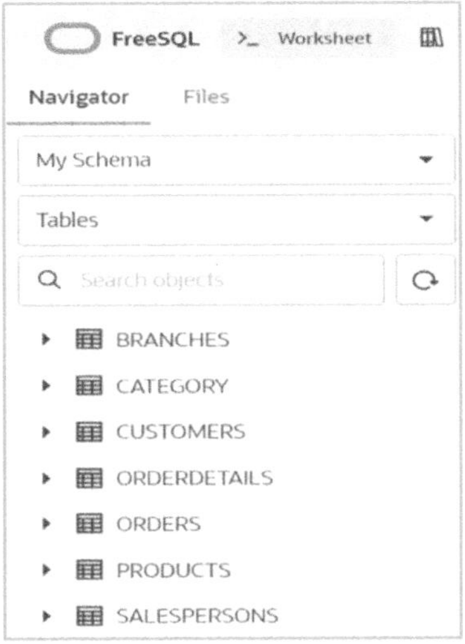

***Figure 2.6**: Tables created schema after script execution*

This completes the setup of the **BDS Training Dataset** in Oracle Free SQL.

Oracle FreeSQL is now ready for use and can be used to perform all exercises provided in this book.

Verifying the Dataset in Oracle FreeSQL

After running the setup script successfully, the tables and data are now created in the Oracle FreeSQL environment.

To verify that the data has been loaded correctly, follow the given steps:

1. In the worksheet, type the following query:

   ```
   SELECT * FROM Branches;
   ```

2. To execute, highlight the query and click the **Run** button on the toolbar (small triangle icon) or press *Ctrl* + *Enter* to execute.

   The results should display a list of branch records with their corresponding details such as `BranchID`, `BranchName`, and `City`.

   This confirms that the dataset setup is complete and ready for use.

Installing Oracle Database XE

Oracle Database Express Edition (XE) is a free, lightweight version of the Oracle Database designed for learning, development, and small-scale applications. It includes all major database features and runs locally on a personal computer, making it ideal for practicing SQL in a persistent environment.

Installing Oracle Database XE provides full administrative control and allows creating and managing database objects that remain available across sessions. The installation process is straightforward and takes only a few minutes.

Prerequisites for Installation

Before starting the installation, ensure that the system meets the following basic requirements for a smooth setup of Oracle Database Express Edition (XE):

- **Administrator Privileges**: The installation must be performed by a user with administrative rights. Log in as a local administrator or ensure the current account belongs to the Administrators group.
- **No Existing XE Service**: Verify that no previous Oracle Database Express Edition service is running on the system to avoid conflicts during installation.
- **Unset Environment Variables**: Temporarily remove any existing `ORACLE_HOME` or `TNS_ADMIN` environment variables. These are typically absent on new installations.

Installing Oracle Database XE

Follow these steps to install Oracle Database Express Edition (XE) on a Windows system:

1. Download the Installer: Visit http://oracle.com/xe and click **Download Oracle Database XE**. The download page appears as shown in Figure 2.7:

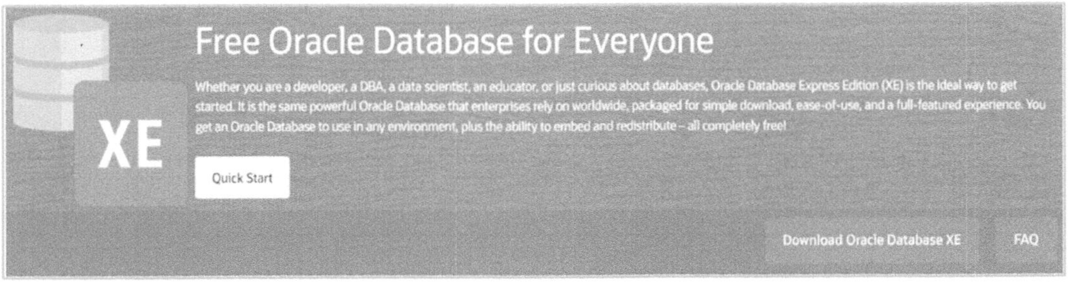

***Figure 2.7**: Oracle Database XE download page on Oracle's website*

2. On the next screen under **Oracle Database XE Downloads**, select **Oracle Database 21c Express Edition for Windows x64**.

***Figure 2.8**: Selecting the Oracle XE version for Windows 64-bit*

This will download the `OracleXE213_Win64.zip` file to the computer. The download may take a few minutes, depending on the internet speed.

3. Extract the files: Unzip the downloaded file. The extracted folder will contain a `setup` file.

Verify the perquisites, then double-click `setup` to start the installer. The `setup` file is shown in Figure 2.9:

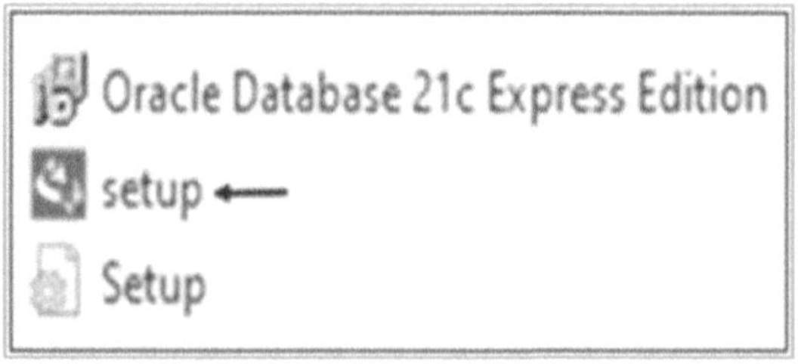

***Figure 2.9**: The setup.exe file to install Oracle XE*

4. Run the Installer: When prompted with "Do you want to allow this app to make changes to your device?", select **Yes**.
5. On the next screen, accept the license agreement as shown here:

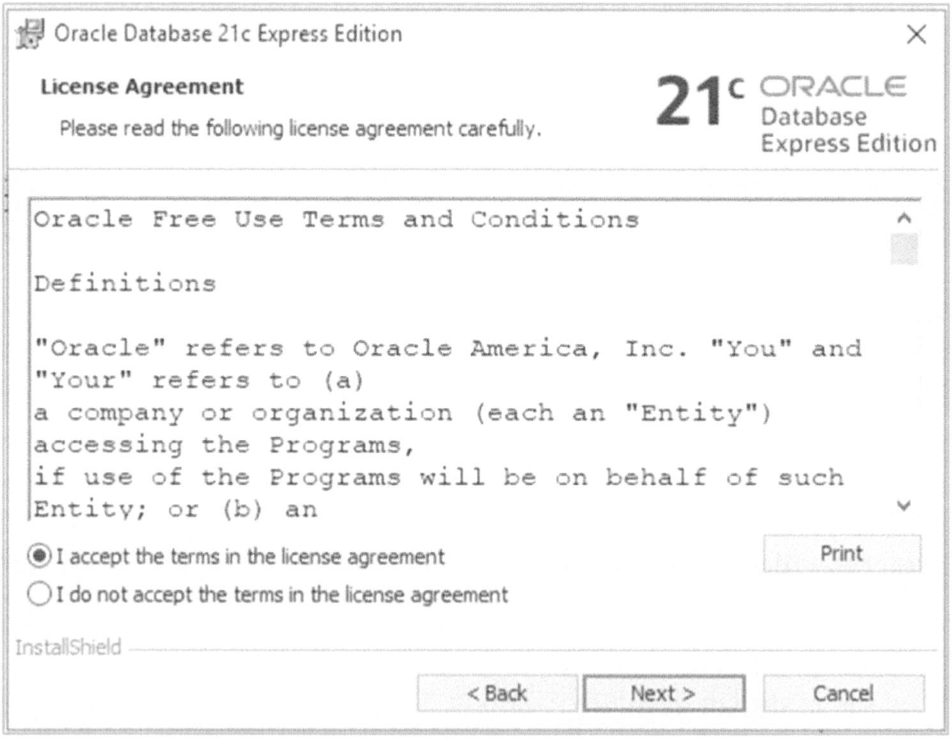

***Figure 2.10**: Oracle XE License Agreement*

6. On the subsequent screen, choose a destination folder (or keep the default), and proceed, as shown in Figure 2.11:

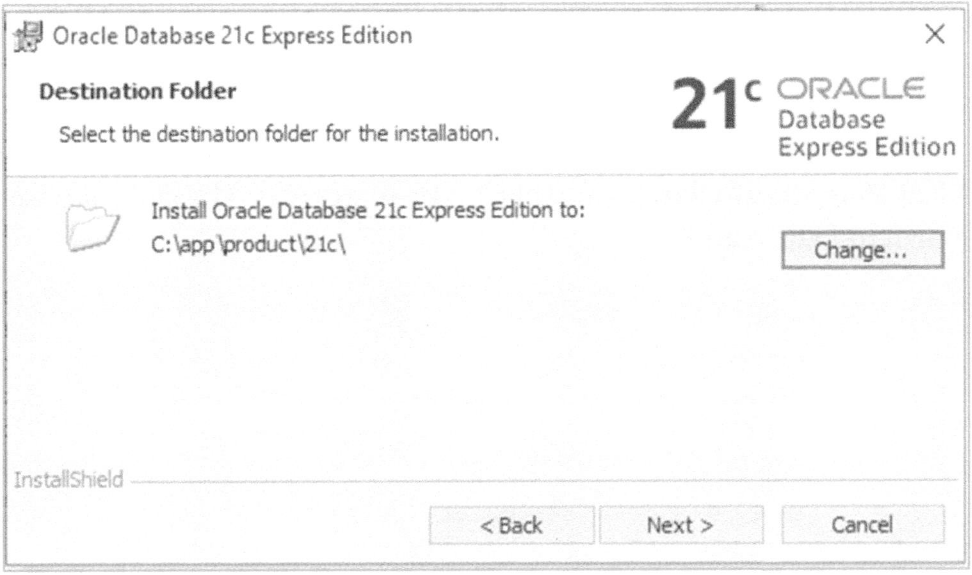

***Figure 2.11**: Selecting the destination folder*

7. Click **Next**.
8. Set administrative password: Enter a single password for the `SYS`, `SYSTEM`, and `PDBADMIN` accounts.
9. For consistency with this book's exercise, use `oracle123` (avoid special characters like "@"). The password screen is shown in Figure 2.12:

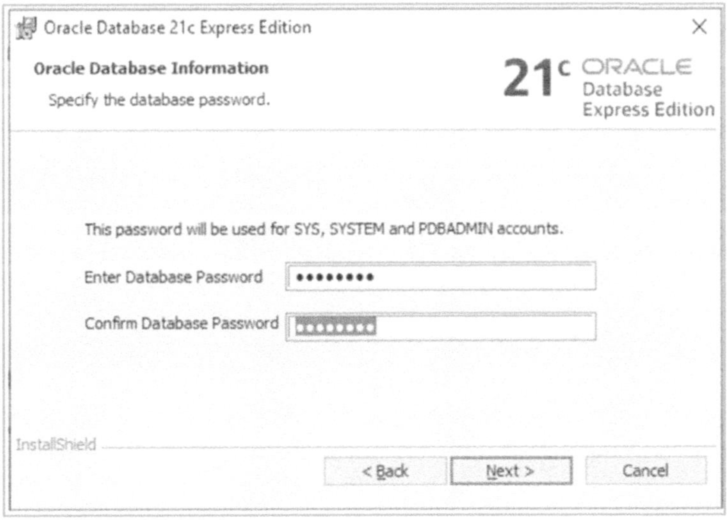

***Figure 2.12**: Providing passwords for the SYS, SYSTEM, and PDBADMIN accounts*

10. Install and complete setup: Review the summary screen, then click **Install** to begin installation. The process may take 20–30 minutes, depending on your system.

    During installation, a Windows Defender Firewall prompt may appear—select **Private networks** and click **Allow access**. The summary screen is shown in Figure 2.13:

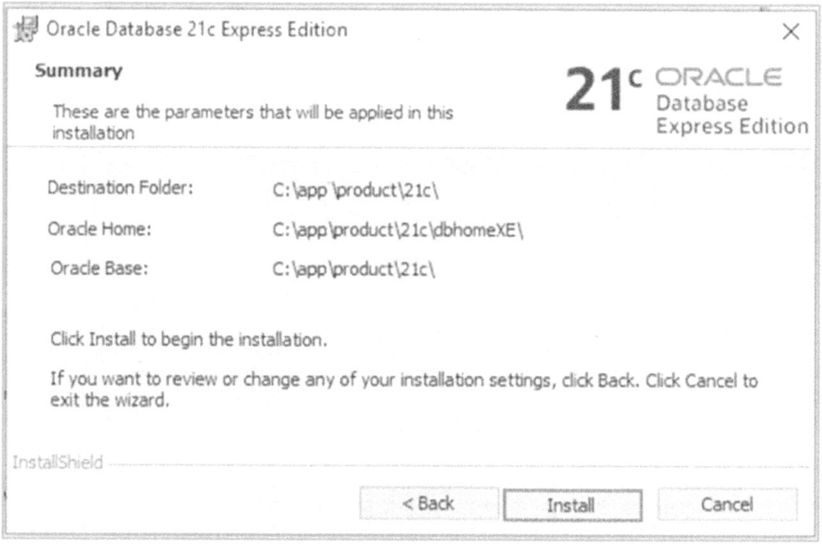

***Figure 2.13**: Installation summary screen*

11. Finish installation: When the installation is complete, the summary screen displays connection details such as hostname, port, and service name, as shown in Figure 2.14. Make a note or take a screenshot for future reference.

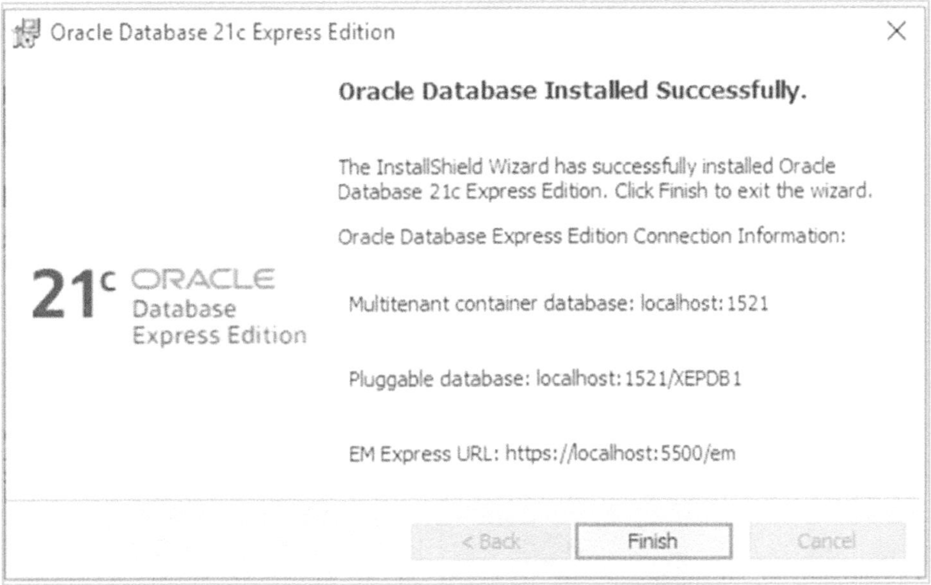

***Figure 2.14**: Oracle Database XE Edition installation completed successfully*

This completes the installation of Oracle Database Express Edition (XE) on the local system.

Verifying and Connecting to Oracle XE

After installing Oracle Database Express Edition (XE), the next step is to verify that the database is running correctly. This can be done using **SQL*Plus**, a command-line tool installed automatically with Oracle XE.

This section also covers creating a user account that will later be used to connect through Oracle SQL Developer.

The steps to connect to the database are as follows:

1. Open SQL*Plus: From the Windows **Start** menu, locate the **Oracle** folder and select **SQL Plus** as shown in Figure 2.15:

***Figure 2.15**: Launching SQL Plus in the command prompt*

SQL Plus will open in a command prompt window.

2. Connect as SYSDBA: At the **Enter user-name:** prompt, type the following:

```
/ as sysdba
```

Press **Enter** to connect to the database as `sysdba`, as shown in Figure 2.16:

```
SQL*Plus: Release 21.0.0.0.0 - Production on Tue Oct 7 18:04:19 2025
Version 21.3.0.0.0

Copyright (c) 1982, 2021, Oracle.  All rights reserved.

Enter user-name: / as sysdba

Connected to:
Oracle Database 21c Express Edition Release 21.0.0.0.0 - Production
Version 21.3.0.0.0
```

***Figure 2.16**: Connecting as sysdba*

The user who installed the database automatically has SYSDBA privileges.

3. List pluggable databases: At the SQL prompt, run the following command:

```
Select name from v$pdbs;
```

The prompt screen with the SQL statement is shown in Figure 2.17:

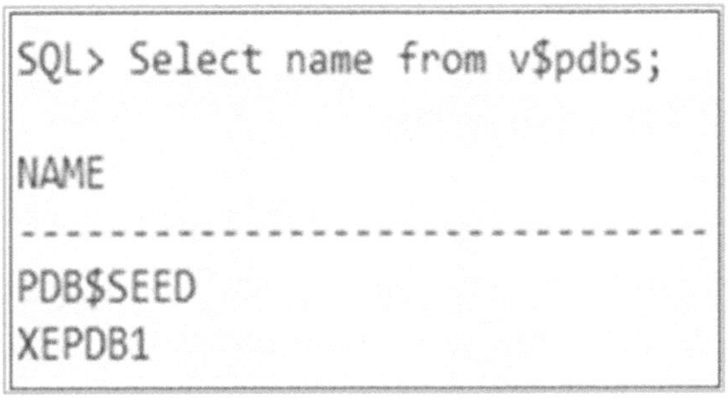

***Figure 2.17**: Getting the list of pluggable databases*

The pluggable database is **XEPDB1**.

4. Connect to the pluggable database: Use the following format to connect:

```
  connect sys/<password>@<hostname>:<portnumber>/<pdb_name> as
sysdba;
```

For example, on my machine it is:

```
connect sys/oracle123@localhost:1521/XEPDB1 as sysdba;
```

Figure 2.18 shows the command:

***Figure 2.18**: Connecting to a pluggable database*

Replace the username, password, host, and port according to your setup.

5. Create a practice user: Always use a separate user account for exercises. Avoid using administrative users such as `SYS` and `SYSTEM` for routine queries.

Create a new user for this book's exercises:

```
CREATE USER bds_train IDENTIFIED by bds_train;
```

6. Grant privileges: Provide the necessary privileges to allow login and object creation:

```
GRANT CONNECT, RESOURCE TO bds_train;
```

The user `bds_train` is now ready to be used in SQL Developer.

Setting Up SQL Developer

Oracle SQL Developer is a free, graphical tool provided by Oracle for working with databases. It allows users to write and execute SQL queries, create and manage database objects, and view data in an intuitive interface.

After installing Oracle Database XE and creating the `bds_train` user, the next step is to configure a connection in SQL Developer. This connection will serve as the primary workspace for running all SQL statements and exercises in this book.

Downloading and Installing SQL Developer

Oracle SQL Developer simplifies database management and SQL development. It is available on Windows, macOS, and Linux systems.

The steps to install SQL Developer (Windows) are as follows:

1. Visit https://www.oracle.com/database/sqldeveloper/technologies/download/
2. Under **SQL Developer Downloads**, locate the version for **Windows 64-bit with JDK 17 included**, as shown in Figure 2.19:

***Figure 2.19**: SQL Developer Windows 64-bit with JDK 17 included*

3. Click **Download** to begin. The file named `sqldeveloper-24.3.1.347.1826-x64.zip` will be saved to your computer.

4. Right-click the ZIP file and select **Extract All**.
5. In the extracted folder, double-click `sqldeveloper.exe` to launch SQL Developer. The file icon is shown in Figure 2.20:

***Figure 2.20**: SQL Developer installation file*

A dialog box may appear asking whether to import preferences from a previous installation. Select **No** to skip this step.

NOTE: SQL Developer does not require a traditional installation. It runs directly from the extracted folder and can be launched anytime by double-clicking `sqldeveloper.exe`. For convenience, create a desktop shortcut or pin it to the taskbar.

SQL Developer will then open the main interface window.

Creating a New Connection in SQL Developer

Follow these steps to connect Oracle SQL Developer to Oracle Database XE:

1. In SQL Developer, click the "+" icon on the left panel to open the **Connections** window, as shown in Figure 2.21:

***Figure 2.21**: Opening the Connections window*

Alternatively, from the menu select **File** > **New**> **Database Connection** to open the New / Select Database Connection dialog box.

2. Enter the connection details: In the dialog box, provide the following connection information:

Table 2.2*: SQL Developer connection details*

Field	**Value**
Connection Name	`BDS_Training_Data`
Username	`bds_train`
Password	`bds_train`
Save Password	√ (check this box)
Connection Type	`Basic`
Role	`Default`
Hostname	`localhost`
Port	`1521`
Service Name	`XEPDB1`

3. Test the connection: Click on the **Test** button to verify the configuration. The status line at the bottom should display "Success" if the connection is valid.
4. Save and connect: Click **Save** to retain the connection details for future use, then click **Connect** to open a new SQL Worksheet.

At this point, Oracle SQL Developer is fully configured and connected to the `bds_train` user in the `XEPDB1` database.

Running SQL Scripts

After establishing a connection in Oracle SQL Developer, the next step is to run the SQL scripts provided with this book.

This script creates the tables and inserts data to generate the **BDS Training Dataset**, which will be used in all examples and exercises throughout the book.

The script file, `BDS_Training_Data_Create_Insert_Scripts.sql`, is located in the **Data** folder included with the downloaded materials.

The steps to run the SQL script are as follows:

1. Open the script file: In SQL Developer, go to **File** > **Open**, and browse to: **Data** > `BDS_Training_Data_Create_Insert_Scripts.sql`.

   Select the file and click **Open**. The script will appear in a new SQL Worksheet tab.
2. Review the script: Scroll through the file to view the `CREATE TABLE` and `INSERT INTO` statements. The script includes tables such as `Orders`, `OrderDetails`, `Customers`, `Products`, `Category`, `SalesPersons`, and `Branches`, along with their related data.
3. Execute the script: To run the entire script, click the **Run Script** button on the toolbar or press **F5**. The **Run Script** button is shown in Figure 2.22:

   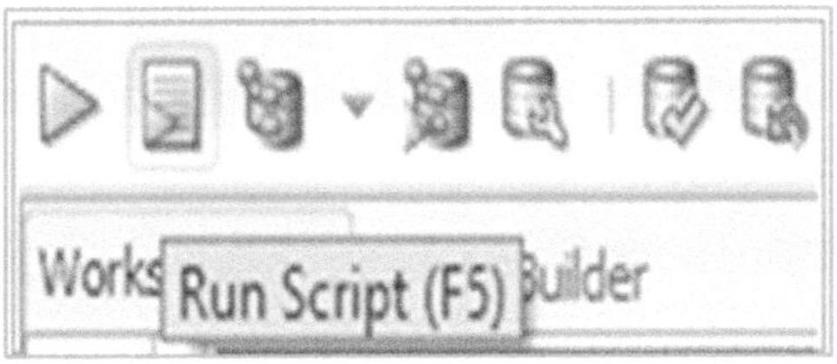

   ***Figure 2.22**: The Run Script button on the toolbar*

   If the **Select Connection** dialog box appears, click **OK**.

   The execution progresses, and messages (such as "Table created" and "Rows inserted") will appear in the **Script output** window.
4. Verify the tables: In the **Connections** pane, expand **BDS_Training_Data** > **Tables** to view newly created tables.

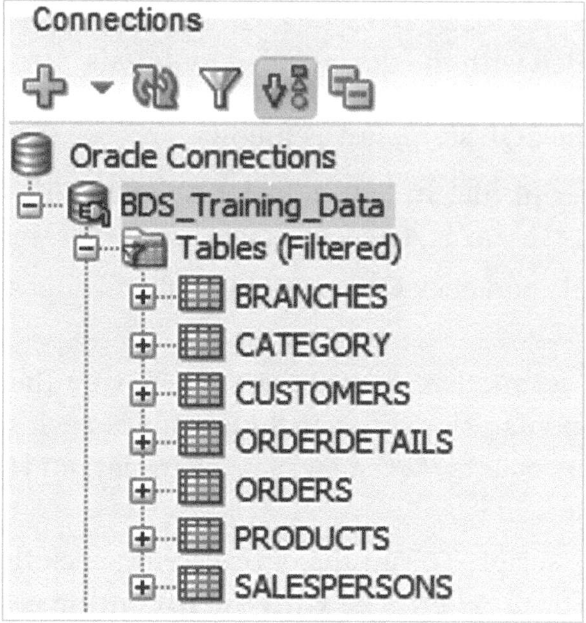

Figure 2.23: *Tables in the Connections pane*

5. Run a sample query: To confirm that the data was loaded correctly, execute the following statement:

```
SELECT * FROM Branches;
```

The query results should display rows of sample data from the `Branches` table as shown in Figure 2.24:

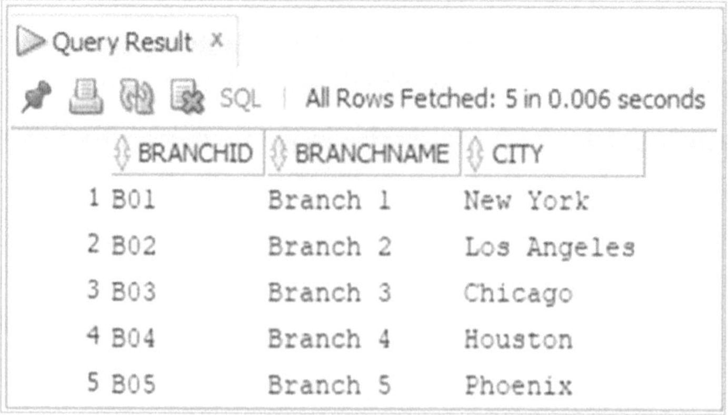

	BRANCHID	BRANCHNAME	CITY
1	B01	Branch 1	New York
2	B02	Branch 2	Los Angeles
3	B03	Branch 3	Chicago
4	B04	Branch 4	Houston
5	B05	Branch 5	Phoenix

Figure 2.24: *Data retrieved from the Branches table*

After successfully executing the script, the **BDS Training Dataset** is now available in Oracle XE and ready for use in all exercises in the upcoming chapters.

Conclusion

This chapter covered the setup of the Oracle SQL learning environment using either Oracle FreeSQL or Oracle Database Express Edition (XE).

The installation and configuration of Oracle SQL Developer were completed, and the BDS Training Dataset was created using the provided SQL scripts.

With the environment ready and verified, all required tables and data are available for hands-on practice.

The next chapter, **Writing SELECT Queries**, introduces techniques for retrieving and analyzing data using the SELECT statement along with key clauses such as WHERE, ORDER BY, and DISTINCT.

Practice Questions

Use the training dataset to complete the following practice questions. These exercises reinforce concepts covered in this chapter.

1. List two key differences between Oracle FreeSQL and Oracle Database Express Edition (XE) and explain when each environment is most suitable.
2. What is Oracle SQL Developer, and why is it used?
3. Describe the steps required to run the script file, `BDS_Training_Data_Create_Insert_Scripts.sql`, in Oracle SQL Developer.
4. Write a SQL query to confirm that data was inserted into the `Customers` table.
5. Explain how data persistence differs between Oracle FreeSQL and Oracle Database XE.

Practice Answers

The answers to the preceding questions are as follows:

Answer 1

Oracle FreeSQL runs in a web browser and requires no local installation, making it suitable for quick practice, demonstrations, and learning SQL concepts.

Oracle Database Express Edition (XE) is installed locally and provides full control over database objects, making it suitable for extended practice and development work where persistent storage is required.

Answer 2

Oracle SQL Developer is a free graphical tool used to connect to Oracle databases. It allows users to write and execute SQL queries, run scripts, and manage database objects using a graphical interface instead of command-line tools.

Answer 3

To run the `BDS_Training_Data_Create_Insert_Scripts.sql` file in Oracle SQL Developer, open the file using **File** > **Open**, then click the **Run Script** button or press **F5**.

After execution, status messages such as "Table created" confirm success, and the created tables appear under the connection in the Tables list.

Answer 4

```
SELECT * FROM Customers;
```

Answer 5

In Oracle XE, data is stored locally in the installed database, so tables and other objects persist across sessions until they are explicitly dropped.

In Oracle FreeSQL, objects are created in a cloud-based practice schema. Objects typically persist across sessions; however, long-term retention is not guaranteed, and the environment may be reset, requiring scripts to be rerun.

Chapter 3
Writing SELECT Queries

Introduction

With the environment configured in the previous chapter, this chapter introduces hands-on SQL development using the Oracle Database.

It introduces the fundamental building block of all SQL querying—the `SELECT` statement—and explains how it is used for retrieving and analyzing data in any relational database.

This chapter demonstrates how to write queries that retrieve specific columns, filter rows using conditions, arrange results in a defined order, and remove duplicate entries using the `DISTINCT` keyword.

This chapter will cover the following topics:

- Understanding Oracle Data Types
- The SELECT Statement
- The WHERE Clause
- The ORDER BY Clause
- The DISTINCT Clause

Understanding Oracle Data Types

Every column in an Oracle database table has a data type, which defines the kind of data it can store—such as text, numbers, or dates. Understanding data types is essential for writing correct SQL queries.

The following table provides the common Oracle data types with descriptions:

***Table 3.1**: Oracle Data types*

Data Type	Description
`CHAR(n)`	Fixed-length character data. It always stores exactly n characters. If a value is shorter, it is padded with spaces.
`VARCHAR2(n)`	Variable-length character data that stores up to *n* characters. Most commonly used for names, codes, and descriptions.
`NUMBER(p,s)`	Numeric data. *p* is the total number of digits (precision), and *s* is the number of digits after the decimal point (scale).
`Date`	Stores date and time values. The default display format is `'DD-MON-YYYY'`.
`LONG`	Stores variable-length character data up to 2 GB. Historically used for large text fields, but now largely replaced by CLOB.
`CLOB`	Stores large blocks of character data. Often used for documents or lengthy descriptions.
`BLOB`	Stores binary large objects such as images or PDF files.

Quoting and Formatting Rules

When writing SQL queries, it is important to use the correct format for different types of data values. Each data type—such as text, numbers, or dates—follows specific quoting and formatting rules in Oracle SQL. Following these rules ensures that queries run without errors and return accurate results.

The following table outlines the quoting and formatting rules of the literal values, along with examples:

***Table 3.2**: Quoting rules*

Data Type	Example	Quoting Rule
CHAR, VARCHAR2	`'New York', 'B01'`	Enclosed in single quotes `'...'`
NUMBER	`1000, 3.50, -42`	Not quoted
DATE	`'07-FEB-2023'`	Enclosed in single quotes and formatted as `'DD-MON-YYYY'`
LONG, CLOB	`'Long text value here...'`	Quoted like strings (not typically queried in full with `SELECT *`)

The DESC Command

To view the structure of a table, including its columns and data types, Oracle SQL provides the `DESC` command (short for DESCRIBE).

This command is useful for verifying the data types associated with each column, particularly when writing `SELECT` queries.

Syntax

```
DESC table_name;
```

Exercise 1: Using the DESC Command

Use the `DESC` command to view the structure of the `Branches` table.

The steps to use the `DESC` command are as follows:

1. Open the SQL Worksheet in Oracle FreeSQL (or Oracle SQL Developer).
2. Type the following command:
   ```
   DESC Branches;
   ```
3. To execute the command, use the appropriate option based on the environment in use:

a. In FreeSQL, highlight the command and click the **Run** button on the toolbar (small rectangle in the middle) or press *Ctrl* + *Enter* to execute.

b. In SQL Developer, press *Ctrl* + *Enter* or click the **Run Statement** (green arrow) icon on the toolbar.

The output of the query is shown in Figure 3.1:

Column	Null?	Type
BRANCHID	NOT NULL	VARCHAR2(100)
BRANCHNAME	-	VARCHAR2(100)
CITY	-	VARCHAR2(100)

***Figure 3.1**: Output of the DESC command*

Query Explanation

- **DESC**: Short for `DESCRIBE`; used to view a table's structure.
- **Branches**: Name of the table being described.

Understanding the Output

The `DESC` command displays the structure of the `Branches` table. The output is explained in the following table:

***Table 3.3**: Description of columns in the `Branches` table*

Column Name	Null?	Data Type	Description
`BRANCHID`	`NOT NULL`	VARCHAR2(10)	Primary identifier for each branch. Stores up to `10` characters. This field must have a value.
`BRANCHNAME`	`(blank)`	VARCHAR2(100)	Name of the branch. Stores up to `100` characters. Optional.
`CITY`	`(blank)`	VARCHAR2(100)	The city where the branch is located. Stores up to `100` characters. Optional.

NOTE: In Oracle, `NULL` means the column can be left empty—no value is required. If a column is marked as `NOT NULL`, a value must be provided when inserting a row.

The `DESC` command is a useful tool for viewing the structure of a table. Try running `DESC` on other tables in the training dataset (such as `Orders`, `OrderDetails`, `SalesPersons`, `Customers`, `Category`, or `Products`) to explore their structure and understand how the data is organized.

The SELECT Statement

The `SELECT` statement is used to retrieve data from one or more tables in a relational database. It forms the foundation of SQL (Structured Query Language) and is one of the most commonly used commands in database operations.

The following are the key features of the `SELECT` statement:

- SQL keywords such as `SELECT`, `FROM`, `WHERE`, and others are not case sensitive. However, they are conventionally written in uppercase to improve readability and distinguish them from table or column names.
- Table and column names in Oracle are also not case sensitive unless they are created using quoted identifiers.
- The `SELECT` statement retrieves rows and columns from a table.
- It can return all rows or a filtered set of rows.
- It can return specific columns or all columns using * wildcard.
- It can be used with clauses like `WHERE`, `ORDER BY`, `GROUP BY`, `JOIN`, and others to refine or organize query results.
- A semicolon (`;`) is commonly used to terminate a `SELECT` statement in Oracle SQL.

Syntax

```
SELECT column1, column2,
FROM table_name
WHERE <condition>
HAVING <condition>
ORDER BY <expression>;
```

Exercise 2: Using the SELECT Statement

Use the `SELECT` statement to retrieve all columns and data from the `Branches` table. This exercise demonstrates how to view the complete contents of a table using a simple query.

The steps to retrieve all columns and data from the `Branches` table are as follows:

1. In the SQL Worksheet of Oracle FreeSQL or SQL Developer, execute the following statement:

   ```
   SELECT * FROM Branches;
   ```

2. To execute the statement, use the appropriate option based on the environment in use:
   a. In FreeSQL, highlight the statement and click the **Run** button on the toolbar or press *Ctrl* + *Enter* to execute.
   b. In SQL Developer, press *Ctrl* + *Enter* or click the **Run Statement** (green arrow) icon on the toolbar.

The output of the query is shown in Figure 3.2:

BRANCHID	BRANCHNAME	CITY
B01	Branch 1	New York
B02	Branch 2	Los Angeles
B03	Branch 3	Chicago
B04	Branch 4	Houston
B05	Branch 5	Phoenix

***Figure 3.2**: All rows from the Branches table*

Query Explanation

- `SELECT *`: Retrieves all columns from the specified table.
- `FROM`: Specifies the `Branches` table as the source of the data.

To understand the data present in all the tables, run a `SELECT` statement on each table. For example:

```
SELECT * FROM Customers;
```

To view the data types and definitions of each column in a table, run the following command:

```
DESC <table_name>;
```

Selecting specific columns

Tables often contain many columns, but only a few may be needed for a particular query. The `SELECT` statement allows retrieving only those columns that are relevant to the task.

Exercise 3: Using SELECT to Retrieve Specific Columns from a Table

Using the `Branches` table, apply the `SELECT` statement to retrieve the `Branchname` and `City` columns.

The steps to retrieve specific columns from the `Branches` table are as follows:

1. In the SQL Worksheet, type the following statement:

   ```
   SELECT Branchname, City
   FROM Branches;
   ```

2. To execute the statement, use the appropriate option based on the environment in use:
   a. In FreeSQL, highlight the statement and click the **Run** button on the toolbar or press *Ctrl* + *Enter* to execute.
   b. In SQL Developer, press *Ctrl* + *Enter* or click the **Run Statement** (green arrow) icon on the toolbar.

The output of the query is shown in Figure 3.3:

BRANCHNAME	CITY
Branch 1	New York
Branch 2	Los Angeles
Branch 3	Chicago
Branch 4	Houston
Branch 5	Phoenix

***Figure 3.3**: Returns specific columns from the table*

The above `SELECT` statement returns the branch names and their corresponding cities.

Using an Alias

When a query is executed, the output displays the default column names as defined in the table. However, in many practical scenarios, it may be necessary to display these column headings with alternative or more user-friendly names.

This can be done by assigning an alias immediately after the column name in the `SELECT` statement. An alias only changes how the column name appears in the query result; it does not modify the actual column name in the underlying table.

Exercise 4: Using an Alias to Rename Columns

Using the `Branches` table, retrieve the `BranchID` and `City` columns. Rename `BranchID` to `BranchNo` and `City` to `Location`.

The steps to rename columns using an alias are as follows:

1. In the SQL Worksheet, execute the following statement:

   ```
   SELECT BranchID as BranchNo, City as Location
   FROM Branches;
   ```

2. To execute the statement, use the appropriate option based on the environment in use:

a. In FreeSQL, highlight the statement and click the **Run** button on the toolbar or press *Ctrl* + *Enter* to execute.

b. In SQL Developer, press *Ctrl* + *Enter* or click the **Run Statement** (green arrow) icon on the toolbar.

The output of the query is shown in Figure 3.4:

BRANCHNO	LOCATION
B01	New York
B02	Los Angeles
B03	Chicago
B04	Houston
B05	Phoenix

Figure 3.4: *Renamed columns*

To provide spaces between the alias name or to display the alias without upper case, include the alias in double quotation marks.

For example:

```
SELECT BranchID as "Branch No", City as "Location"
FROM Branches;
```

The output of the above statement is shown in Figure 3.5:

Branch No	Location
B01	New York
B02	Los Angeles
B03	Chicago
B04	Houston
B05	Phoenix

Figure 3.5: *Column headers displayed with spaces and non-upper case*

The preceding query displays column headers using the specified aliases, including spaces and mixed-case text as defined within the double quotation marks.

The WHERE Clause

The `WHERE` clause is used to filter rows in a table based on specified conditions. It instructs the database to return only those records that meet the defined condition. Without a `WHERE` clause, SQL returns all rows from the table.

Syntax

```
SELECT column1, column2,
FROM table_name
WHERE <condition>;
```

Exercise 5: Using the WHERE Clause

Using the `Customers` table, retrieve all rows where the `Segment` value is `Corporate`.

The steps to retrieve rows based on a condition using the WHERE clause are as follows:

1. In the SQL Worksheet, execute the following statement:

   ```
   SELECT * FROM Customers
   WHERE Segment = 'Corporate';
   ```

   NOTE: When using the `WHERE` condition, string comparisons are case-sensitive.
   `WHERE Segment = 'Corporate'` — is correct
   `WHERE Segment = 'corporate'` — is incorrect
   Always match the case exactly as it appears in the table data. For example, in the Customers table, the segment Corporate is stored with an uppercase **C**, so using all lowercase will not return any rows.

2. To execute the statement, use the appropriate option based on the environment in use:

   a. In FreeSQL, highlight the statement and click the **Run** button on the toolbar or press *Ctrl* + *Enter* to execute.

   b. In SQL Developer, press *Ctrl* + *Enter* or click the **Run Statement** (green arrow) icon on the toolbar.

The output of the query is shown in Figure 3.6:

CUSTOMERID	CUSTOMERNAME	REGION	SEGMENT
C005	Kimberly Robinson	Pennsylvania	Corporate
C016	Lisa Jackson	Washington	Corporate
C031	Troy Liu	Kentucky	Corporate
C033	Elizabeth Fowler	Rhode Island	Corporate
C035	Tamara George	New York	Corporate
C039	Beth Keller	Oklahoma	Corporate
C040	Joseph Obrien	Indiana	Corporate
C041	Nicole Vaughn	Virginia	Corporate
C044	Kevin Hall	Iowa	Corporate
C047	John Ryan	Washington	Corporate
C049	Cheryl Davis	Nevada	Corporate
C050	Jason Shields	Arkansas	Corporate

Figure 3.6*: Rows returned only for Segment Corporate*

TIP*: Break SQL conditions into smaller steps to improve clarity and debugging:*

1. *Start with the base query:*

   ```
   SELECT * from Customers;
   ```

   This displays all rows and columns from the `Customers` *table. It also helps confirm how values (for example,* `'Corporate'`*) are stored in the data.*

2. *Add the condition to the query:*

   ```
   SELECT * FROM Customers WHERE Segment = 'Corporate';
   ```

This narrows the result to only those records where the segment is `'Corporate'`*.*

Exercise 6: Using the WHERE Clause (Another Example)

Using the `SalesPersons` table, retrieve the `SalesPersonName`, `Location`, and `BranchID` columns for those assigned to branch `'B05'`. Also, rename `SalesPersonName` to `Emp Name` in the output.

The steps to retrieve salesperson details based on a condition are as follows:

1. In the SQL Worksheet, execute the following statement:

```
SELECT SalesPersonName AS "Emp Name", Location, BranchID
FROM SalesPersons
WHERE BranchID = 'B05';
```

TIP: *If unsure about the column names in a table, run the* `DESC` *command on that table or execute a* `Select *` *query to view its structure.*

2. To execute the statement, use the appropriate option based on the environment in use:
   a. In FreeSQL, highlight the statement and click the **Run** button on the toolbar or press *Ctrl* + *Enter* to execute.
   b. In SQL Developer, press *Ctrl* + *Enter* or click the **Run Statement** (green arrow) on the toolbar.

The output of the query is shown in Figure 3.7:

Emp Name	LOCATION	BRANCHID
Paul Carrillo	Port Ronaldburgh	B05
Jesse Rogers	Ramirezchester	B05
Kylie Williams	Stanleyland	B05
David Martinez	West David	B05

Figure 3.7: *Salespersons working in Branch B05*

The query retrieves the salespersons working in branch `'B05'`, along with their locations and branch IDs.

The ORDER BY Clause

The `ORDER BY` clause sorts the query results based on one or more columns. This makes it easier to read and understand the output by organizing the data in a specific order. By default, the sorting is done in ascending order *(A–Z, 1–9)*, but it can be explicitly set to descending *(Z–A, 9–1)*.

Sorting can be done in the following ways:

- **Ascending order** (A to Z, 1 to 9) – this is the default behavior.
- **Descending order** (Z to A, 9 to 1)

Without the `ORDER BY` clause, SQL may return results in no particular order, often reflecting the sequence in which the data was inserted into the table.

Syntax

```
SELECT column1, column2
FROM table_name
ORDER BY <expression>;
```

If the query contains a `WHERE` clause, it will come before `ORDER BY`.

Exercise 7: Using the ORDER BY Clause

Using the `Category` table, retrieve the `Category` and `SubCategory` columns, sorted alphabetically by `SubCategory`.

The steps to retrieve the category details sorted alphabetically by `SubCategory` are as follows:

1. First, run the SQL to retrieve `Category` and `SubCategory` columns.
   In the SQL Worksheet, execute the following statement:

   ```
   SELECT Category, SubCategory
   FROM Category;
   ```

   This query return rows in no particular order.
2. Now, execute the query with the `Order By` clause:

```
SELECT Category, SubCategory
FROM Category
ORDER BY SubCategory;
```

The query returns rows in the default ascending order, as shown in Figure 3.8:

CATEGORY	SUBCATEGORY
Technology	Accessories
Office Supplies	Binders
Furniture	Bookcases
Furniture	Chairs
Technology	Computers
Office Supplies	Paper
Technology	Phones
Office Supplies	Storage
Furniture	Tables
Technology	-

***Figure 3.8**: Columns sorted in ascending order*

3. To display the columns in descending order, specify the sort direction explicitly. Type the following statement to sort the results in descending order:

```
SELECT Category, Subcategory
FROM Category
ORDER BY SubCategory DESC;
```

This query returns the results in descending order of `SubCategory`.

***TIP**: Use `ASC` or `DESC` after any column name in the `ORDER BY` clause to control the sorting order.*

Exercise 8: Using WHERE and ORDER BY in a SELECT Statement

Using the `Category` table, retrieve the `Category` and `SubCategory` columns where the `Category` value is `'Office Supplies'`. Sort the results alphabetically by `SubCategory`.

Execute the following statement to use the `WHERE` and `ORDER BY` clauses in a `SELECT` statement:

```
SELECT Category, Subcategory
FROM Category
WHERE Category = 'Office Supplies'
ORDER BY SubCategory;
```

The output of the query is shown in Figure 3.9:

CATEGORY	SUBCATEGORY
Office Supplies	Binders
Office Supplies	Paper
Office Supplies	Storage

***Figure 3.9**: Output using WHERE and ORDER BY*

The `ORDER BY` clause helps organize query results in a logical sequence, either ascending (default) or descending. It is useful when presenting sorted reports or improving the readability of large datasets.

The Distinct Clause

The `DISTINCT` clause is used to return only unique values in the result set. When a column contains duplicate entries, `DISTINCT` ensures that each value appears only once in the output.

Syntax

```
SELECT DISTINCT column-name
FROM table_name;
```

Exercise 9: Using the DISTINCT Clause

Using the `Customers` table, apply the `DISTINCT` clause to list all unique `Segment` values.

Execute the following statement to use the DISTINCT clause to list unique segments:

```
SELECT DISTINCT Segment
FROM Customers;
```

The output of the query is shown in Figure 3.10:

SEGMENT
Home Office
Consumer
Corporate

***Figure 3.10**: Distinct segments in the Customers table*

The DISTINCT clause is useful when summarizing or exploring data to understand the range of unique entries in a column.

Conclusion

This chapter introduced the foundational concepts required for working with Oracle SQL. It began with an overview of Oracle data types, explaining how different kinds of data are stored and managed within relational tables.

The chapter then covered techniques for retrieving and organizing data using the SELECT statement, applying filters with the WHERE clause, sorting results using ORDER BY, and removing duplicate records with the DISTINCT clause.

Together, these concepts form the core of SQL querying and establish a strong foundation for effective data retrieval.

With these fundamentals in place, the next chapter, **Working with Conditions and Operators**, builds on this knowledge by demonstrating how to create more precise and flexible queries using logical and comparison operators.

Practice Questions

Use the training dataset to complete the following practice questions. These exercises reinforce concepts covered in this chapter.

1. Using the `Orders` table, retrieve all orders placed by customer `'C008'`.
2. Display all unique ship modes used in the `Orders` table.
3. Find orders shipped from branch `'B03'`.
4. List customer names and regions for customers in the Segment '`Consumer`'.
5. Show the distinct combinations of `Category` and `SubCategory` from the `Category` table.

Practice Answers

The answers to the preceding questions are as follows:

Answer 1

```
SELECT *
FROM Orders
WHERE CustomerID = 'C008';
```

Answer 2

```
SELECT DISTINCT ShipMode
FROM Orders;
```

Answer 3

```
SELECT *
FROM Orders
WHERE BranchID = 'B03';
```

Answer 4

```
SELECT CustomerName, Region
FROM Customers
WHERE Segment = 'Consumer';
```

Answer 5

```
SELECT DISTINCT Category, SubCategory
FROM Category;
```

Chapter 4
Working with Conditions and Operators

Introduction

Building on the concepts introduced in the previous chapter, this chapter explores how **conditions** and **operators** make SQL queries more precise and meaningful.

Instead of retrieving all records from a table, these tools allow filtering data to extract only the rows that meet specific criteria—such as customers from a certain region, orders placed after a given date, or products within a defined price range.

By mastering these techniques, queries become more accurate, targeted, and efficient, making it easier to analyze large datasets by focusing on relevant information.

This chapter will cover the following topics:

- Using Comparison Operators
- Using Logical Operators
- Perform Pattern Matching
- Handling NULL Values
- Filtering Data Using Lists and Ranges

Using Comparison Operators

Comparison operators are used in SQL to filter rows based on specific criteria. They include symbols such as `=`, `!=`, `<>`, `<`, `>`, `<=`, and `>=`, and are typically used in the `WHERE` clause of a query. These operators allow the database to compare column values to a given value and return only the rows that meet the condition.

The following table summarizes the most commonly used comparison operators in Oracle SQL:

Table 4.1: *SQL comparison operators*

Operator	**Description**	**Example**	**Result**
=	Equal to	`WHERE Region = 'Ohio'`	Returns rows where `Region` is exactly `Ohio`
!= or <>	Not equal to	`WHERE Category <> 'Furniture'`	Returns rows where `Category` is anything except `Furniture`
<	Less than	`WHERE Sales < 10`	Returns rows where `Sales` is less than `10`
>	Greater than	`WHERE Sales > 130`	Returns rows where Sales is more than `130`
<=	Less than or equal to	`WHERE Sales <= 10.89`	Returns rows where Sales is less than or exactly equal to `10.89`
>=	Greater than or equal to	`WHERE Sales >= 10.89`	Returns rows where Sales is greater than or exactly equal to `10.89`

Exercise 1: Using the Equal (=) Operator

Using the `Customers` table, retrieve all customers from the `'Ohio'` region.

The steps to use the Equal operator (=) are as follows:

1. In the SQL Worksheet, execute the following statement:

```
SELECT CustomerID, CustomerName, Region
FROM Customers
WHERE Region = 'Ohio';
```

2. To execute the statement, use the appropriate option based on the environment in use:
   c. In FreeSQL, click the **Run** button on the toolbar or press *Ctrl* + *Enter* to execute.
   d. In SQL Developer, press *Ctrl* + *Enter* or click the **Run Statement** (green arrow) icon on the toolbar.

The output of the query is shown in Figure 4.1:

CUSTOMERID	CUSTOMERNAME	REGION
C002	Brian Yang	Ohio
C009	Renee Blair	Ohio

***Figure 4.1**: Customers in the Ohio Region*

Query Explanation

- `SELECT`: Retrieves three columns—`CustomerID`, `CustomerName`, and `Region`.
- `FROM`: Specifies the `Customers` table to query.
- `WHERE`: Filters the results to only include customers from the `'Ohio'` region.

This example demonstrates how the `WHERE` clause filters data based on specific criteria, such as customers from the *Ohio* region.

Exercise 2: Using the Not Equal (<>) Operator

Using the `Category` table, retrieve all `Category` and `SubCategory` values where the `Category` is not equal to `'Furniture'`.

The steps to use the Not Equal (<>) operator are as follows:

1. In the SQL Worksheet, execute the following statement:

```
SELECT Category, SubCategory
FROM Category
WHERE Category <> 'Furniture';
```

2. To execute the statement, use the appropriate option based on the environment in use:

   a. In FreeSQL, click the **Run** button on the toolbar or press *Ctrl* + *Enter*.

   b. In Oracle SQL Developer, press *Ctrl* + *Enter* or click the **Run Statement** (green arrow) icon on the toolbar.

   The output of the query is shown in Figure 4.2:

CATEGORY	SUBCATEGORY
Technology	Phones
Technology	Computers
Technology	Accessories
Office Supplies	Binders
Office Supplies	Paper
Office Supplies	Storage
Technology	-

***Figure 4.2**: Category and SubCategory excluding Furniture*

Query Explanation

- `SELECT`: Selects the `Category` and `SubCategory` columns.
- `FROM`: Specifies the table category from which the columns are selected.
- `WHERE`: Specifies the <> condition to exclude the records where the `Category` value is `'Furniture'`.

This example demonstrates how the <> operator filters out specific values, helping retrieve all records that do not match the given condition.

Exercise 3: Using the Less Than (<) Operator

Using the `OrderDetails` table, retrieve the `OrderID`, `ProductID`, and `Sales` columns where `Sales` is less than `30`.

In the SQL Worksheet, execute the following statement to use the Less Than (<) operator:

```
SELECT OrderID, ProductID, Sales
FROM OrderDetails
WHERE Sales < 30;
```

The output of the query is shown in Figure 4.3:

ORDERID	PRODUCTID	SALES
O1007	P0004	25.62
O1024	P0013	14.33
O1010	P0026	23.69
O1014	P0030	28.02
O1021	P0017	28.65
O1022	P0031	7.17
O1023	P0003	23.88
O1024	P0046	11.63

***Figure 4.3**: Output where Sales is less than 30*

Query Explanation

- **`SELECT`**: Retrieves `OrderID`, `ProductID`, and `Sales` columns.
- **`FROM`**: Specifies the `OrderDetails` table from where the columns are selected.
- **`WHERE`**: Filters records that match the criteria of `Sales < 30`.

The < operator is useful for comparing numeric values. The next exercise explores how to use the > operator to retrieve records greater than a specified amount.

Exercise 4: Using the Greater Than (>) Operator

Using the `OrderDetails` table, retrieve the `OrderID`, `ProductID`, and `Sales` columns where `Sales` is greater than `240`.

In the SQL Worksheet, execute the following statement to use the Greater Than (>) operator:

```
SELECT OrderID, ProductID, Sales
FROM OrderDetails
WHERE Sales > 240;
```

The output of the query is shown in Figure 4.4:

ORDERID	PRODUCTID	SALES
01007	P0049	267.08
01033	P0024	278.16
01009	P0024	242.12
01015	P0036	321.62
01026	P0029	245.94

Figure 4.4*: Output where Sales is greater than 240*

Query Explanation

- `SELECT`: Retrieves the required columns.
- `FROM`: Specifies the `OrderDetails` table from which the columns are selected.
- `WHERE`: Filters records that match the criteria of `Sales > 240`.

This query displays all order details where the sales amount is greater than 240. In the next exercise, the less than or equal to (<=) operator is used to include both lower and equal values in the results.

Exercise 5: Using the Less Than or Equal To (<=) Operator

Using the `OrderDetails` table, retrieve the `OrderID`, `ProductID`, and `Sales` columns where `Sales` is less than or equal to `30`.

In the SQL Worksheet, execute the following statement to use the Less Than or Equal To (<=) operator:

```
SELECT OrderID, ProductID, Sales
FROM OrderDetails
WHERE Sales <= 30;
```

The output of the query is shown in Figure 4.5:

ORDERID	PRODUCTID	SALES
O1007	P0004	25.62
O1024	P0013	14.33
O1010	P0026	23.69
O1014	P0030	28.02
O1021	P0017	28.65
O1022	P0031	7.17
O1023	P0003	23.88
O1024	P0046	11.63

Figure 4.5*: Output after using the less than or equal to condition*

Reader Exercise*: The greater than or equal to (>=) operator works in the same way as the less than or equal to (<=) operator explained above. Try using the >= operator to retrieve records where the* `Sales` *value is greater than or equal to a specified amount.*

Comparison operators in SQL are used to filter data based on specific conditions. Operators such as =, !=, <, >, <=, and >= help return rows that match particular values or fall within defined ranges.

Using Logical Operators

Logical operators are used to combine multiple conditions within a SQL query, allowing for more precise and flexible data filtering. They provide greater control over which rows are included or excluded based on one or more criteria.

The three primary logical operators in SQL are `AND`, `OR`, and `NOT`, described as follows:

- `AND` returns rows where *all* specified conditions are true.
- `OR` returns rows where *at least one* condition is true.
- `NOT` reverses a condition, returning rows that do *not* meet the specified criteria.

The following table summarizes the commonly used logical operators along with examples and their expected outcomes.

***Table 4.2**: Logical Operators in SQL*

Operator	**Description**	**Example**	**Result**
`AND`	Returns rows where both conditions are true	`WHERE Region = 'Ohio' AND Segment = 'Consumer'`	Returns records where `Region` is `Ohio` and `Segment` is `Consumer`
`OR`	Returns rows where at least one condition is true	`WHERE Category = 'Furniture' OR Subcategory = 'Phones'`	Returns records where either the `Category` is `Furniture` or the `Subcategory` is `Phones`
`NOT`	Reverses a condition, returning rows that do not match the specified condition	`WHERE NOT Category = 'Furniture'`	Returns all records where `Category` is not `Furniture`

AND Operator

The `AND` operator allows you to combine two or more conditions in a `WHERE` clause. A record is returned only when *all* conditions evaluate to true.

Exercise 6: Using the AND Operator

Using the `Customers` table, retrieve the `CustomerID`, `CustomerName`, `Region`, and `Segment` columns for customers from the `'Ohio'` region who belong to the `'Consumer'` segment.

In the SQL Worksheet, execute the following statement to use the `AND` operator:

```
SELECT CustomerID, CustomerName, Region, Segment
FROM Customers
WHERE Region = 'Ohio' AND Segment = 'Consumer';
```

The output of the query is shown in Figure 4.6:

CUSTOMERID	CUSTOMERNAME	REGION	SEGMENT
C002	Brian Yang	Ohio	Consumer

***Figure 4.6**: Output after using the AND operator*

This query returns customers meeting both conditions specified in the `WHERE` clause.

The next exercise demonstrates how the `OR` operator can be used to retrieve records that satisfy either of the specified conditions.

OR Operator

The `OR` operator is used to combine multiple conditions in a `WHERE` clause. A row is returned when any one of the specified conditions is true.

Exercise 7: Using the OR Operator

Using the `Category` table, retrieve the `Category` and `Subcategory` columns where the `Category` is `'Furniture'` or the `SubCategory` is `'Phones'`.

In the SQL Worksheet, execute the following statement to use the `OR` operator:

```
SELECT Category, SubCategory
FROM Category
WHERE Category = 'Furniture' or Subcategory = 'Phones';
```

The output of the query is shown in Figure 4.7:

CATEGORY	SUBCATEGORY
Furniture	Chairs
Furniture	Tables
Furniture	Bookcases
Technology	Phones

***Figure 4.7**: Output after using the OR operator*

This query retrieves the rows that satisfy either of the specified conditions, returning categories related to `Furniture` or `Phones`. The next exercise introduces the `NOT` operator, which is used to exclude records that match a specific condition.

NOT Operator

The `NOT` operator is used to negate a condition in a `WHERE` clause. It returns rows that do not meet the specified condition.

Exercise 8: Using the NOT Operator

Using the `Category` table, retrieve the `Category` and `Subcategory` columns where the `Category` is not `'Furniture'`.

In the SQL Worksheet, execute the following statement to use the NOT operator:

```
SELECT Category, SubCategory
FROM Category
WHERE NOT Category = 'Furniture';
```

The output of the query is shown in Figure 4.8:

CATEGORY	SUBCATEGORY
Technology	Phones
Technology	Computers
Technology	Accessories
Office Supplies	Binders
Office Supplies	Paper
Office Supplies	Storage
Technology	-

***Figure 4.8**: Output after using the NOT operator*

In the output, all the categories except `'Furniture'` are displayed. The `NOT` operator excludes rows that match the specified condition.

Logical operators—`AND`, `OR`, and `NOT`—provide flexibility in filtering data by combining or reversing conditions. They refine query results by determining how multiple conditions are evaluated.

`AND` returns rows that meet all specified conditions, `OR` returns rows that meet any of the conditions, and `NOT` excludes rows that meet the specified condition. Together, these operators are essential for creating complex and precise data filters in SQL.

Perform Pattern Matching

The `LIKE` operator is used in SQL to search for patterns in text data instead of matching exact values. It is useful when only part of a value is known — such as a starting letter, ending word, or a sequence of characters within a string. Common examples include finding names that begin with `'A'` or cities that contain the word `'York'`.

The `LIKE` operator works with the following two special wildcard characters:

- `%` (percent sign): It matches any number of characters, including none.
- `_` (underscore): It matches exactly one character.

By combining `LIKE` with these wildcards, SQL queries can handle a wide range of pattern-matching scenarios in a simple and efficient way.

Syntax

```
SELECT column1, column2, ...
FROM table_name
WHERE column LIKE 'pattern';
```

Exercise 9: Using the LIKE Operator

Using the `Customers` table, retrieve the `CustomerID` and `CustomerName` columns where the names start with the letter `'A'`.

Execute the following statement to use the `LIKE` operator with the wildcard character (%):

```
SELECT CustomerID, CustomerName
FROM Customers
WHERE CustomerName LIKE 'A%';
```

The output of the query is shown in Figure 4.9:

CUSTOMERID	CUSTOMERNAME
C001	Allison Hill
C020	Austin Gentry
C025	Ann Williams

***Figure 4.9**: Customers with names starting with the letter A*

The query retrieves all customers whose name can be of any length but starts with the letter `'A'`.

Exercise 10: Using the LIKE Operator – Finding Names Ending with Specific Characters

Using the `Customers` table, retrieve the `CustomerID` and `CustomerName` columns where the names end with `'son'`.

Execute the following statement to use the `LIKE` operator with `%` to find names ending with specific characters:

```
SELECT CustomerID, CustomerName
FROM Customers
WHERE CustomerName LIKE '%son';
```

The output of the query is shown in Figure 4.10:

CUSTOMERID	CUSTOMERNAME
C003	Javier Johnson
C005	Kimberly Robinson
C016	Lisa Jackson
C017	Joel Nelson
C019	Crystal Johnson

***Figure 4.10**: Customers with names ending with 'son'*

The query retrieves all customers whose name can be of any length but ends with the letters `'son'`.

Exercise 11: Using the LIKE Operator with the Underscore (_) Wildcard

Using the `Customers` table, retrieve the `CustomerName` and `Region` columns where the `Region` is exactly four characters long.

Execute the following statement to use the `LIKE` operator with the underscore wildcard:

```
SELECT CustomerName, Region
FROM Customers
WHERE Region LIKE '____';
```

The query uses four underscores (_)in the `LIKE` condition to represent exactly four characters.

The output of the query is shown in Figure 4.11:

CUSTOMERNAME	REGION
Allison Hill	Iowa
Brian Yang	Ohio
Renee Blair	Ohio
Daniel Adams	Utah
Juan Dunlap	Utah
Kevin Hall	Iowa

***Figure 4.11**: Output where the Region is exactly four characters long*

The query retrieves all customers where the region is exactly four characters long.

NOTE: The **LIKE** operator can also combine both wildcards in a single condition.
For example:

```
SELECT * from Customers WHERE CustomerName LIKE '_a%';
```

This condition retrieves all customers whose names have **'a'** as the **second character**, followed by any number of additional characters.

The `LIKE` operator enables pattern-based searching in SQL, allowing flexible filtering when only part of a text value is known. By using `%` for multiple characters and _ for a single character, SQL makes it easy to perform text-based queries for names, keywords, and partial matches.

Handling NULL Values

In SQL, `NULL` represents a value that is missing, unknown, or not applicable. It is different from a zero (`0`), which is an actual numeric value. In Oracle SQL, empty strings (`''`) are also treated as `NULL`.

Because `NULL` means the value is "unknown" or "not present", regular comparison operators like `=` or `!=` do not work as expected.

Use the following conditions to check for the `NULL` values:

- `IS NULL`: Returns the rows where the column contains no value.
- `IS NOT NULL`: Returns the rows where the column has any value (excluding `NULL`, including `0`).

These conditions are useful for identifying incomplete records, cleaning data, or filtering out missing values from query results.

Syntax

```
SELECT column1, column2, ...
FROM table_name
WHERE column IS NULL;
```

```
SELECT column1, column2, ...
FROM table_name
WHERE column IS NOT NULL;
```

Exercise 12: Using IS NULL

Using the `Category` table, retrieve the `Category` and `SubCategory` columns where the `SubCategory` value is `NULL`.

Execute the following statement to use `IS NULL` to find rows with `NULL` values:

```
SELECT Category, SubCategory
FROM Category
WHERE SubCategory IS NULL;
```

The output of the query is shown in Figure 4.12:

CATEGORY	SUBCATEGORY
Technology	-

***Figure 4.12**: Category where SubCategory is NULL*

The query returns one record from the `Category` table where `SubCategory` has a `NULL` value.

Exercise 13: Using IS NOT NULL

Using the `Category` table, retrieve the `Category` and `SubCategory` columns where `SubCategory` values are present (that is, `IS NOT NULL`).

Execute the following statement to use `IS NOT NULL` to find rows with non-null values:

1. In the SQL Worksheet, execute the following statement:

```
SELECT Category, SubCategory
FROM Category
WHERE SubCategory IS NOT NULL;
```

   The output of the query is shown in Figure 4.13:

CATEGORY	SUBCATEGORY
Furniture	Chairs
Furniture	Tables
Furniture	Bookcases
Technology	Phones
Technology	Computers
Technology	Accessories
Office Supplies	Binders
Office Supplies	Paper
Office Supplies	Storage

***Figure 4.13**: Category where SubCategory is Not NULL*

The output excludes the `'Technology'` category, which has a `NULL` value in the `SubCategory` column.

In SQL, missing or unknown values are represented by `NULL`, which indicates the absence of a value—different from zero or an empty string. Standard comparison operators such as = and <> cannot be used with NULL values. Instead, the conditions `IS NULL` and `IS NOT NULL` are used to check whether a value is missing. These conditions are commonly used to identify the missing data and exclude blank values from query results.

Filtering Data Using Lists and Ranges

In SQL, operators such as `IN`, `NOT IN`, and `BETWEEN` are used to filter data based on lists of values or ranges. These operators reduce the need to write multiple comparison conditions and make queries easier to read and maintain. They are commonly used when checking whether a column value matches one of several possible values or falls within a specified range.

The following table summarizes how each of these operators works, along with examples that demonstrate their usage:

***Table 4.3**: Using IN, NOT IN, and BETWEEN*

Operator	**Description**	**Example**	**Result**
`IN`	Checks if a value matches any value in a given list	`WHERE Region IN ('Florida', 'Hawaii, Indiana')`	Returns rows where `Region` is either `'Florida'` or `'Hawaii'` or `'Indiana'`
`NOT IN`	Checks if a value does **not** match any value in a given list	`WHERE BranchID NOT IN ('B01', 'B03')`	Returns rows where `BranchID` is not `'B01'` or `'B03'`
`BETWEEN`	Checks if a value falls within a specified range (inclusive)	`WHERE Sales BETWEEN 125 AND 150`	Returns rows where `Sales` is greater than or equal to `125` and less than or equal to `150`

IN Operator

The `IN` operator is used to check whether a value matches any value in a given list. It simplifies multiple `OR` conditions in a `WHERE` clause.

Exercise 14: Using the IN Operator

Using the `Customers` table, retrieve the `CustomerID`, `CustomerName`, and `Region` columns for customers residing in the regions `'Florida'`, `'Indiana'`, or `'Hawaii'`.

Execute the following statement to use the IN operator:

```
SELECT CustomerID, CustomerName, Region
FROM Customers
WHERE Region IN ('Florida', 'Hawaii', 'Indiana');
```

The output of the query is shown in Figure 4.14:

CUSTOMERID	CUSTOMERNAME	REGION
C003	Javier Johnson	Indiana
C006	Sean Blake	Hawaii
C014	Jesse Flowers	Hawaii
C022	Maria Thomas	Florida
C024	Kevin Cox	Florida
C030	Gina Carter	Hawaii
C040	Joseph Obrien	Indiana

Figure 4.14*: Output after using the IN operator*

The query returns customer details for only the specified regions using the `IN` operator.

NOT IN Operator

The `NOT IN` operator is used to exclude rows that match any value in a specified list. It returns all rows except those containing the listed values.

Exercise 15: Using the NOT IN Operator

Using the `Branches` table, retrieve all rows except those with the `BranchID` values `'B01'` and `'B03'`.

In the SQL Worksheet, execute the following statement:

```
SELECT *
FROM Branches
WHERE BranchID NOT IN ('B01','B03');
```

The output of the query is shown in Figure 4.15:

BRANCHID	BRANCHNAME	CITY
B02	Branch 2	Los Angeles
B04	Branch 4	Houston
B05	Branch 5	Phoenix

***Figure 4.15**: Output after using the NOT IN operator*

The query returns all branch details while excluding rows with the `BranchID` values `'B01'` and `'B03'`.

BETWEEN Operator

The `BETWEEN` operator is used to filter rows based on a range of values. It returns records where the column value is greater than or equal to the lower limit and less than or equal to the upper limit.

Exercise 16: Using the BETWEEN Operator

Using the `OrderDetails` table, retrieve the `OrderID` and `Sales` columns where the `Sales` values are between `150` and `200`. Sort the results in ascending order by `Sales`.

Execute the following statement in the SQL Worksheet to use the `BETWEEN` operator:

```
SELECT OrderID, Sales
FROM OrderDetails
WHERE Sales between 150 and 200
ORDER BY Sales;
```

The output of the query is shown in Figure 4.16:

ORDERID	SALES
01002	150.13
01004	161.27
01008	161.5
01007	163.18
01024	175.07
01010	181.3
01025	191.16

***Figure 4.16**: Output after using the BETWEEN operator*

The query returns order details where the `Sales` values fall between `150` and `200`, inclusive of both limits.

SQL operators like `IN`, `NOT IN`, and `BETWEEN` simplify data filtering by allowing comparisons against lists or a range of values. The `IN` operator matches values within a list, `NOT IN` excludes those values, and `BETWEEN` retrieves values that fall within a defined range. These operators are commonly used to simplify conditions when working with large datasets.

Conclusion

This chapter covered essential techniques for filtering data in SQL. It introduced comparison operators to evaluate conditions, logical operators to combine multiple criteria, and pattern matching to search within text values.

The chapter also explained how to handle missing data using NULL checks and demonstrated the use of list and range-based filtering with IN, NOT IN, and BETWEEN. Together, these features allow queries to return only the data that meets specific requirements.

The next chapter, **Functions and Expressions**, introduces built-in functions and shows how they can be used to calculate values and transform query results.

Practice Questions

Use the training dataset to complete the following practice questions. These exercises reinforce concepts covered in this chapter.

1. Using the `Orders` table, retrieve the `OrderID`, `CustomerID`, and `ShipMode` columns where `ShipMode` is `'Express'`.
2. Using the `Products` table, retrieve the `ProductName`, `CategoryID`, and `UnitPrice` columns where `CategoryID` is equal to `8`, and `UnitPrice` is greater than `19`. Sort the results by `UnitPrice`.
3. Using the `Customers` table, retrieve the `CustomerID` and `CustomerName` columns where the `CustomerName` starts with `'A'` and contains the letter `'n'`.
4. Using the `SalesPersons` table, retrieve the `SalesPersonName`, `Position`, and `BranchID` columns where there are no `BranchID` values (i.e., `NULL`).
5. Using the `OrderDetails` table, retrieve `OrderID`, `ProductID`, and `Sales` columns where `ProductID` ends with a number `'7'` and `Sales` is between `80` and `130`. Sort the results first by `OrderID` and then by `Sales`.

Practice Answers

The answers to the preceding questions are as follows:

Answer 1

```
SELECT OrderID, CustomerID, ShipMode
FROM Orders
WHERE ShipMode = 'Express';
```

Answer 2

```
SELECT ProductName, CategoryID, UnitPrice
FROM Products
WHERE CategoryID = '8' AND UnitPrice > 19
ORDER BY 3;
```

NOTE: In the preceding query, `ORDER BY 3` is used to sort the results by the third column in the `SELECT` list, which is `UnitPrice`. Instead of specifying the column name directly, SQL allows using the column's position number in the `SELECT` clause.

Answer 3

```
SELECT CustomerID, CustomerName
FROM Customers
WHERE CustomerName LIKE 'A%n%';
```

Answer 4

```
SELECT SalesPersonName, Position, BranchID
FROM SalesPersons
WHERE BranchID IS NULL;
```

Answer 5

```
SELECT OrderID, ProductID, Sales
FROM OrderDetails
WHERE ProductID like '%7'
AND Sales BETWEEN 80 AND 130
ORDER BY 1,3;
```

Chapter 5
Functions and Expressions

Introduction

In SQL, functions and expressions are used to modify and analyze data directly within a query. Instead of simply displaying raw data, functions enable transformations such as converting text to uppercase, rounding numbers, formatting dates, or handling missing values.

SQL provides built-in functions for different purposes — text functions for working with strings, numeric functions for performing calculations, date functions for managing and formatting dates, and conditional functions for applying logical operations. Together, these features make SQL a powerful tool for transforming and presenting data effectively.

This chapter will cover the following topics:

- Functions in SQL
- Applying Text Functions
- Applying Number Functions
- Working with Dates in Oracle
- Writing Conditional Expressions

Functions in SQL

In SQL, functions are built-in operations that perform a specific task and return a single value. These tasks may include performing calculations, transforming data, aggregating rows, or manipulating strings and dates.

Functions can be used within a `SELECT` statement as well as in clauses such as `WHERE`, `GROUP BY`, `ORDER BY`, and even in `HAVING`.

Purpose of Functions

SQL functions are commonly used to:

- Simplify repetitive logic (for example, rounding numbers or converting text to uppercase).
- Aggregate values (for example, total sales or average order value).
- Transform data for reporting (for example, formatting a date or extracting part of a string).
- Improve query readability and efficiency.

Types of SQL Functions

SQL functions generally fall into two main categories:

- **Scalar Functions**:

  These functions operate on a single value and return a single value. They can be used wherever an expression is permitted in SQL. Examples include:

  - `UPPER('hello') returns 'HELLO'`
  - `ROUND(123.456, 2) returns 123.46`
  - `LENGTH('Skyline Cafe') returns 12`
- **Aggregate Functions**:

  These functions operate on a set of rows and return a single summary value. They are commonly used with the `GROUP BY` clause. Examples include:

  - `SUM(Sales)` returns total sales
  - `AVG(Profit)` returns average score
  - `COUNT(*)` returns count of rows

Syntax of Functions

Functions are written by specifying the function name followed by parentheses ( ). The values or expressions on which the function operates are placed within the parentheses. Function names are not case sensitive.

Syntax

```
SELECT Function_name(<value>)
FROM table_name;
```

Using the DUAL Table for Function Examples

In Oracle, the `DUAL` table is commonly used when a query needs to evaluate expressions or execute functions without retrieving data from an application table. The `DUAL` table is a built-in Oracle table that contains exactly **one row** and **one column**. It is primarily used to test expressions, call functions, and return calculated or constant values.

The `DUAL` table is used to:

- Test or demonstrate SQL functions such as `UPPER`, `ROUND`, or `SYSDATE`
- Return a constant or calculated values
- Perform quick checks or validation of expressions

NOTE: When the required data is not available in the `BDS_Training_Data` schema, the `DUAL` table is used to demonstrate function syntax and behavior.

Functions enhance the power of SQL by simplifying complex operations, enabling data transformation, summarization, and formatting within queries.

Applying Text Functions

Text (or string) functions in Oracle SQL are used to manipulate and analyze character data. These functions are commonly used when working with columns that store names, codes, or other text-based information. They support tasks such as text formatting, substring extraction, and evaluating text length.

The following table summarizes some of the most commonly used text functions in Oracle SQL, along with examples and their expected results:

***Table 5.1a**: Character Case and Length Functions*

Function	Description	Example	Result
`UPPER(text)`	Converts all characters to uppercase	`UPPER('oracle')`	ORACLE
`LOWER(text)`	Converts all characters to lowercase	`LOWER('ORACLE')`	oracle
`INITCAP(text)`	Converts the first letter of each word to uppercase	`INITCAP('oracle sql')`	Oracle Sql
`LENGTH(text)`	Returns the number of characters in a string	`LENGTH('Skyline')`	7
`INSTR(text, substring)`	Returns the position of a substring within a string	`INSTR('Skyline Cafe', 'Cafe')`	9

The next group of text functions focuses on extracting parts of strings, padding values, and replacing text segments.

***Table 5.1b**: Substring, Padding, and Replacement Functions*

Function	Description	Example	Result
`SUBSTR(text, start, len)`	Extracts a substring starting at a specified position for a given length	`SUBSTR('Skyline', 1, 3)`	Sky
`TRIM(text)`	Removes leading and trailing spaces	`TRIM(' Hello ')`	Hello
`LPAD(text, len, pad)`	Pads the left side of a string with a specified character until the desired length is reached	`LPAD('45', 5, '0')`	00045
`RPAD(text, len, pad)`	Pads the right side of a string with a specified character until the desired length is reached	`RPAD('45', 5, '0')`	45000

Function	Description	Example	Result
`REPLACE(text, old, new)`	Replaces part of a string with another string	`REPLACE('Branch A', 'Branch', 'Dept')`	Dept A
`CONCAT(str1, str2)`	Joins two strings together	`CONCAT('Sky', 'line')`	Skyline

These functions help present text in a consistent format, support data cleaning, and enable detailed string-based analysis within SQL queries.

UPPER() and LOWER() Functions

The `UPPER()` and `LOWER()` functions are text functions used to convert character data into uppercase and lowercase, respectively. These functions are commonly used to standardize text values and to perform case-insensitive comparisons in SQL queries.

Exercise 1: Using the UPPER() and LOWER() Functions

Using the `Orders` table, retrieve the unique `ShipMode` values and display them in both uppercase and lowercase.

Execute the following statement to use the `Upper()` and `Lower()` functions:

```
SELECT DISTINCT ShipMode, UPPER(ShipMode), LOWER(ShipMode)
FROM Orders;
```

The output of the query is shown in Figure 5.1:

SHIPMODE	UPPER(SHIPMODE)	LOWER(SHIPMODE)
Two-Day	TWO-DAY	two-day
Same-Day	SAME-DAY	same-day
Standard	STANDARD	standard
Priority	PRIORITY	priority
Express	EXPRESS	express

***Figure 5.1**: Output using the Upper() and Lower() functions*

Query Explanation

- `SELECT`: Retrieves the columns.
- `DISTINCT ShipMode`: Returns the unique list of `ShipMode` values.
- `UPPER(ShipMode)`: Converts the values in the `ShipMode` column to uppercase.
- `LOWER(ShipMode)`: Converts the values in the `ShipMode` column to lowercase.
- `FROM`: Specifies the `Orders` table from which the columns are selected.

LENGTH() Function

The `LENGTH()` function is used to return the number of characters in a text string. It is useful for analyzing or filtering data based on the length of values in a column.

Exercise 2: Using the LENGTH() Function

Using the `Branches` table, retrieve the `BranchID` values and display the length of each `BranchID`.

Execute the following statement to use the `LENGTH()` function:

```
SELECT BranchID, Length(BranchID)
FROM Branches;
```

The output of the query is shown in Figure 5.2:

BRANCHID	LENGTH(BRANCHID)
B01	3
B02	3
B03	3
B04	3
B05	3

***Figure 5.2**: Output using the Length() function*

The `LENGTH()` function can be used to validate data consistency. For example, if `BranchID` values are required to be three characters long, this function can quickly identify any records that do not meet this rule.

SUBSTR() Function

The `SUBSTR()` function is used to extract a portion of a text string, starting from a specified position and returning a defined number of characters. It is useful for analyzing or formatting specific segments of text values.

Exercise 3: Using the SUBSTR() Function

Using the `Orders` table, retrieve the unique `ShipMode` values and display the first five characters of each value.

Execute the following statement to use the `SUBSTR()` function:

```
SELECT DISTINCT ShipMode, SUBSTR(ShipMode,1,5)
FROM Orders;
```

The output of the query is shown in Figure 5.3:

SHIPMODE	SUBSTR(SHIPMODE,1,5)
Express	Expre
Standard	Stand
Same-Day	Same-
Priority	Prior
Two-Day	Two-D

Figure 5.3: *Output using the SUBSTR() function*

Query Explanation

- `SELECT`: Retrieves specific columns from a table.
- `DISTINCT ShipMode`: Returns a unique list of `ShipMode` values.
- `SUBSTR(ShipMode, 1, 5)`: Extracts a substring from the `ShipMode` value, starting at position `1` and returning the next `5` characters.
- `FROM`: Specifies the `Orders` table as the source of data.

INITCAP() Function

The `INITCAP()` function converts the first letter of each word in a string to uppercase and the remaining letters to lowercase. It is commonly used to format names, titles, or sentences in proper case.

Exercise 4: Using the INITCAP() Function

Use the `INITCAP()` function with the `DUAL` table to convert the sentence `'welcome to oracle tutorial'` so that the first letter of each word is capitalized.

Execute the following statement to use the `INITCAP()` function:

```
SELECT INITCAP('welcome to oracle tutorial') AS ProperCase
FROM DUAL;
```

The output of the query is shown in Figure 5.4:

PROPERCASE
Welcome To Oracle Tutorial

***Figure 5.4**: Output using the INITCAP() function*

Query Explanation

- `SELECT`: Retrieves the specific columns from a table.
- `INITCAP()`: Converts the first letter of each word in the specified text to uppercase.
- `FROM`: Specifies the `Dual` table as the source of data.

TRIM() Function

The `TRIM()` function is used to remove unwanted spaces or specified characters from the beginning and/or end of a string. It is commonly used to clean text data before processing or comparison.

Exercise 5: Using the TRIM() Function

Use the `TRIM()` function with the `DUAL` table to remove the leading and trailing spaces from the text `'  welcome '`.

Execute the following statement to use the `TRIM()` function:

```
SELECT TRIM(' welcome ') AS Trimmed
FROM DUAL;
```

The output of the query is shown in Figure 5.5:

TRIMMED
welcome

***Figure 5.5**: Output using the TRIM() function*

The `TRIM()` function removes the leading and trailing spaces around the word '`welcome`', ensuring the result is clean and properly formatted.

LPAD() and RPAD() Functions

The `LPAD()` and `RPAD()` functions are used to pad a string with specified characters to a defined length. The `LPAD()` function adds characters to the **left** of a string, while `RPAD()` adds characters to the **right**. These functions are often used to align data or create uniform string lengths in output.

Exercise 6: Using LPAD() and RPAD() Functions

Using the `Branches` table, apply the `LPAD()` and `RPAD()` functions within a single query to add two zeros to the left and right of each `BranchID`. Display the original `BranchID`, the left-padded version, and the right-padded version.

Execute the following statement to use `LPAD()` and `RPAD()` functions:

```
SELECT BranchID
      LPAD(BranchID,5,0) AS LeftPadded,
      RPAD(BranchID,5,0) AS RightPadded
FROM Branches;
```

The output of the query is shown in Figure 5.6:

BRANCHID	LEFTPADDED	RIGHTPADDED
B01	00B01	B0100
B02	00B02	B0200
B03	00B03	B0300
B04	00B04	B0400
B05	00B05	B0500

***Figure 5.6**: Output using the LPAD() and RPAD() functions*

Query Explanation

- `SELECT`: Retrieves the specific columns from a table.
- `LPAD(BranchID,5,'0')`: Pads the `BranchID` with zeros on the left side until the total length is 5 characters. For example, '`B01`' becomes '`00B01`'.
- `RPAD(BranchID,5,'0')`: Pads the `BranchID` with zeros on the right side until the total length is 5 characters. For example, `'B01'` becomes `'B0100'`.
- `FROM`: Specifies the `Branches` table as the source of data.

REPLACE() Function

The `REPLACE()` function is used to substitute all occurrences of a specified substring within a string with a new substring. It is used to update or clean text data by replacing unwanted words or characters.

Exercise 7: Using the REPLACE() Function

Using the `Branches` table, display the `BranchName` along with a new column `'New BranchName'` that replaces the word `'Branch'` with `'Dept'`.

Execute the following statement to use the `REPLACE()` function:

```
SELECT BranchName,
REPLACE(BranchName, 'Branch', 'Dept') AS "New BranchName"
FROM Branches;
```

The output of the query is shown in Figure 5.7:

BRANCHNAME	New BranchName
Branch 1	Dept 1
Branch 2	Dept 2
Branch 3	Dept 3
Branch 4	Dept 4
Branch 5	Dept 5

***Figure 5.7**: Output using the REPLACE() function*

Query Explanation

- `SELECT`: Retrieves the specified columns for output.
- **`BranchName`**: Displays the original name of each branch.
- **`REPLACE(BranchName, 'Branch', 'Dept')`**: Replaces every occurrence of the word `'Branch'` with `'Dept'`.
- **`AS "New BranchName"`**: Assigns a custom column alias **`New BranchName`** for readability in the output.
- **`FROM`**: Indicates that the data is being selected from the `Branches` table.

INSTR() Function

The `INSTR()` function is used to find the position of a specified substring within a string. It returns a numeric value indicating where the substring first occurs. If the substring is not found, the function returns `0`.

Exercise 8: Using the INSTR() Function

Using the `SalesPersons` table, write a query to display the distinct `Position` values and show the position of the letter `'M'` in each position title.

Execute the following statement to use the `INSTR()` function:

```
SELECT DISTINCT Position,
      INSTR (Position,'M') AS CharacterPosition
FROM SalesPersons;
```

The output of the query is shown in Figure 5.8:

POSITION	CHARACTERPOSITION
Senior Sales	0
Regional Manager	10
Store Manager	7
Sales Associate	0
Sales Executive	0
Director	0

Figure 5.8: *Output using the INSTR() function*

Query Explanation

- **`SELECT`**: Specifies the columns to retrieve in the result set.
- **`DISTINCT Position`**: Ensures that each position appears only once in the result set.
- **`INSTR(Position, 'M')`**: Searches for the letter `'M'` within each `Position` value and returns its first occurrence. If `'M'` is not found, it returns `0`.

- **AS CharacterPosition**: Assigns an alias to the result of the `INSTR()` function for readability.
- **FROM**: Indicates that the data is being retrieved from the `SalesPersons` table.

CONCAT() Function and || Operator

The `CONCAT()` function and the `||` (concatenation) operator are used to join two or more strings into a single string. The `CONCAT()` function can combine **two expressions** at a time, while the `||` operator can concatenate **multiple expressions** in a single statement.

Exercise 9: Using CONCAT() Function and || Operator

Using the `Branches` table, write a query to display the `BranchID`, `BranchName`, and two new columns combining them as `'B01Branch 1'` and `'B01-Branch1'`.

Execute the following statement to use the `CONCAT()` function and `||` Operator:

```
SELECT BranchID, BranchName,
      CONCAT(BranchID,BranchName) AS "Using Concat",
      BranchID||'-'||BranchName AS "Using ||"
FROM Branches;
```

The output of the query is shown in Figure 5.9:

BRANCHID	BRANCHNAME	Using Concat	Using ||
B01	Branch 1	B01Branch 1	B01-Branch 1
B02	Branch 2	B02Branch 2	B02-Branch 2
B03	Branch 3	B03Branch 3	B03-Branch 3
B04	Branch 4	B04Branch 4	B04-Branch 4
B05	Branch 5	B05Branch 5	B05-Branch 5

Figure 5.9*: Output using the CONCAT() function and the || operator*

Query Explanation

- `SELECT`: Specifies the columns to be displayed in the result set.
- `BranchID`: Retrieves the unique identifier of each branch.
- `BranchName`: Retrieves the name of each branch.
- `CONCAT(BranchID, BranchName) AS "Using Concat"`: Combines `BranchID` and `BranchName` into a single string without any separator. The result is labeled as `"Using Concat"` in the output.
- `BranchID || '-' || BranchName AS "Using ||"`: Uses the concatenation operator (`||`)to concatenate `BranchID` and `BranchName` with a hyphen (-) in between. The result is labeled as `"Using ||"`.
- `FROM`: Specifies that the data is being selected from the `Branches` table.

Text functions in SQL are powerful tools for cleaning, formatting, and manipulating string data. Whether converting text to uppercase, lowercase, or proper case; trimming spaces; replacing characters; or combining columns, these functions ensure that data is presented accurately and consistently in reports and queries.

Applying Number Functions

Oracle SQL provides a set of numeric functions designed to perform operations on numeric values. These functions handle tasks such as rounding numbers to specific decimal places, removing fractional parts, calculating remainders, and performing other mathematical operations. They are commonly used in financial calculations, data formatting, and analytical queries to ensure that numeric results are accurate and consistent.

The following table lists some of the most commonly used numeric functions in Oracle, along with a brief description, example, and expected result.

***Table 5.2**: Commonly Used Numeric Functions in Oracle*

Function	Description	Example	Result
`ABS(n)`	Returns the absolute (positive) value of `n`	`ABS(-10)`	`10`
`SIGN(n)`	Returns `-1, 0, or 1` based on sign of `n`	`SIGN(-15)`	`-1`
`CEIL(n)`	Returns the smallest integer ≥ `n`	`CEIL(3.14)`	`4`
`FLOOR(n)`	Returns the largest integer ≤ `n`	`FLOOR(3.9)`	`3`
`ROUND(n, d)`	Rounds `n` to `d` decimal places	`ROUND(123.456, 2)`	`123.46`
`TRUNC(n, d)`	Truncates `n` to `d` decimal places	`TRUNC(123.456, 2)`	`123.45`
`MOD(n, m)`	Returns the remainder when `n` is divided by `m`	`MOD(10, 3)`	`1`
`POWER(n, m)`	Returns `n` raised to the power of `m`	`POWER(2, 3)`	`8`
`SQRT(n)`	Returns the square root of `n`	`SQRT(25)`	`5`
`EXP(n)`	Returns `e` raised to the power of `n`	`EXP(1)`	`2.71828...`
`LN(n)`	Returns the natural logarithm of `n`	`LN(10)`	`2.30258...`
`LOG(b, n)` (Oracle 21c+)	Returns log of `n` base `b`	`LOG(10, 100)`	`2`

ABS() and SIGN() Functions

The `ABS()` function returns the absolute (positive) value of a number, while the `SIGN()` function returns `-1`, `0`, or `1` depending on whether the number is negative, zero, or positive. These functions are useful for mathematical and conditional calculations.

Exercise 10: Using ABS() and SIGN() Functions

Use the `DUAL` table to write a query that displays the absolute value and sign of `-10`.

Execute the following statement to use the `ABS` and `SIGN` function:

```
SELECT ABS(-10) AS AbsoluteValue,
SIGN(-10) AS SignValue
FROM Dual;
```

The output of the query is shown in Figure 5.10:

ABSOLUTEVALUE	SIGNVALUE
10	-1

***Figure 5.10**: Output using the ABS() and SIGN() functions*

Query Explanation

- **`SELECT`**: Specifies the values and expressions to be returned in the result.
- **`ABS(-10) AS AbsoluteValue`**: Uses the `ABS()` (absolute value) function to return the non-negative version of `-10`, which is `10`. The result is labeled as `AbsoluteValue`.
- **`SIGN(-10) AS SignValue`**: It returns the sign of `-10`:
  - `-1` if the number is negative,
  - `0` if the number is zero,
  - `1` if the number is positive

  In this case, the function returns `-1` and the results is labeled as `SignValue`.
- **`FROM`**: It specifies Oracle's special one-row table `DUAL`, which is used when no data is required from the actual table.

CEIL() and FLOOR() Functions

The `CEIL()` and `FLOOR()` functions are used to round numeric values in opposite directions. The `CEIL()` function returns the smallest integer that is greater than or equal to a given number, while the `FLOOR()` function returns the largest integer that is less than or equal to the number. These functions are often used in financial calculations, pricing, and statistical rounding.

Exercise 11: Using the CEIL() and FLOOR() Functions

Using the `OrderDetails` table, write a query to display the original `Sales` values, along with their ceiling and floor values, for records where `Sales` is greater than `240`.

Execute the following statement to use the `CEIL()` and `FLOOR()` functions:

```
SELECT Sales,
      CEIL(Sales) AS CeilValue,
      FLOOR(Sales) AS FloorValue
FROM OrderDetails
WHERE Sales > 240;
```

The output of the query is shown in Figure 5.11:

SALES	CEILVALUE	FLOORVALUE
267.08	268	267
278.16	279	278
242.12	243	242
321.62	322	321
245.94	246	245

***Figure 5.11**: Output using the CEIL() and FLOOR() functions*

Query Explanation

- `SELECT`: Specifies the columns to retrieve in the result set.
- `Sales`: Displays the original `Sales` value from each record in the `OrderDetails` table.
- `CEIL(Sales) AS CeilValue`: Returns the smallest integer that is greater than or equal to the `Sales` value. The result is labeled as `CeilValue`.
- `FLOOR(Sales) AS FloorValue`: Returns the largest integer that is less than or equal to the `Sales` value. The result is labeled as `FloorValue`.
- `FROM`: Indicates that the data is being retrieved from the `OrderDetails` table.
- `WHERE Sales > 240`: Filters the results to include only those records where the `Sales` value is greater than `240`.

ROUND(), TRUNC(), and MOD() Functions

The `ROUND()`, `TRUNC()`, and `MOD()` functions are used to perform numeric manipulations in SQL. Their purposes are described as follows:

- The `ROUND()` function rounds a number to a specified number of decimal places.
- The `TRUNC()` function truncates a number to a specified number of decimal places without rounding.
- The `MOD()` function returns the remainder when one number is divided by another.

These functions are often used for financial, mathematical, and analytical calculations.

Exercise 12: Using ROUND(), TRUNC(), and MOD() Functions

Using the `OrderDetails` table, retrieve rows where the `Sales` amount is greater than `240`. Display the following columns:

- `Sales` – the original sales amount

- `ROUND(Sales)` – the sales amount rounded to the nearest whole number
- `TRUNC(Sales,1)` – the sales amount truncated to 1 decimal place
- `MOD(Sales,5)` – the remainder when the sales amount is divided by 5

Execute the following statement to use the `ROUND()`, `TRUNC()`, and `MOD()` functions:

```
SELECT Sales,
      ROUND(Sales, 0) AS Rounded,
      TRUNC(Sales, 1) AS Truncated,
      MOD(Sales, 5) AS Remainder
FROM OrderDetails
WHERE Sales > 240;
```

The output of the query is shown in Figure 5.12:

SALES	ROUNDED	TRUNCATED	REMAINDER
267.08	267	267	2.08
278.16	278	278.1	3.16
242.12	242	242.1	2.12
321.62	322	321.6	1.62
245.94	246	245.9	0.94

***Figure 5.12**: Output using the ROUND(), TRUNC(), and MOD() functions*

Query Explanation

- **`SELECT`**: Specifies the columns to be included in the result set.
- **`Sales`**: Displays the original `Sales` amount from the `OrderDetails` table.
- **`ROUND(Sales, 0) AS Rounded`**: Rounds the `Sales` value to the nearest whole number (`0` decimal places). The result is labeled as `Rounded`.
- **`TRUNC(Sales, 1) AS Truncated`**: Removes digits after the first decimal place without rounding. The result is labeled as `Truncated`.
- **`MOD(Sales, 5) AS Remainder`**: Calculates the remainder when the `Sales` value is divided by `5`. The result is labeled as `Remainder`.
- **`FROM`**: Specifies the `OrderDetails` table as the source table.

- **`WHERE Sales > 240`**: Filters the result set to include only those rows where the `Sales` value is greater than `240`.

POWER(), SQRT(), EXP(), and LN() Functions

The `POWER()`, `SQRT()`, `EXP()`, and `LN()` functions are mathematical functions in SQL used to perform exponential and logarithmic calculations. Their purposes are summarized as follows:

- The `POWER()` function raises a number to a specified exponent.
- The `SQRT()` function returns the square root of a number.
- The `EXP()` function raises the mathematical constant *e* (approximately 2.71828) to the power of a given number.
- The `LN()` function returns the natural logarithm (base *e*) of a number.

These functions are used in scientific, statistical, and financial computations.

Exercise 13: Using the POWER(), SQRT(), EXP(), and LN() Functions

Using the `OrderDetails` table, write a query that displays the following values for records where the `UnitPrice` is greater than `40`:

- `UnitPrice` – the original unit price
- `POWER(UnitPrice, 2)` – the square of the unit price
- `SQRT(UnitPrice)` – the square root of the unit price
- `EXP(UnitPrice)` – the exponential value of the unit price
- `LN(UnitPrice)` – the natural logarithm of the unit price

Round all the function results to two decimal places using the `ROUND` function.

Execute the following statement to use the `POWER()`, `SQRT()`, `EXP()`, and `LN()` functions:

```
SELECT UnitPrice,
      ROUND(POWER(UnitPrice, 2), 2) AS Squared,
      ROUND(SQRT(UnitPrice), 2) AS SquareRoot,
      ROUND(EXP(UnitPrice), 2) AS Exponential,
      ROUND(LN(UnitPrice), 2) AS NaturalLog
      FROM OrderDetails
WHERE UnitPrice > 40;
```

The output of the query is shown in Figure 5.13:

UNITPRICE	SQUARED	SQUAREROOT	EXPONENTIAL	NATURALLOG
46.98	2207.12	6.85	25301994664331355020\u200b9.77	3.85
42.66	1819.88	6.53	3365135824271407081.72	3.75
46.75	2185.56	6.84	20103284971171326815\u200b4.69	3.84
47.51	2257.2	6.89	4298637620772671962\u200b03.2	3.86
45.88	2104.97	6.77	84223023836390047492.83	3.83
46.41	2153.89	6.81	143089216325193364286.5	3.84

***Figure 5.13**: Output using the POWER(), SQRT(), EXP(), and LN() functions*

Query Explanation

- **`SELECT`**: Specifies the columns to be included in the result set.
- **`UnitPrice`**: Retrieves the `UnitPrice` value from the `OrderDetails` table.
- **`ROUND(POWER(UnitPrice, 2), 2) AS Squared`**: Calculates the square of `UnitPrice` using the `POWER()` function and rounds the result to two decimal places. The result is labeled as `Squared`.
- **`ROUND(SQRT(UnitPrice), 2) AS SquareRoot`**: Calculates the square root of `UnitPrice` using the `SQRT()` function and rounds the result to two decimal places. The result is labeled as `SquareRoot`.
- **`ROUND(EXP(UnitPrice), 2) AS Exponential`**: Calculates the exponential value of `UnitPrice` using the `EXP()` function (that is, `e` raised to the power of `UnitPrice`), and rounds the result to two decimal places. The result is labeled as `Exponential`.

- **`ROUND(LN(UnitPrice), 2) AS NaturalLog`**: Calculates the natural logarithm (base `e`) of `UnitPrice` using the LN() function and rounds the result to two decimal places. The result is labeled as `NaturalLog`.
- **`FROM`**: Specifies that the data is being retrieved from the `OrderDetails` table.
- **`WHERE UnitPrice > 40`**: Filters the result set to include only rows where `UnitPrice` is greater than `40`.

LOG() Function

The `LOG()` function returns the logarithm of a number for a specified base. It accepts two arguments: the base and the number.

For example, `LOG(10, 100)` returns `2` because $10^2 = 100$.

This function is used in mathematical and scientific calculations involving exponential relationships.

Exercise 14: Using the LOG() Function

Using the `DUAL` table, write a query to calculate the logarithm of `100` with base `10` and display the result.

Execute the following statement to use the LOG() Function:

```
SELECT LOG(10, 100) AS LogResult
FROM DUAL;
```

The output of the query is shown in Figure 5.14:

LOGRESULT
2

***Figure 5.14**: Output using the LOG() function*

Query Explanation

- **`SELECT`**: Specifies the expression to be displayed in the result set.

- `LOG(10, 100) AS LogResult`: Calculates the logarithm of 100 with base 10. This determines the power to which 10 must be raised to produce 100. The result is labeled as `LogResult`.
- `FROM`: Uses Oracle's built-in `DUAL` table to execute the expression without referencing an actual user-defined table.

Number functions are essential for performing mathematical calculations, formatting numeric values, and supporting analytical operations. Whether rounding figures, computing remainders, or applying advanced mathematical expressions, these functions help ensure accurate and meaningful numeric results in SQL queries.

Working with Dates in Oracle

In Oracle, the `DATE` data type stores both date and time information down to the second. A `DATE` value includes the following components:

- Century, Year, Month, and Day
- Hour, Minute, Second

Example of a full `DATE` value:

```
15-AUG-2024 03:45:00 PM
```

NOTE: In Oracle SQL, date values must be enclosed in **single quotes** and often require explicit formatting using the `TO_DATE()` function to ensure accurate comparison and storage.

Oracle provides a comprehensive set of built-in date functions that support date extraction, formatting, manipulation, and calculation of date values.

The following table lists some of the most commonly used date functions in Oracle, along with their descriptions, example usage, and typical results:

***Table 5.3**: Commonly used Date Functions in Oracle*

Function	Description	Example	Result
`SYSDATE`	Returns current system date and time	`SELECT SYSDATE FROM DUAL;`	`30-JUL-2025 04:20:00 PM`
`CURRENT_DATE`	Returns current date and time in session time zone	`SELECT CURRENT_DATE FROM DUAL;`	`30-JUL-2025 04:20:00 PM`
`SYSTIMESTAMP`	Returns date and time with time zone and fractional seconds	`SELECT SYSTIMESTAMP FROM DUAL;`	`30-JUL-25 16.20.00.123 456`
`TO_DATE(string, format)`	Converts text to date using a format model	`TO_DATE('31-12-2025', 'DD-MM-YYYY')`	`31-DEC-2025`
`TO_CHAR(date, format)`	Converts date to text in a given format	`TO_CHAR(SYSDATE, 'YYYY-MM-DD')`	`2025-07-30`
`ADD_MONTHS(date, n)`	Adds n months to a date	`ADD_MONTHS(SYSDATE, 2)`	`30-SEP-2025`
`MONTHS_BETWEEN(d1, d2)`	Returns months between two dates	`MONTHS_BETWEEN('31-AUG-2025', '30-JUN-2025')`	`2`
`NEXT_DAY(date, 'DAY')`	Returns next given weekday after date	`NEXT_DAY(SYSDATE, 'MONDAY')`	`04-AUG-2025`
`LAST_DAY(date)`	Returns last day of month for a given date	`LAST_DAY(SYSDATE)`	`31-JUL-2025`
`ROUND(date, 'fmt')`	Rounds date to specified unit (for example, month)	`ROUND(SYSDATE, 'MONTH')`	`01-AUG-2025`
`TRUNC(date, 'fmt')`	Truncates a date to specified unit	`TRUNC(SYSDATE, 'MONTH')`	`01-JUL-2025`
`EXTRACT(YEAR FROM date)`	Extracts year component from a date value	`EXTRACT(YEAR FROM SYSDATE)`	`2025`

SYSDATE, CURRENT_DATE, and SYSTIMESTAMP Functions

The SYSDATE, CURRENT_DATE, and SYSTIMESTAMP functions are used to retrieve the current date and time in Oracle, each serving specific purpose as follows:

- SYSDATE returns the current date and time from the database server's system clock.
- CURRENT_DATE returns the current date and time according to the user's session time zone.
- SYSTIMESTAMP returns the current date and time including fractional seconds and time zone information.

These functions are commonly used for logging transactions, tracking system activity, and performing date-based calculations.

Exercise 15: Using the SYSDATE, CURRENT_DATE and SYSTIMESTAMP Functions

Use the DUAL table to write a query that displays:

- The current date and time using SYSDATE
- The current date and time in the user's session time zone using CURRENT_DATE
- The full timestamp, including fractional seconds and time zone using SYSTIMESTAMP

Execute the following statement to use the SYSDATE, CURRENT_DATE, and SYSTIMESTAMP functions:

```
SELECT
  SYSDATE AS SystemDateTime,
  CURRENT_DATE AS SessionDateTime,
  SYSTIMESTAMP AS SystemTimestamp
FROM DUAL;
```

The output of the query is shown in Figure 5.15:

SYSTEMDATETIME	SESSIONDATETIME	SYSTEMTIMESTAMP
14-OCT-25	14-OCT-25	14-OCT-25 09.52.33.691787 PM +00:00

Figure 5.15*: Output using the SYSDATE(), CURRENT_DATE(), and SYSTIMESTAMP() functions*

NOTE: Values will differ based on system clock and session time zone settings.

Query Explanation

- `SELECT`: Specifies the columns and expressions to be retrieved in the result set.
- `SYSDATE AS SystemDateTime`: Retrieves the current date and time from the database server's system clock. It does not include fractional seconds or time zone.
- `CURRENT_DATE AS SessionDateTime`: Retrieves the current date and time based on the user session's time zone. It may differ from `SYSDATE` if the session is configured with a different time zone.
- `SYSTIMESTAMP AS SystemTimestamp`: Returns the current timestamp with fractional seconds and time zone information. It provides higher precision than `SYSDATE`.
- `FROM`: Specifies Oracle's special one-row, one-column table `DUAL`, used when selecting values or expressions that are not associated to any specific data table.

LAST_DAY, ADD_MONTHS, and NEXT_DAY Functions

Oracle provides the following built-in date functions to simplify common date calculations and support time-based analysis:

- `LAST_DAY` returns the last day of the month for a given date. It is useful for identifying month-end reporting periods or billing cycles.

- ADD_MONTHS adds or subtracts a specified number of months to a given date. It is commonly used to calculate future or past dates, such as payment due dates or contract expirations.
- NEXT_DAY returns the date of the next specified weekday after a given date. It is often used to find the next business day or a specific day of the week following a transaction.

These functions, along with date arithmetic (for example, ShipDate - OrderDate), enable powerful date calculations and transformations in Oracle.

Exercise 16: Using Date Arithmetic and LAST_DAY, ADD_MONTHS, and NEXT_DAY Functions

Using the Orders table, write a query to display the following details for each order where BranchID = 'B04':

- OrderID, OrderDate, ShipDate, and BranchID
- ShipDate - OrderDate – the number of days taken to ship the order
- LAST_DAY(OrderDate) – the last day of the order month
- ADD_MONTHS(OrderDate, 2) – the order date plus two months
- NEXT_DAY(OrderDate, 'MONDAY') – the next Monday after the order date

Execute the following statement to use the Date Arithmetic and Date functions:

```
SELECT OrderID, OrderDate, ShipDate, BranchID,
      ShipDate - OrderDate AS DaysToShip,
      LAST_DAY(OrderDate) AS EndOfMonth,
      ADD_MONTHS(OrderDate, 2) AS OrderPlus2Months,
      NEXT_DAY(OrderDate, 'MONDAY') AS NextMonday
FROM Orders
WHERE BranchID = 'B04';
```

The output of the query is shown in Figure 5.16:

ORDERID	ORDERDATE	SHIPDATE	BRANCHID	DAYSTOSHIP	ENDOFMONTH	ORDERPLUS2MONTHS	NEXTMONDAY
01023	03-APR-25	09-APR-25	B04	6	30-APR-25	03-JUN-25	07-APR-25
01029	10-AUG-25	16-AUG-25	B04	6	31-AUG-25	10-OCT-25	11-AUG-25

***Figure 5.16**: Output using the Date Arithmetic functions*

Query Explanation

- **`SELECT`**: Retrieves order details from the `Orders` table for `BranchID = 'B04'`.
- **`ShipDate - OrderDate AS DaysToShip`**: Subtracts `OrderDate` from `ShipDate` to calculate the number of days taken to ship the order. The result is labeled `DaysToShip`.
- **`LAST_DAY(OrderDate) AS EndOfMonth`**: Returns the last date of the month in which the order was placed.
- **`ADD_MONTHS(OrderDate, 2) AS OrderPlus2Months`**: Adds two months to the `OrderDate` using the `ADD_MONTHS` function.
- **`NEXT_DAY(OrderDate, 'MONDAY') AS NextMonday`**: Finds the next Monday that occurs after the given `OrderDate`.
- **`FROM`**: Specifies that the data is being retrieved from the `Orders` table.
- **`WHERE BranchID = 'B04'`**: Filters results to include only orders processed by the branch `'B04'`.

ROUND and TRUNC Functions on Dates

The `ROUND` and `TRUNC` functions can also be used with date values in Oracle to simplify or standardize date representations. Their purposes are as follows:

- `ROUND` rounds a date to the nearest unit specified by a format model (for example, month or year).
- `TRUNC` truncates a date to the beginning of the specified unit without rounding.

These functions are useful for generating reports based on months, quarters, or years where precise time components are not required.

Exercise 17: Using the ROUND and TRUNC Functions on Dates

Using the `Orders` table, write a query to display the following details for each order, filtering records where `BranchID = 'B04'`:

- `OrderID`, `OrderDate`, and `BranchID`
- `ROUND(OrderDate, 'MONTH')` –the order date rounded to the nearest month
- `TRUNC(OrderDate, 'MONTH')` – the order date truncated to the first day of the month
- `TRUNC(OrderDate, 'YEAR')` – the order date truncated to the first day of the year

Execute the following statement to use the `ROUND` and `TRUNC` functions:

```
SELECT
  OrderID,  OrderDate, BranchID,
  ROUND(OrderDate, 'MONTH') AS RoundedToMonth,
  TRUNC(OrderDate, 'MONTH') AS StartOfMonth,
  TRUNC(OrderDate, 'YEAR')  AS StartOfYear
FROM Orders
WHERE BranchID = 'B04';
```

The output of the query is shown in Figure 5.17:

ORDERID	ORDERDATE	BRANCHID	ROUNDEDTOMONTH	STARTOFMONTH	STARTOFYEAR
O1023	03-APR-25	B04	01-APR-25	01-APR-25	01-JAN-25
O1029	10-AUG-25	B04	01-AUG-25	01-AUG-25	01-JAN-25

***Figure 5.17**: Output using the ROUND() and TRUNC() functions*

Query Explanation

- **`SELECT`**: Specifies the list of columns and expressions to return in the result set.
- **`ROUND(OrderDate, 'MONTH') AS RoundedToMonth`**: Rounds `OrderDate` to the nearest month:
  - If the day is 16 or later, it rounds up to the first day of the next month.

  - If the day is 15 or earlier, it rounds down to the first day of the current month.

  The result is displayed with the alias `RoundedToMonth`.

- **`TRUNC(OrderDate, 'MONTH') AS StartOfMonth`**: Truncates `OrderDate` to the first day of the current month. The result is displayed with the alias `StartOfMonth`.
- **`TRUNC(OrderDate, 'YEAR') AS StartOfYear`**: Truncates `OrderDate` to the first day of the year (January 1st). The result is displayed with the alias `StartOfYear`.
- **`FROM`**: Specifies that the data is retrieved from the `Orders` table.
- **`WHERE BranchID = 'B04'`**: Filters the results to include only orders from branch `'B04'`.

TO_DATE Function

The `TO_DATE` function converts a character string into an Oracle `DATE` value using a specified date format model. This conversion allows Oracle to recognize the value as a valid date, enabling accurate comparisons, sorting, and date arithmetic. If the format model does not match the string, Oracle returns an error.

Example:

```
TO_DATE('01-AUG-2025', 'DD-MON-YYYY')
```

This converts the text `'01-AUG-2025'` into a date value representing August 1, 2025.

Exercise 18: Using the TO_DATE() Function

Using the `DUAL` table, write a query to convert the date represented as the string `'01/AUG/2025'` into an Oracle `Date` value.

NOTE: Character strings representing a date should be explicitly converted to Oracle `DATE` value to enable reliable date comparison and date arithmetic operations.

Execute the following statement to use the `TO_DATE` function:

```
SELECT TO_DATE('01-AUG-2025', 'DD-MON-YYYY') AS ConvertedDate
FROM dual;
```

The output of the query is shown in Figure 5.18:

CONVERTEDDATE
01-AUG-25

***Figure 5.18**: Output using the TO_DATE() function*

NOTE: The output format of a `DATE` value depends on the session's `NLS_DATE_FORMAT`. Oracle FreeSQL may display dates in a format such as MM/DD/YYYY, HH:MI:SS AM. Internally, Oracle stores the full date and time value regardless of how it is displayed.

Query Explanation

- **`SELECT`**: Specifies the columns or expressions to include in the result set.
- **`TO_DATE('01-AUG-2025', 'DD-MON-YYYY')`**: Converts the string `'01-AUG-2025'` into an Oracle `DATE` value. The format model `'DD-MON-YYYY'` defined how Oracle interprets the string:
  - `DD`: two-digit day (`01`)
  - `MON`: three-letter month abbreviation (`AUG`)
  - `YYYY`: four-digit year (`2025`)
- **`AS ConvertedDate`**: Assigns the alias `ConvertedDate` to the resulting column for readability.
- **`FROM`**: Uses Oracle's special one-row `DUAL` table, which is used to evaluate expressions or functions that are not associated with a specific table.

TO_CHAR Function

The `TO_CHAR` function converts a DATE or NUMBER value into a character string using a specified format model.

When used with dates, it allows customization of how a date is displayed—for example, by showing the full month name, year, or time components.

This function is commonly used in reporting, data formatting, and string concatenation, where date values must appear in a specific textual format.

Example:

`TO_CHAR(SYSDATE, 'Month YYYY')` returns a value like `'August 2025'`.

Exercise 19: Using the TO_CHAR Function

Using the `Orders` table, write a query to display `OrderID`, `OrderDate`, and use the `TO_CHAR` function to create a new column that shows the month and year of each order in the format `'Month YYYY'`. Filter the results to include only those rows where the `BranchID = 'B04'`.

NOTE: An Oracle `Date` value must be converted to a string using the `TO_CHAR` function to display it in a customized format.

Execute the following statement to use the `TO_CHAR` function:

```
SELECT OrderID, OrderDate,
   TO_CHAR(OrderDate, 'Month YYYY') AS Formatted_MonthYear
  FROM Orders
WHERE BranchID = 'B04';
```

The output of the query is shown in Figure 5.19:

ORDERID	ORDERDATE	FORMATTED_MONTHYEAR
O1023	03-APR-25	April 2025
O1029	10-AUG-25	August 2025

***Figure 5.19**: Output using the TO_CHAR() function*

Query Explanation

- `SELECT`: Retrieves specific columns from the `Orders` table.
- `TO_CHAR(OrderDate, 'Month YYYY') AS Formatted_MonthYear`: Converts `OrderDate` (stored in Oracle's internal date format) into a formatted character string showing the month and year. The result is labeled `FormattedMonthYear`.
- `FROM`: Specifies the `Orders` table as the source of data.
- `WHERE`: Filters the results to include only orders placed by `BranchID 'B04'`.

Using EXTRACT and TO_CHAR in Date Analysis

The `EXTRACT` function retrieves a specific component, such as year, month, or day, from a `DATE` or `TIMESTAMP` value and returns it as a numeric result.

The `TO_CHAR` function, when applied to a date, converts it into a character string based on the specified format model.

While `EXTRACT` is used for numerical extraction (for example, `EXTRACT(YEAR FROM OrderDate)`), `TO_CHAR()` is suited for textual representation, such as displaying the full day name (`TO_CHAR(OrderDate, 'DAY')`).

Together, these functions support both numerical and descriptive analysis of date values in SQL.

Exercise 20: Using the EXTRACT and TO_CHAR Functions for date analysis

Using the `Orders` table, write a query to display the following:

- `OrderID` and `OrderDate`
- `EXTRACT(YEAR FROM OrderDate)`: the year extracted from the order date
- `EXTRACT(MONTH FROM OrderDate)`: the month extracted from the order date
- `TO_CHAR(OrderDate, 'DAY')`: the name of the day of the week from the order date
- Filter the result to include only rows where `BranchID = 'B04'`

Execute the following statement to use the `EXTRACT()` and `TO_CHAR()` functions:

```
SELECT OrderID, OrderDate,
      EXTRACT(YEAR FROM OrderDate) AS OrderYear,
      EXTRACT(MONTH FROM OrderDate) AS OrderMonth,
      TO_CHAR(OrderDate, 'Day') AS DayOfWeek
FROM Orders
WHERE BranchID = 'B04';
```

The output of the query is shown in Figure 5.20:

ORDERID	ORDERDATE	ORDERYEAR	ORDERMONTH	DAYOFWEEK
O1023	03-APR-25	2025	4	Thursday
O1029	10-AUG-25	2025	8	Sunday

***Figure 5.20**: Output using the EXTRACT() and TO_CHAR() functions*

Query Explanation

- **`SELECT`**: Specifies the columns and expressions to return in the result set.
- **`EXTRACT(YEAR FROM OrderDate) AS OrderYear`**: Extracts the year from `OrderDate` (for example, 2025) and labels the result as `OrderYear`.
- **`EXTRACT(MONTH FROM OrderDate)`**: Extracts the numeric month (for example, 1 for January) and labels the result as `OrderMonth`.
- **`TO_CHAR(OrderDate, 'Day') AS DayOfWeek`**: Converts `OrderDate` into a character string displaying the full day of the week (for example, Monday). The result is labeled as `DayOfWeek`.
- **`FROM`**: Specifies the `Orders` table as the data source.
- **`WHERE BranchID = 'B04'`**: Filters the results to include only orders placed by `BranchID 'B04'`.

Oracle's set of date functions makes it possible to extract, format, and manipulate date values to support a wide range of business needs. Tasks such as calculating delivery timelines, aligning reports to specific months or years, or converting between string and date formats rely heavily on these functions when building accurate SQL queries.

Writing Conditional Expressions

In addition to text, number, and date functions, Oracle SQL provides conditional expressions that allow queries to return different results based on logical conditions. These expressions are essential for handling NULL values, evaluating conditions, and generating derived columns.

Conditional expressions make SQL more expressive by enabling row-level decision-making. Common conditional expressions include:

- `NVL`: It replaces NULL values
- `CASE`: It is used for multi-branch conditional logic
- `DECODE`: It provides simplified, Oracle-specific conditional evaluation

The following table summarizes the most commonly used conditional expressions in Oracle:

***Table 5.4**: Commonly Used Conditional Expressions in Oracle*

Function/Exp	Description	Example	Result
`NVL(expr1, expr2)`	Replaces `NULL` in `expr1` with `expr2`	`NVL(Sales, 0)`	Returns `Sales` if not null, else `0`
`NVL2(expr1, expr2, expr3)`	Returns `expr2` if `expr1` is not `NULL`; otherwise returns `expr3`	`NVL2(Discount, 'Yes', 'No')`	`'Yes'` if Discount is not null
`CASE WHEN ... THEN ... ELSE ... END`	Performs conditional logic like IF-THEN-ELSE	`CASE WHEN Sales > 500 THEN 'High' ELSE 'Low' END`	`'High'` or `'Low'` depending on value
`DECODE(expr, val1, res1, ..., default)`	Oracle-specific function for simple conditional evaluations	`DECODE(Status, 'A', 'Active', 'I', 'Inactive', 'Other')`	`'Active'`, `'Inactive'`, or `'Other'`

NVL Function

The NVL function replaces NULL values with a specified replacement value. It takes the following two arguments:

- The first expression (expr1) is evaluated to determine if it contains a NULL value.
- If expr1 is NULL, the second expression (expr2) is returned; otherwise, the original value of expr1 is returned.

This function is commonly used to handle missing or undefined data in query results and to ensure consistent output during calculations or reporting.

Exercise 21: Using the NVL Function

Using the Category table, replace any NULL values in the SubCategory column with 'No SubCategory' for categories 'Furniture' and 'Technology'.

In the dataset, one of the SubCategory values under the 'Technology' category is NULL. The objective is to replace this value with 'No SubCategory' in the query output.

Execute the following statement to use the NVL function:

```
SELECT Category, SubCategory,
       NVL(SubCategory, 'No SubCategory') AS SubCategoryLabel
FROM Category
WHERE Category IN ('Furniture','Technology');
```

The output of the query is shown in Figure 5.21:

CATEGORY	SUBCATEGORY	SUBCATEGORYLABEL
Furniture	Chairs	Chairs
Furniture	Tables	Tables
Furniture	Bookcases	Bookcases
Technology	Phones	Phones
Technology	Computers	Computers
Technology	Accessories	Accessories
Technology	-	No SubCategory

***Figure 5.21**: Output using the NVL() function*

Query Explanation

- `SELECT`: Specifies the columns to retrieve from the `Category` table.
- `NVL(SubCategory, 'No SubCategory') AS SubCategoryLabel`: Replaces any NULL values in the `SubCategory` column with the string `'No SubCategory'`. The result is displayed under the alias `SubCategoryLabel`.
- `FROM`: Indicates that the data is being retrieved from the `Category` table.
- `WHERE`: Filters the result to include only rows where the `Category` is either `'Furniture'` or `'Technology'`.

NVL2 Function

The `NVL2` function extends the functionality of `NVL` by allowing different results to be returned depending on whether a column contains a NULL value or not. It accepts the following three arguments:

- `expr1`: The expression to evaluate for a NULL value.
- `expr2`: The value returned if `expr1` is not NULL.
- `expr3`: The value returned if `expr1` is NULL.

In other words, if `expr1` has a value, Oracle returns `expr2`; if `expr1` is NULL, it returns `expr3`.

Exercise 22: Using the NVL2 Function

Using the `SalesPersons` table, write a query to display:

- `SalesPersonName`, `Position`, and `BranchID`
- A new column named `Branch_Assigned` that returns `'Yes'` if the corresponding `BranchID` is not NULL, and `'No'` if it is NULL
- Only rows for salespersons `'Julie Alexander'`, `'Lena Carter'`, and `'Edgar Raymond'`

Execute the following statement to use the `NVL2()` function:

```
SELECT
      SalesPersonName, Position, BranchID,
      NVL2(BranchID, 'Yes', 'No') AS Branch_Assigned
FROM  SalesPersons
WHERE SalesPersonName in ('Julie Alexander','Lena Carter','Edgar
Raymond');
```

The output of the query is shown in Figure 5.22:

SALESPERSONNAME	POSITION	BRANCHID	BRANCH_ASSIGNED
Edgar Raymond	Store Manager	B03	Yes
Julie Alexander	Regional Manager	B02	Yes
Lena Carter	Sales Executive	-	No

***Figure 5.22**: Output using the NVL2() function*

Query Explanation

- `SELECT`: Specifies the columns and expressions to be retrieved in the result set.

- **`NVL2(BranchID, 'Yes', 'No') AS Branch_Assigned`**: Uses the `NVL2()` function to check the `BranchID` column:
    - If `BranchID` is **not NULL**, it returns `'Yes'`, indicating that the salesperson is assigned to a branch.
    - If `BranchID` is **NULL**, it returns `'No'`, indicating no branch assignment. The result is labeled as `Branch_Assigned`.
- **`FROM`**: Specifies the `SalesPersons` table as the data source.
- **`WHERE`**: Filters the records to include only the three specified salespersons: `'Julie Alexander'`, `'Lena Carter'`, and `'Edgar Raymond'`.

CASE Expression

The `CASE` expression in Oracle SQL performs conditional logic within a query, similar to an IF-THEN-ELSE structure in programming languages. It evaluates conditions sequentially and returns a value when the first condition is met. If no condition matches, an optional `ELSE` clause specifies the default value.

There are two types of `CASE` expressions:

- Simple CASE: Compares single expression to multiple possible values.
- Searched CASE: Evaluates multiple independent Boolean conditions (commonly used in reporting and categorization).

Exercise 23: Using the CASE expression

Using the `OrderDetails` table, write a query to display the following:

- `OrderID`, `ProductID`, and `Sales`
- A new column named `SalesCategory` with the following logic:
    - `'Medium'` if `Sales` is greater than `125` and less than `140`
    - `'High'` if `Sales` is greater than `140` and less than `150`
    - `'Excellent'` for all other values

Execute the following statement to use the `CASE` expression:

```
SELECT OrderID, ProductID, Sales,
      CASE
        WHEN Sales > 125 AND Sales < 140 THEN 'Medium'
        WHEN Sales > 140 AND Sales < 150 THEN 'High'
        ELSE 'Excellent'
     END AS SalesCategory
FROM OrderDetails
WHERE SALES BETWEEN 130 and 160
ORDER BY Sales;
```

The output of the query is shown in Figure 5.23:

ORDERID	PRODUCTID	SALES	SALESCATEGORY
O1001	P0017	136.94	Medium
O1013	P0050	146.05	High
O1002	P0009	150.13	Excellent

***Figure 5.23**: Output using the CASE expression*

Query Explanation

- **`SELECT`**: Specifies the columns to retrieve from the `OrderDetails` table.
- **`CASE`**: Used to assign a custom label (`SalesCategory`) based on the value of `Sales`:
  - Returns `'Medium'` when `Sales` is greater than `125` and less than `140`
  - Returns `'High'` when `Sales` is greater than `140` and less than `150`
  - Returns `'Excellent'` for all other values within the filtered range
- **`FROM`**: Specifies the `OrderDetails` table as the data source.
- **`WHERE`**: Filters the rows to include only those where `Sales` value is between `130` and `160` (inclusive).
- **`ORDER BY`**: Sorts the result set in ascending order of the `Sales` values.

DECODE Function

The `DECODE` function in Oracle provides a simplified way to perform conditional evaluations, similar to a series of IF-THEN-ELSE statements.

It compares an expression to a list of possible values and returns a corresponding result when a match is found. If no match is found, an optional default value can be returned.

Exercise 24: Using the DECODE function

Using the `Orders` table, write a query to display:

- A unique list of `ShipMode` values
- A new column named `DeliveryType` defined as follows:
    - `'Fast'` when `ShipMode = 'Priority'`
    - `'Expedited'` when `ShipMode = 'Express'`
    - `'Regular'` when `ShipMode = 'Standard'`
    - `'Other'` for all other shipping modes

Execute the following statement to use the `DECODE()` function:

```
SELECT DISTINCT ShipMode,
       DECODE(ShipMode,
              'Priority', 'Fast',
              'Express', 'Expedited',
              'Standard', 'Regular',
              'Other') AS DeliveryType
FROM Orders;
```

The output of the query is shown in Figure 5.24:

SHIPMODE	DELIVERYTYPE
Same-Day	Other
Priority	Fast
Two-Day	Other
Express	Expedited
Standard	Regular

***Figure 5.24**: Output using the DECODE() function*

Query Explanation

- `SELECT DISTINCT`: Retrieves a unique list of `ShipMode` values along with their corresponding delivery type labels.
- `DECODE()`: Acts like an IF–THEN–ELSE structure to assign custom labels based on the value of `ShipMode`:
    - Returns `'Fast'` when `ShipMode = 'Priority'`
    - Returns `'Expedited'` when `ShipMode = 'Express'`
    - Returns `'Regular'` when `ShipMode = 'Standard'`
    - Returns `'Other'` for all other values

  The result is labeled as `DeliveryType`.
- `FROM`: Specifies that the data is being retrieved from the `Orders` table.

Conditional expressions like `NVL`, `NVL2`, `CASE`, and `DECODE` enhance SQL queries by enabling dynamic logic based on data values. These functions are essential for handling missing data, categorizing results, and applying custom display labels directly within a query. Mastering conditional expressions leads to more flexible, readable, and meaningful SQL output, particularly in reporting and data transformation tasks.

Conclusion

This chapter explored how SQL functions can transform and enhance data retrieval. It began by introducing the concepts of functions and their usage in SQL, followed by text functions for modifying and formatting string values and numeric functions for performing calculations and rounding numeric data.

The chapter also covered Oracle-specific date functions used to manipulate date and time values. Finally, it demonstrated the use of conditional expressions such as NVL, NVL2, CASE, and DECODE to apply logical conditions within SQL queries.

Mastering these functions provides the foundation for writing more dynamic, readable, and meaningful SQL queries.

The next chapter, **Data Aggregation and GROUP BY**, focuses on summarizing and grouping data to derive analytical insights.

Practice Questions

Use the training dataset to complete the following practice questions. These exercises reinforce concepts covered in this chapter.

1. Using the `Customers` table, retrieve a distinct list of `Segment` values. Create a new column called `NewSegment` that displays only the first four characters of the Segment using the `SUBSTR()` function.
2. Using the `Customers` table, apply the `INSTR()` and `SUBSTR()` functions to split the `CustomerName` column into two new columns: `FirstName` and `LastName`.
3. Using the `Orders` table and the `OrderDate` column, create new columns that display the year, quarter, month name, day of the month, weekday name, and day of the week number.

4. Using the `OrderDetails` table, display the `Profit` column and create a new column named `ProfitCategory` with the following logic:
   - `'Excellent'` if `Profit` > `60`
   - `'High'` if `Profit` > `50` and ≤ `60`
   - `'Medium'` if `Profit` > `40` and ≤ `50`
   - `'Low'` for all other values
5. Using the `SalesPersons` table, retrieve distinct `Position` values and create a new column named `RoleType` using the `DECODE` function with the following logic:
   - `'Field Role'` if `Position` = `'Sales Executive'`
   - `'Management'` if `Position` = `'Sales Manager'`
   - `'Support'` if `Position` = `'Sales Analyst'`
   - `'Other'` for any other `Position` values

   Sort the results by Position.

Practice Answers

The answers to the preceding questions are as follows:

Answer 1

```
SELECT DISTINCT Segment,
      SUBSTR(Segment,1,4) AS NewSegment
FROM Customers;
```

Answer 2

```
SELECT CustomerName,
      SUBSTR(CustomerName,1,INSTR(CustomerName,' ')-1) AS FirstName,
      SUBSTR(CustomerName, INSTR(CustomerName, ' ') + 1) AS LastName
FROM Customers;
```

NOTE: A query explanation is provided for this question because it combines multiple string functions (`INSTR()` and `SUBSTR()`) in a single expression.

Query Explanation

This query splits the full customer name into first and last names using a combination of `INSTR()` and `SUBSTR()` functions:

- **`CustomerName`**: Displays the original full name from the `Customers` table.
- **`INSTR(CustomerName, ' ')`**: Finds the position of the first space in the string
- **`SUBSTR(CustomerName, 1, INSTR(CustomerName, ' ') - 1)`**: Extracts the first name, starting at position 1 and ending before the space.
- **`SUBSTR(CustomerName, INSTR(CustomerName, ' ') + 1)`**: Extracts the last name, starting just after the space until the end of the string.

Answer 3

```
SELECT OrderID, OrderDate,
             EXTRACT(YEAR FROM OrderDate) AS OrderYear,
             TO_CHAR(OrderDate, 'Q') AS QuarterNumber,
             TO_CHAR(OrderDate, 'Month') AS MonthName,
             EXTRACT(DAY FROM OrderDate) AS DayOfMonth,
             TO_CHAR(OrderDate, 'Day') AS WeekdayName,
             TO_CHAR(OrderDate, 'D') AS DayOfWeekNumber
FROM Orders;
```

Answer 4

```
SELECT Profit,
             CASE
               WHEN Profit > 60 THEN 'Excellent'
               WHEN Profit > 50 AND Profit <= 60 THEN 'High'
               WHEN Profit > 40 AND Profit <= 50 THEN 'Medium'
                  …
                  …
               ELSE 'Low'
             END AS ProfitCategory
      FROM OrderDetails
      ORDER BY Profit DESC;
```

Answer 5

```
SELECT DISTINCT Position,
             DECODE(Position,
                    'Sales Executive', 'Field Role',
                    'Sales Manager', 'Management',
                    'Sales Analyst', 'Support',
                    'Other') AS RoleType
      FROM SalesPersons
      ORDER BY Position;
```

Chapter 6

Data Aggregation and GROUP BY

Introduction

In data analysis, summarizing large volumes of data into meaningful insights is a key step toward decision-making. Oracle SQL provides powerful set of aggregation functions that allow calculation of totals, averages, counts, minimums, and maximums across rows of data. To summarize data effectively, records are often grouped based on one or more columns using the GROUP BY clause.

In addition, Oracle allows filtering of grouped results using the HAVING clause, which enables the inclusion or exclusion of groups based on specific aggregate conditions.

This chapter demonstrates how to compute aggregate values, group data using GROUP BY, and further refine results with the HAVING clause.

This chapter will cover the following topics:

- Introduction to Aggregation
- Common Aggregation Functions
- Using the GROUP BY Clause
- Filtering Groups with HAVING

Introduction to Aggregation

Aggregation is the process of summarizing detailed data into meaningful totals or statistics. Unlike functions such as `UPPER()`, `LOWER()`, `ROUND()`, or `TO_CHAR()`, which operate on individual rows, aggregation functions operate on a set of rows and return a single summary value.

Instead of analyzing data row by row, aggregate functions summarize data at a group or summary level—for example, calculating totals, finding averages, or identifying maximum or minimum values.

In SQL, data is aggregated using functions such as `SUM()`, `AVG()`, `COUNT()`, `MIN()`, and `MAX()`. These functions operate on groups of rows to produce summarized results that form the foundation for reporting and analysis.

Example

In the `OrderDetails` table, each row contains a `Sales` value associated with a specific `OrderID`. The table may contain hundreds of rows with different sales amounts. Applying the following statement aggregates all sales values into a single result:

```
SELECT SUM(Sales) AS TotalSales
FROM OrderDetails;
```

The query returns a single value—such as **5398.44**—representing the total sales across all orders.

Aggregation becomes even more powerful when combined with the `GROUP BY` clause, which enables summarizing data by categories such as `OrderID`, `ProductID`, or `BranchID`.

Common Aggregation Functions

Oracle SQL provides several built-in aggregation functions that are essential for summarizing data. These functions operate on multiple rows and return a single summarized result.

The following table summarizes the most frequently used aggregation functions along with their descriptions and examples:

***Table 6.1**: Common Aggregation Functions in Oracle*

Function	Description	Example	Result
SUM(column)	Returns the total sum of a numeric column	`SUM(Sales)`	Total of all `Sales` values
AVG(column)	Calculates the average of numeric values	`AVG(Sales)`	Average `Sales` of all products
COUNT(*)	Counts all rows in a table, including those with `NULL` values	`COUNT(*)`	Total number of rows from a table
COUNT(column)	Counts only non-NULL values in a column	`COUNT(ShipDate)`	Number of orders with `ShipDate`
COUNT(DISTINCT column)	Counts unique (non-NULL) values in a column	`COUNT(DISTINCT CustomerID)`	Number of distinct `CustomerID` entries
MIN(column)	Returns the smallest value in the specified column	`MIN(Sales)`	Lowest `Sales` amount
MAX(column)	Returns the largest value in the specified column	`MAX(Sales)`	Highest `Sales` among all orders

SUM() Function

The `SUM()` function is used to calculate the total of all numeric values in a specified column.

Exercise 1: Using the SUM Function

Using the `OrderDetails` table, write a query to display the total `Sales` value and assign an alias `TotalSales` to the result.

Execute the following statement to use the `SUM()` function:

```
SELECT SUM(Sales) AS TotalSales
FROM OrderDetails;
```

The output of the query is shown in Figure 6.1:

TOTALSALES
4682.14

***Figure 6.1**: Output using the SUM() function*

Query Explanation

- **`SELECT`**: Specifies the column to be returned—in this case, the result of the `SUM()` function.
- **`SUM(Sales)`**: Adds all numeric values in the `Sales` column.
- **`AS TotalSales`**: Assigns an alias to the result column.
- **`FROM`**: Specifies the `OrderDetails` table from which the column is retrieved.

AVG() Function

The `AVG()` function calculates the average of all numeric values in a specified column. It is often combined with the `ROUND()` function to make the result more readable in reports or dashboards.

Exercise 2: Using the AVG() Function

Using the `OrderDetails` table, write a query to display the average value of the `UnitPrice` column. Assign an alias `AveragePrice` to the result.

The steps to use the `AVG()` function are as follows:

1. In the SQL Worksheet, type the following statement:

   ```
   SELECT AVG(UnitPrice) AS AveragePrice
   FROM OrderDetails;
   ```

The output may display the result with more than two decimal places (for example, `25.90279069767`).

2. To round the result to two decimal places, use the `ROUND()` function as shown here:

```
SELECT ROUND(AVG(UnitPrice), 2) AS AveragePrice
FROM OrderDetails;
```

This revised query returns the average unit price rounded to two decimal places (for example, `25.9`), making the output more suitable for reporting and presentation.

The output of the query is shown in Figure 6.2:

AVERAGEPRICE
25.9

***Figure 6.2**: Output using the AVG() function*

Query Explanation

- **`SELECT`**: Specifies the column to be returned.
- **`AVG(UnitPrice)`**: Calculates the average of all values in the `UnitPrice` column.
- **`ROUND(..., 2)`**: Rounds the result of the `AVG()` function to two decimal places.
- **`AS AveragePrice`**: Assigns an alias to the result column.
- **`FROM`**: Specifies the `OrderDetails` table from which the column is retrieved.

COUNT() Function

The `COUNT()` function is used to count the number of rows or specific values in a table. It has three common variations:

- **`COUNT(*)`**: Counts all rows in a table, including those with `NULL` values.
- **`COUNT(column)`**: Counts only the non-null values in the specified column.
- **`COUNT(DISTINCT column)`**: Counts the number of unique (non-null) values in a column.

Exercise 3: Using the COUNT() Function Variations

Using the `SalesPersons` table, determine:

- The total number of salespersons.
- The number of branch IDs assigned to salespersons.
- The number of distinct branches.

Execute the following statements to use different `COUNT()` variations:

```
SELECT
  COUNT(*) AS "Total SalesPersons",
  COUNT(BranchID) AS "With BranchAssigned",
  COUNT(DISTINCT BranchID) AS "Unique Branches"
FROM SalesPersons;
```

The output of the query is shown in Figure 6.3:

Total SalesPersons	With BranchAssigned	Unique Branches
53	50	5

***Figure 6.3**: Output using the COUNT() functions*

Query Notes

- **`COUNT(*)`**: Counts all rows in the `SalesPersons` table, including those with `NULL` values.
- **`COUNT(BranchID)`**: Counts only rows where `BranchID` is not `NULL` (that is, salespersons assigned to a branch).
- **`COUNT(DISTINCT BranchID)`**: Counts the number of unique, non-`NULL` branch values.

MIN() and MAX() Functions

The `MIN()` and `MAX()` functions are used to identify the smallest and largest values in a specified column. They are commonly applied to numeric or date columns to determine value ranges or extremes within a dataset.

Exercise 4: Using the MIN() and MAX() Functions

Using the `OrderDetails` table, find the smallest and largest `Sales` amounts.

Execute the following statements in the SQL Worksheet to use the `MIN()` and `MAX()` functions:

```
SELECT
  MIN(Sales) AS "Minimum Sale",
  MAX(Sales) AS "Maximum Sale"
FROM OrderDetails;
```

The output of the query is shown in Figure 6.4:

Minimum Sale	Maximum Sale
7.17	321.62

***Figure 6.4**: Output using the MIN() and MAX() functions*

Query Notes

- **`MIN(Sales)`**: Returns the smallest sales value from the `Sales` column.
- **`MAX(Sales)`**: Returns the largest sales value from the `Sales` column.

Aggregation functions such as `SUM()`, `AVG()`, `COUNT()`, `MIN()`, and `MAX()` are essential for summarizing data in SQL queries. They perform calculations across multiple rows and return meaningful aggregated results for analysis and reporting.

Using the GROUP BY Clause

The `GROUP BY` clause is used when aggregated results need to be summarized by one or more columns.

Instead of applying aggregate functions such as `SUM()`, `AVG()`, or `COUNT()` across the entire result set, `GROUP BY` divides the data into subsets based on the specified column(s) and then applies the aggregation to each group individually.

This clause is commonly used with aggregate functions to produce summarized reports and derive meaningful insights from detailed data.

Things to Remember

When working with the `GROUP BY` clause, keep the following key points in mind to ensure correct and meaningful results:

- Columns that are not part of an aggregate function must be listed in the `GROUP BY` clause.
- The `GROUP BY` clause divides rows into groups based on one or more columns.
- SQL applies grouping after rows are retrieved and filtered.
- The `GROUP BY` clause appears after `WHERE` and before the `ORDER BY`.
- Aggregations functions such as `SUM()`, `COUNT()`, `AVG()`, `MIN()`, and `MAX()` are commonly used with `GROUP BY`.
- Grouping can be performed using a single column or multiple columns.

Syntax

```
SELECT column1, aggregate_function(column2)
FROM table_name
WHERE <condition>
GROUP BY column1
HAVING <condition>
ORDER BY <expression>;
```

Exercise 5: Determine the Number of Orders Placed from Each Branch

Using the `Orders` table, write a query to display each `BranchID` along with the total number of orders associated with it. Use the `GROUP BY` clause to group the results by branch.

Execute the following statement to find the number of orders placed from each branch:

```
SELECT BranchID, COUNT(OrderID) AS TotalOrders
FROM Orders
GROUP BY BranchID;
```

The output of the query is shown in Figure 6.5:

BRANCHID	TOTALORDERS
B02	6
B03	5
B05	7
B01	8
B04	2

Figure 6.5: *Total number of Orders grouped by BranchID*

Query Notes

- **`BranchID`**: Identifies each branch in the `Orders` table.
- **`COUNT(OrderID)`**: Counts all orders in each branch.
- **`GROUP BY BranchID`**: Groups the rows by branch so that the order count is calculated separately for every `BranchID`.

Exercise 6: Determine the Number of Salespersons in Each Branch

Using the `SalesPersons` table, write a query to display each `BranchID` along with the total number of `SalesPersons` associated with it.

Execute the following statement to find the number of salespersons in each branch:

```
SELECT BranchID, Count(*) AS TotalSalesPersons
FROM SalesPersons
GROUP BY BranchID;
```

The output of the query is shown in Figure 6.6:

BRANCHID	TOTALSALESPERSONS
B02	12
B03	14
-	3
B05	4
B01	9
B04	11

***Figure 6.6**: Total number of SalesPersons grouped by BranchID*

Query Notes

- **`COUNT(*)`**: Counts all rows in each branch, giving the total number of salespersons per branch.
- **`GROUP BY BranchID`**: Groups the data by `BranchID` so that the count is calculated separately for each branch.

Exercise 7: Determine the Number of Salespersons in Each Position

Using the `SalesPersons` table, write a query to display each `Position` along with the total number of salespersons holding that position. Sort the results in descending order based on the count. This exercise demonstrates how to use `ORDER BY` with `GROUP BY`.

Execute the following statement to find the number of salespersons in each position:

```
SELECT Position, COUNT(*) AS TotalSalesPersons
FROM SalesPersons
GROUP BY Position
ORDER BY 2 DESC;
```

The output of the query is shown in Figure 6.7:

POSITION	TOTALSALESPERSONS
Sales Associate	15
Regional Manager	13
Store Manager	12
Senior Sales	10
Sales Executive	2
Director	1

***Figure 6.7**: Total number of SalesPersons grouped by Position*

Query Notes

- `COUNT(*)`: Counts all rows in each group, representing the total number of salespersons in that position.
- `GROUP BY Position`: Groups the rows by position so that the count is calculated for each position separately.
- `ORDER BY 2 DESC`: Sorts the results in descending order of `TotalSalesPersons` (the second column in the `SELECT` list).

Exercise 8: Count the Number of Orders for Each Branch and Shipping Mode

Using the `Orders` table, write a query to display `BranchID`, `ShipMode`, and the total number of orders for each combination of branch and shipping mode. This exercise demonstrates how to use two columns with the `GROUP BY` clause.

Execute the following statement in the SQL Worksheet to count the number of orders for each branch and shipping mode:

```
SELECT BranchID, ShipMode, COUNT(*) AS TotalOrders
FROM Orders
GROUP BY BranchID, ShipMode
ORDER BY ShipMode;
```

The output of the query is shown in Figure 6.8:

BRANCHID	SHIPMODE	TOTALORDERS
B01	Express	4
B02	Express	2
B03	Express	1
B05	Express	1
B01	Priority	1
B03	Priority	1
B05	Priority	2
B03	Same-Day	3
B04	Same-Day	1
B05	Same-Day	1
B01	Standard	2
B05	Standard	2
B01	Two-Day	1
B02	Two-Day	4
B04	Two-Day	1
B05	Two-Day	1

***Figure 6.8**: Count of Orders for each Branch and Shipping Mode*

Query Notes

- `COUNT(*)`: Counts all rows in each group, representing the total number of orders for every `BranchID–ShipMode` combination.
- `GROUP BY BranchID, ShipMode`: Groups the data first by `BranchID` and then by shipping mode to calculate counts per combination.
- `ORDER BY ShipMode`: Sorts the results by shipping mode in ascending order.

The `GROUP BY` clause is essential for summarizing data by organizing rows into meaningful groups. When used with aggregate functions, it produces grouped results that help generate summarized insights.

Filtering Groups with Having

The `HAVING` clause is used to filter grouped results after aggregation has been performed.

While the `WHERE` clause filters individual rows *before* grouping, `HAVING` filters aggregated results *after* the `GROUP BY` clause is applied.

The `HAVING` clause is typically used with aggregate functions such as `SUM()`, `COUNT()`, `AVG()`, `MIN()`, and `MAX()` to return only those groups that meet specific conditions.

Syntax

```
SELECT column1, aggregate_function(column2)
FROM table_name
GROUP BY column1
HAVING condition;
```

Things to Remember

- `HAVING` is similar to the `WHERE` clause, but it filters aggregated results instead of individual rows.
- `WHERE` filters raw data *before* grouping while `HAVING` filters data *after* aggregation.
- `HAVING` is most commonly used in queries that include a `GROUP BY` clause.
- Conditions in `HAVING` usually involve aggregate functions such as `SUM()`, `AVG()`, or `COUNT()`.
- The `HAVING` clause appears *after* `GROUP BY` and *before* `ORDER BY` in a SQL query.

Rules for Using Aliases in Clauses

Understanding the order in which SQL statements are processed helps explain why some clauses can or cannot use column aliases.

The following table outlines the typical SQL query processing order and indicates whether column aliases can be used in each clause.

***Table 6.2**: SQL Query Processing Order*

Step	**Clause**	**Purpose**	**Can Use Column Alias**
1	`FROM`	Identifies the source tables or views	No
2	`WHERE`	Filters rows before grouping or aggregation	No
3	`GROUP BY`	Groups rows into sets for aggregation	No
4	`HAVING`	Filters groups after aggregation	No
5	`SELECT`	Selects columns, calculates expressions, and assigns aliases	Yes *(aliases are defined here)*
6	`ORDER BY`	Sorts the final result set	Yes *(can use aliases from* `SELECT`*)*

Exercise 9: Branches with More Than Five Orders

Using the `Orders` table, list the `BranchID` values and the number of `OrderID` values for each branch, but include only those branches where the total number of orders exceeds five.

This exercise demonstrates how to use the `HAVING` clause with `GROUP BY` to filter aggregated results.

Execute the following statement in the SQL Worksheet to find branches with more than five orders:

```
SELECT BranchID, COUNT(OrderID) AS TotalOrders
FROM Orders
GROUP BY BranchID
HAVING COUNT(OrderID) > 5;
```

The output of the query is shown in Figure 6.9:

BRANCHID	TOTALORDERS
B02	6
B05	7
B01	8

***Figure 6.9**: Branches with more than 5 Orders*

Query Notes

- `COUNT(OrderID)`: Counts the total number of orders in each branch.
- `GROUP BY BranchID`: Groups all orders by `BranchID`, so the count is calculated per branch.
- `HAVING COUNT(OrderID) > 5`: Filters the results to include only branches with more than five orders.

Exercise 10: Identifying Higher-Paying Positions in the Organization

Using the `SalesPersons` table, display each `Position` and its average salary, but include only those positions where the average salary is greater than 6,000. Sort the results in descending order of average salary.

This exercise demonstrates how to use the `HAVING` clause with the `AVG()` function to filter grouped results.

Execute the following statement to display positions and their average salary (above 6,000):

```
SELECT Position, ROUND(AVG(Salary), 2) AS AvgSalary
FROM SalesPersons
GROUP BY Position
HAVING AVG(Salary) > 6000
ORDER BY AvgSalary DESC;
```

The output of the query is shown in Figure 6.10:

POSITION	AVGSALARY
Director	82000
Regional Manager	59498.15
Store Manager	57336.83
Sales Executive	55000
Senior Sales	51746
Sales Associate	51067.13

Figure 6.10*: Average Salary by Position with Average Salary above 6,000*

Query Notes

- `ROUND(AVG(Salary), 2)`: Calculates the average salary for each position and rounds it to two decimal places.
- `GROUP BY Position`: Groups the data by position so that the average salary is calculated for each role individually.
- `HAVING AVG(Salary) > 6000`: Filters the results to include only positions where the average salary exceeds 6,000.
- `ORDER BY AvgSalary DESC`: Sorts the positions from highest to lowest average salary.

Finding Duplicates in a Table

In many real-world scenarios, it is necessary to identify *duplicate records* in a table. Duplicates can occur due to data entry errors, importing data from multiple sources, or business rules that allow multiple entries with the same values.

Identifying such duplicates is important for maintaining data integrity and ensuring accurate reporting.

The standard SQL approach for identifying duplicates involves grouping rows by the column(s) that define a duplicate and using the `HAVING` clause to filter groups that occur more than once.

Syntax

```
SELECT column1, column2, ..., COUNT(*) AS DuplicateCount
FROM table_name
GROUP BY column1, column2, ...
HAVING COUNT(*) > 1
ORDER BY DuplicateCount DESC;
```

Explanation

- **`column1, column2, ...`**: Refers to the column(s) that define a duplicate.
- **`COUNT(*) AS DuplicateCount`**: Counts how many times each combination of values occurs.
- **`GROUP BY column1, column2, ...`**: Groups the rows based on the specified columns.
- **`HAVING COUNT(*) > 1`**: Filters the results to include only combinations that appear more than once.
- **`ORDER BY DuplicateCount DESC`**: Sorts the results so the most frequent duplicates appear first.

Exercise 11: Find Customers Who Have Placed More Than One Order

Using the `Orders` table, write a query to display `CustomerID` values and the total number of orders (`OrderCount`) for customers who have placed more than one order. This exercise demonstrates how to use the `HAVING` clause to find duplicate entries by identifying customers who appear more than once in the table.

Execute the following statement to find customers who have placed more than one order:

```
SELECT CustomerID,
       COUNT(*) AS OrderCount
FROM Orders
GROUP BY CustomerID
HAVING COUNT(*) > 1
ORDER BY OrderCount DESC, CustomerID;
```

The output of the query is shown in Figure 6.11:

CUSTOMERID	ORDERCOUNT
C023	4
C010	3
C017	3
C030	3
C046	3
C048	2

***Figure 6.11**: Output showing Customers with more than one Order*

Query Notes

- `COUNT(*)`: Counts the total number of orders placed by each customer.
- `GROUP BY CustomerID`: Groups the data so that the count is calculated for each customer individually.
- `HAVING COUNT(*) > 1`: Filters the results to include only customers who have placed more than one order.
- `ORDER BY OrderCount DESC, CustomerID`: Sorts the results by the total number of orders (highest first) and then by `CustomerID` alphabetically or numerically.

The `HAVING` clause is a powerful tool for refining grouped results by applying conditions to aggregated data. It enables filtering of summarized data that cannot be handled using the `WHERE` clause.

Conclusion

This chapter introduced the concept of aggregation in SQL and explained how it can be used to summarize data effectively. It explored common aggregation functions such as SUM(), AVG(), COUNT(), MIN(), and MAX(), along with practical techniques for grouping data using the GROUP BY clause. The chapter also covered filtering aggregated results using the HAVING clause to refine the output based on conditions applied to grouped data.

Together, these concepts form a strong foundation for generating summarized and insightful query results.

The next chapter, **Combining Data with Joins**, explores how to combine data from multiple tables to answer more complex analytical questions.

Practice Questions

Use the training dataset to complete the following practice questions. These exercises reinforce concepts covered in this chapter.

1. Using the `Customers` table, find the number of customers in each region.
2. Using the `SalesPersons` table, list the `BranchID` values and the total salary payable for each Branch.
3. Using the `SalesPersons` table, display each `Position` and its average salary, rounded to two decimal places. Exclude the *Director* position from the results.
4. Using the `SalesPersons` table, list each `Position` along with the highest salary for that position. Include only those positions where the maximum salary is greater than or equal to 5,000.
5. Using the `SalesPersons` table, display each `BranchID` along with the total salary, highest salary, lowest salary, and average salary (rounded to two decimal places). Include only those branches where the average salary is greater than 1,000. Sort the results by average salary in ascending order.

Practice Answers

The answers to the preceding questions are as follows:

Answer 1

```
SELECT Region, COUNT(*) AS CustomerCount
FROM Customers
GROUP BY Region;
```

Answer 2

```
SELECT BranchID, SUM(Salary) AS TotalSal
FROM SalesPersons
GROUP BY BranchID;
```

Answer 3

```
SELECT Position, Round(AVG(Salary),2) AS AvgSal
FROM SalesPersons
WHERE Position <>'Director'
GROUP BY Position;
```

Answer 4

```
Select Position, MAX(Salary) AS MaxSal
FROM SalesPersons
GROUP BY Position
HAVING MAX(Salary) >=5000;
```

Answer 5

```
SELECT BranchID,
SUM(Salary) AS TotalSal,
MAX(Salary) AS MaxSal,
      MIN(Salary) AS MinSal,
ROUND(Avg(Salary),2) AS AvgSal
FROM SalesPersons
GROUP BY BranchID
HAVING Avg(Salary) > 1000
ORDER BY AVGSAL;
```

Chapter 7
Combining Data with Joins

Introduction

In a relational database, data is stored across multiple related tables to reduce redundancy and maintain accuracy. For example, customer details are stored in a `Customers` table, while orders are stored in an `Orders` table. These tables are linked using a common key, such as `CustomerID`.

To view related information together, SQL uses *joins* to connect data from different tables based on matching values in their key columns. Joins make it possible to retrieve meaningful results, such as displaying each order along with the customer who placed it. Joins are fundamental for analyzing data spread across multiple tables.

This chapter will cover the following topics:

- Understanding Joins
- INNER JOIN
- OUTER JOIN
- CROSS JOIN
- SELF JOIN
- Best Practices for Using Joins

Understanding Joins

In a relational database, related data is often stored in separate tables. This design minimizes redundancy, maintains data integrity, and simplifies updates. However, retrieving meaningful information often requires combining data from these tables. The `JOIN` operation in SQL allows data from multiple tables to be combined based on a related column, typically a **primary key** in one table and a **foreign key** in another.

Example from the Training Dataset:

- The `Customers` table contains customer details.
- The `Orders` table stores information about orders placed by customers.

Both tables share the `CustomerID` column, which serves as the link between them and allows the data to be joined and viewed as a single result set.

Need for Joins in SQL

Without joins, working with multiple tables would require running separate queries and manually matching results, which is inefficient and error-prone.

Joins are essential because they:

- Combine related rows from different tables into a single result set.
- Allow querying across multiple entities (such as `Customers`, `Orders`, and `Products`) in a single `SQL` statement.
- Enable complex analysis and reporting by linking data across multiple relationships.

Role of Keys in Joins

Primary keys and foreign keys play a central role in defining relationships between tables. They ensure that data stored in different tables can be accurately linked, making joins reliable and meaningful.

To understand how joins work, it's important to understand the following two key types that establish such relationships:

- **Primary Key**: A column (or set of columns) that uniquely identifies each row in a table.
- **Foreign Key**: A column in one table whose values correspond to the primary key in another table, establishing a relationship between the two.

  The following Figure 7.1 illustrates the relationship between the `Customers` and `Orders` tables, where the `CustomerID` column serves as the connecting key between them:

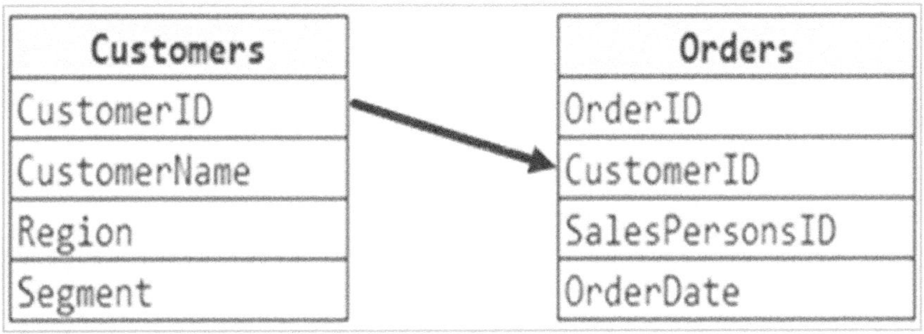

***Figure 7.1**: Relationship between Customers and Orders tables through the CustomerID column*

As shown in the preceding figure, `CustomerID` is the primary key in the `Customers` table and a foreign key in the `Orders` table. These two tables can be joined on `CustomerID` to retrieve customer details along with their orders.

NOTE: In Oracle SQL, joins do not require primary key or foreign key constraints to be formally defined in the database. A join works as long as the columns contain logically related values. For example, even if `Orders.CustomerID` is not declared as a foreign key; it can still be joined to `Customers.CustomerID` when the values match.

Understanding how primary and foreign keys function is the first step toward performing joins effectively. However, these keys are not mandatory for creating joins—SQL joins operate on any columns that contain related or matching values.

Identifying Join Columns

When working with unfamiliar tables, identifying the correct columns for joins is an essential first step. Before performing a join, ensure that the columns are logically and structurally compatible. This can be done by:

- **Checking column names**: Look for columns with the same or similar names across tables (for example, `CustomerID` in both `Orders` and `Customers`).
- **Comparing data types**: Ensure that the columns being joined have compatible data types (for example, both are `NUMBER` or both are `VARCHAR2`).
- **Testing for uniqueness**: The primary key column contains unique values, while the foreign key column may contain repeating values.
- **Reviewing sample data**: Compare the actual values in each column to confirm that they correspond correctly between the two tables.

Types of Joins in Oracle SQL

Oracle SQL supports several types of joins, each serving a specific purpose in combining data from multiple tables:

- **INNER JOIN**: Returns only the rows that have matching values in both tables.
- **LEFT OUTER JOIN**: Returns all rows from the left table and the matching rows from the right table; unmatched rows from the right table appear as `NULL`.
- **RIGHT OUTER JOIN**: Returns all rows from the right table and the matching rows from the left table; unmatched rows from the left table appear as `NULL`.
- **FULL OUTER JOIN**: Returns both matched and unmatched rows from each table.
- **CROSS JOIN**: Returns all possible combinations of rows from the joined tables (Cartesian product)
- **SELF JOIN**: Joins a table to itself to compare rows within the same table.

The sections that follow will explore each join type in detail, using examples from the `BDS_Training_Data` dataset.

INNER JOIN

An INNER JOIN, also known as an **Equi Join**, returns only the rows that have matching values in both tables being joined. If no match is found between the rows in the two tables, those rows are excluded from the result set.

The following diagram illustrates how an INNER JOIN returns only the matching rows between two tables:

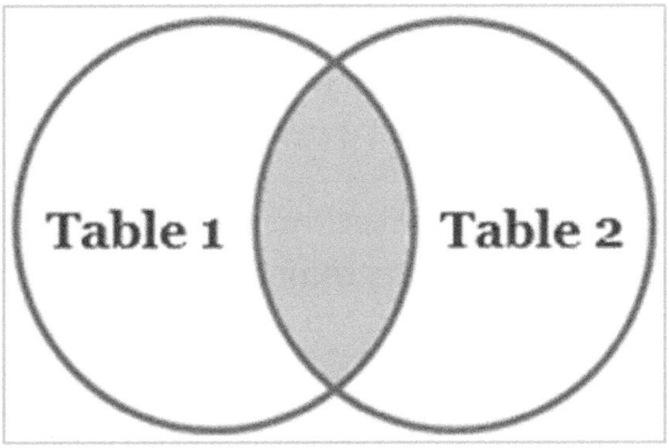

***Figure 7.2**: INNER JOIN returns only the matching rows between both tables*

The INNER JOIN:

- Returns only the rows where a match exists in both tables based on the join condition.
- Excludes rows that do not have a corresponding match in the other table.

INNER JOIN is the most common type of join and is used when the goal is to retrieve data that exists in both related tables.

Syntax

```
SELECT table1.column1, table1.column2, table2.column3
FROM table1
INNER JOIN table2
ON table1.common_column = table2.common_column;
```

In the above syntax:

- `table1.column1, table2.column3` specifies qualified column names, using the table name before the column name to avoid ambiguity.
- `INNER JOIN` specifies the type of join being performed.
- `ON table1.common_column = table2.common_column` defines the join condition that relates the two tables.

Exercise 1: Using INNER JOIN Between Tables

Using the `Customers` and `Orders` tables, retrieve the `CustomerID`, `CustomerName`, `Segment`, `OrderID`, and `OrderDate` for customers in the `Corporate` segment who have placed orders.

Execute the following statement to create an INNER JOIN between the `Customers` and `Orders` tables:

```
SELECT Customers.CustomerID,
      Customers.CustomerName,
      Customers.Segment,
      Orders.OrderID, Orders.OrderDate
FROM Customers
INNER JOIN Orders
      ON Customers.CustomerID = Orders.CustomerID
WHERE Customers.Segment = 'Corporate';
```

The output of the query is shown in Figure 7.3:

CUSTOMERID	CUSTOMERNAME	SEGMENT	ORDERID	ORDERDATE
C049	Cheryl Davis	Corporate	O1002	05-JAN-24
C044	Kevin Hall	Corporate	O1028	02-JUN-25

***Figure 7.3**: INNER JOIN between Customers and Orders tables*

Query Explanation

- **`SELECT`**: Specifies the columns to be returned (`CustomerID`, `CustomerName`), and `Segment` from the `Customers` table, and `OrderID` and `OrderDate` from the `Orders` table.
- **`FROM`**: Specifies the `Customers` table as the primary table in the query.
- **`INNER JOIN Orders`**: Combines rows from the `Customers` table with matching rows from the `Orders` table.
- **`ON Customers.CustomerID = Orders.CustomerID`**: Defines the join condition by matching rows where the `CustomerID` values are equal.
- **`WHERE`**: Filters the results to include only customers whose `Segment` is `Corporate`.

Table Aliases

When a query involves multiple tables, it is common for different tables to contain columns with the same name. For example, `BranchID` appears in both the `SalesPersons` and `Branches` tables in the `BDS_Training_Data` dataset.
This can cause ambiguity when Oracle SQL cannot determine which table's column is being referenced.

To avoid ambiguity, column names are **qualified** using the table name or a shorter **alias**. Although using the full table name eliminates confusion, it can make queries lengthy and harder to read. In such cases, *table aliases* provide a cleaner and more efficient solution.

A table alias is a temporary, short name assigned to a table within a query. Using aliases makes the SQL statements:

- Easier to read and understand
- Faster to write
- Less prone to typing errors
- Easier to maintain, especially when working with multiple joins

Syntax

```
SELECT t1.column1, t2.column2
FROM table1 t1
INNER JOIN table2 t2
ON t1.common_column = t2.common_column;
```

In the above syntax:

- The table aliases `t1` and `t2` are placed immediately after the table names.
- Once assigned, the alias replaces the table name throughout the query.
- Aliases are valid only within the query in which they are defined.

Exercise 2: Using Table Aliases in Joins

Using the `SalesPersons` and `Branches` tables, retrieve `SalesPersonID`, `SalesPersonName`, `Position`, `BranchName`, and `City` for all salespersons who hold the *Senior Sales* position and are assigned to either branch `'B01'` or `'B04'`.

Execute the following statement to display senior salespersons in selected branches:

```
SELECT S.SalesPersonID,
       S.SalesPersonName, S.Position,
       B.BranchName, B.City
FROM SalesPersons S
INNER JOIN Branches B
      ON S.BranchID = B.BranchID
WHERE B.BranchID in ('B01','B04')
AND S.Position = 'Senior Sales';
```

The output of the query is shown in Figure 7.4:

SALESPERSONID	SALESPERSONNAME	POSITION	BRANCHNAME	CITY
SP001	Kimberly Ball	Senior Sales	Branch 4	Houston
SP028	Cynthia Wells	Senior Sales	Branch 4	Houston
SP029	Pamela Jackson	Senior Sales	Branch 4	Houston
SP049	Ashley Jones	Senior Sales	Branch 1	New York
SP050	Robert Avery	Senior Sales	Branch 1	New York

***Figure 7.4**: INNER JOIN displays Senior salespersons in selected branches*

Query Notes

- `S` and `B` are table aliases assigned to `SalesPersons` and `Branches`, respectively, to make the query shorter and easier to read.
- **`INNER JOIN`** combines rows from both tables where `BranchID` values match.
- **`ON S.BranchID = B.BranchID`** defines the join condition by matching rows where `BranchID` values are the same in both tables.
- **`WHERE B.BranchID IN ('B01', 'B04')`** filters the results to only the specified branches.
- **`AND S.Position = 'Senior Sales'`** further filters the results to include only salespersons holding the `Senior Sales` position.

Exercise 3: Using INNER JOIN with Three Tables

Using the `Orders`, `Customers`, and `SalesPersons` tables, retrieve `OrderID`, `OrderDate`, `CustomerName`, `SalesPersonName`, and `BranchName` for all orders handled by branch `'B02'`.

Execute the following statement to display orders from branch `B02` with Customer and Salesperson details:

```
SELECT O.OrderID, O.OrderDate, C.CustomerName,
       S.SalesPersonName, B.BranchName
FROM Orders O
INNER JOIN Customers C
      ON O.CustomerID = C.CustomerID
INNER JOIN SalesPersons S
      ON O.SalesPersonID = S.SalesPersonID
INNER JOIN Branches B
      ON S.BranchID = B.BranchID
WHERE B.BranchID = 'B02';
```

The output of the query is shown in Figure 7.5:

ORDERID	ORDERDATE	CUSTOMERNAME	SALESPERSONNAME	BRANCHNAME
01001	04-JAN-23	Laura Kennedy	Trevor Young	Branch 2
01010	25-JAN-23	Austin Gentry	Joseph Coleman	Branch 2

***Figure** 7.5: Orders from branch B02 with Customer and Salesperson details*

Query Notes

- **`Orders O`** is the primary table, with related tables joined using aliases for clarity.
- **`INNER JOIN Customers C`** links each order to the customer who placed it using `CustomerID`.
- **`INNER JOIN SalesPersons S`** connects each order to the salesperson who handled it using `SalesPersonID`.
- **`INNER JOIN Branches B`** associates each salesperson to their branch through `BranchID`.
- **`WHERE B.BranchID = 'B02'`** filters the results to include only orders handled by branch `B02`.

Choosing the First Table in a Multi-Join Query

In multi-table joins, the first table in the `FROM` clause often sets the logical context of the query. Although Oracle's optimizer determines the actual execution order, choosing an appropriate starting table helps produce SQL code that is clearer, more readable, and easier to maintain.

The following are the guidelines for selecting the first table:

1. **Start with the main subject of the query**:
    - If retrieving a list of orders, begin with the `Orders` table.
    - If the focus is on customer details, begin with the `Customers` table.
2. **Follow the relationship chain**:
    - Each subsequent JOIN must connect to a table that is already included in the query.
3. **Consider filtering logic**:
    - If a filter applies primarily to one table, placing that table first can improve readability.
4. **Understand the role of the optimizer**:
    - Although Oracle may reorder joins for performance, choosing a logical sequence improves human readability and reduces errors.

Example

If the goal is to list all orders with customer and branch details, it is logical to begin with the `Orders` table, since it directly links to both `Customers` and `SalesPersons` (and through `SalesPersons` to `Branches`).

OUTER JOIN

An OUTER JOIN returns both the matching rows between two tables and the unmatched rows from one or both tables, depending on the type of outer join used. Unlike an INNER JOIN, which includes only rows that have matching values in both tables, an OUTER JOIN ensures that unmatched data is also included in the result set.

OUTER JOIN is particularly useful when all records from one table must be included, even when related data is missing in the other table.

Types of Outer Joins in Oracle SQL:

- **LEFT OUTER JOIN**: Returns all rows from the left table and the matching rows from the right table. Rows from the left table with no match appear with `NULL` values in the right table's columns.
- **RIGHT OUTER JOIN**: Returns all rows from the right table and the matching rows from the left table. Rows from the right table with no match appear with `NULL` values in the left table's columns.
- **FULL OUTER JOIN**: Returns all rows from both tables. Matched rows appear once, while unmatched rows from each table contain `NULL` values for missing columns.

Key Differences Between INNER and OUTER Joins

Before exploring the types of outer joins, it is helpful to understand how they differ from inner joins:

- **INNER JOIN**: Returns only rows with matching values in both tables.
- **OUTER JOIN**: Includes unmatched rows from one or both tables, depending on the join type.

The following sections explain each type of outer join in detail.

LEFT OUTER JOIN

A **LEFT OUTER JOIN** returns all rows from the left table specified in the `FROM` clause, along with the matching rows from the right table.

If no match is found in the right table, `NULL` values are returned for its columns.

The following diagram illustrates how a LEFT OUTER JOIN returns all rows from the left table and only the matching rows from the right table:

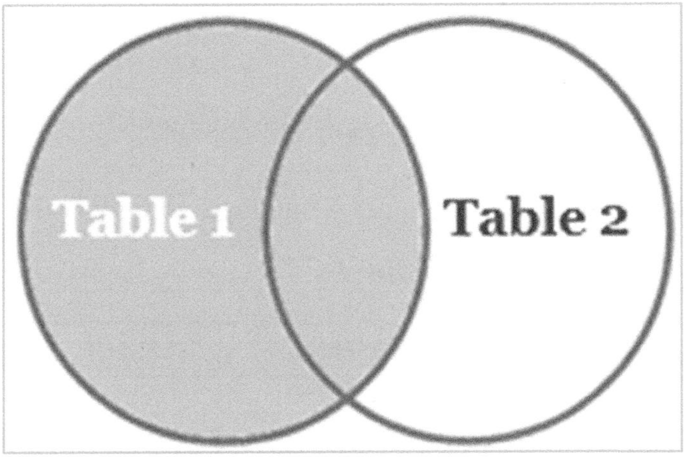

***Figure 7.6**: LEFT OUTER JOIN between the two tables*

This type of join is useful when the primary focus is on the left table's data, while still including related information from the right table whenever available.

Syntax

```
SELECT table1.column1, table1.column2, table2.column3
FROM table1
LEFT OUTER JOIN table2
ON table1.common_column = table2.common_column;
```

Exercise 4: Using LEFT OUTER JOIN

Using the `Customers` and `Orders` tables, retrieve `CustomerID`, `CustomerName`, and `Segment` for all the customers in the `Corporate` segment, along with their `OrderID` values. Ensure that customers without any orders are also included in the results.

In this exercise, the `Customers` table serves as the left table, returning all records for customers in the `Corporate` segment. Matching rows from the `Orders` table are included where available, while `NULL` is displayed for customers who have no corresponding orders.

Execute the following statement to display all `Customers` and `OrderID` values for the `Corporate` Segment:

```
SELECT C.CustomerID, C.CustomerName,
      C.Segment, O.OrderID
FROM Customers C
LEFT OUTER JOIN Orders O
      ON C.CustomerID = O.CustomerID
WHERE C.Segment = 'Corporate'
ORDER BY C.CustomerID;
```

The output of the query is shown in Figure 7.7:

CUSTOMERID	CUSTOMERNAME	SEGMENT	ORDERID
C005	Kimberly Robinson	Corporate	-
C016	Lisa Jackson	Corporate	-
C031	Troy Liu	Corporate	-
C033	Elizabeth Fowler	Corporate	-
C035	Tamara George	Corporate	-
C039	Beth Keller	Corporate	-
C040	Joseph Obrien	Corporate	-
C041	Nicole Vaughn	Corporate	-
C044	Kevin Hall	Corporate	O1028
C047	John Ryan	Corporate	-
C049	Cheryl Davis	Corporate	O1002
C050	Jason Shields	Corporate	-

***Figure** 7.7: Customers in the Corporate Segment with their Orders*

Query Notes

- **`Customers C`** serves as the left table, returning all customer records in the `Corporate` Segment.

- `LEFT OUTER JOIN Orders O` includes matching orders where available; unmatched customers show `NULL` for `OrderID`.
- `ON C.CustomerID = O.CustomerID` defines the join condition between customers and their orders.
- `WHERE C.Segment = 'Corporate'` filters customers to the `Corporate` Segment.
- `ORDER BY C.CustomerID` sorts the results by `CustomerID` in ascending order.

RIGHT OUTER JOIN

A **RIGHT OUTER JOIN** is the opposite of a LEFT OUTER JOIN. It returns all rows from the right table specified in the `FROM` clause, along with the matching rows from the left table. If no matching rows exist in the left table, `NULL` values are returned for its columns.

The following diagram illustrates how a RIGHT OUTER JOIN returns all rows from the right table and only the matching rows from the left table:

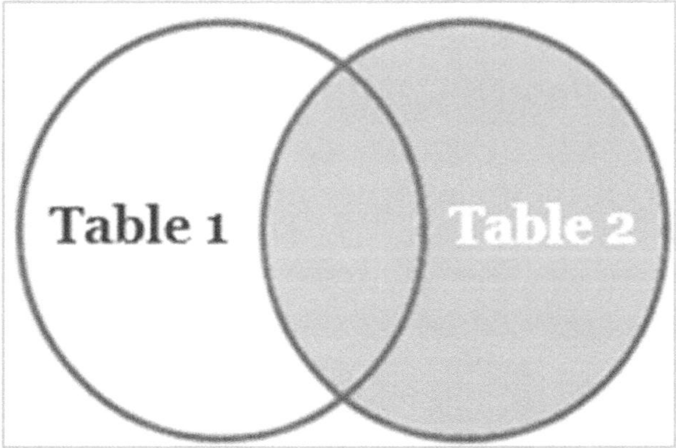

Figure 7.8: *RIGHT OUTER JOIN between the two tables*

This type of join is useful when the focus is to retain all rows from the right table while still retrieving related data from the left table, where available.

Syntax

```
SELECT table1.column1, table1.column2, table2.column3
FROM table1
RIGHT OUTER JOIN table2
ON table1.common_column = table2.common_column;
```

Exercise 5: Using RIGHT OUTER JOIN

Using the `Customers` and `Orders` tables, retrieve `CustomerID`, `CustomerName`, and `Segment` from the `Customers` table, along with the `OrderID` from the `Orders` table. This query demonstrates how a RIGHT OUTER JOIN returns all rows from the `Orders` table (the right table) and only the matching records from the `Customers` table.

Execute the following statement to display all orders and their matching customers:

```
SELECT C.CustomerID, C.CustomerName,
       C.Segment, O.OrderID
FROM Customers C
RIGHT OUTER JOIN Orders O
ON C.CustomerID = O.CustomerID
ORDER BY O.OrderID;
```

The output of the query is shown in Figure 7.9:

CUSTOMERID	CUSTOMERNAME	SEGMENT	ORDERID
C048	Laura Kennedy	Consumer	O1001
C049	Cheryl Davis	Corporate	O1002
C017	Joel Nelson	Consumer	O1003
C009	Renee Blair	Home Office	O1004
C010	Thomas Miller	Consumer	O1005
C025	Ann Williams	Home Office	O1007
C030	Gina Carter	Home Office	O1008
C013	Bobby Hall	Home Office	O1009
C020	Austin Gentry	Consumer	O1010
C008	Brandon Davis	Consumer	O1013
C048	Laura Kennedy	Consumer	O1014
C043	Jocelyn Wright	Consumer	O1015
C023	Justin Baker	Home Office	O1017
C046	Shannon Jones	Consumer	O1021
C046	Shannon Jones	Consumer	O1022
C046	Shannon Jones	Consumer	O1023
C042	Zachary	Consumer	O1024
C045	Michael Brown	Consumer	O1025
C030	Gina Carter	Home Office	O1026
C030	Gina Carter	Home Office	O1027
C044	Kevin Hall	Corporate	O1028
C023	Justin Baker	Home Office	O1029
C023	Justin Baker	Home Office	O1030
C023	Justin Baker	Home Office	O1031
C010	Thomas Miller	Consumer	O1032
C010	Thomas Miller	Consumer	O1033
C017	Joel Nelson	Consumer	O1034
C017	Joel Nelson	Consumer	O1035

***Figure 7.9**: All Orders from the Orders table with matching Customer details*

NOTE: The query output contains 28 rows. For readability, the results are displayed in two parts within the figure.

Query Notes

- `RIGHT OUTER JOIN Orders O` retrieves all rows from the `Orders` table (right table) and only the matching rows from the `Customers` table.
- `ON C.CustomerID = O.CustomerID` defines the join condition between two tables.
- `ORDER BY O.OrderID` sorts the results by `OrderID` in ascending order.

The result shows that a RIGHT OUTER JOIN includes every order from the `Orders` table, returning customer details only where a matching `CustomerID` exists.

FULL OUTER JOIN

A **FULL OUTER JOIN** combines the results of both a LEFT OUTER JOIN and a RIGHT OUTER JOIN. It ensures that:

- All rows from the left table are included, even when no matching rows exist in the right table.
- All rows from the right table are included, even when no matching rows exist in the left table.

Rows without a corresponding match on either side appear with `NULL` values in the columns where related data is missing.

The following diagram illustrates how a FULL OUTER JOIN returns all rows from both tables, including matching and non-matching rows:

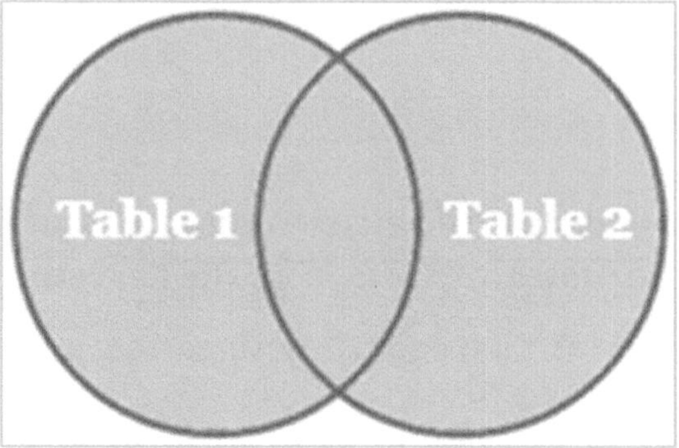

***Figure 7.10**: FULL OUTER JOIN between the two tables*

Syntax

```
SELECT column_list
FROM table1
FULL OUTER JOIN table2
ON table1.common_column = table2.common_column;
```

Exercise 6: Using FULL OUTER JOIN

Using the `Orders` and `OrderDetails` tables, display all `OrderID` values along with their corresponding `CustomerID` and `Sales` amounts. Ensure that:

- Orders without matching sales details are still included.
- Sales records without a corresponding order are also included.

Execute the following statement to display all `OrderID` values with corresponding customer IDs and sales amounts:

```
SELECT O.OrderID, O.CustomerID, OD.Sales
FROM Orders O
FULL OUTER JOIN OrderDetails OD
ON O.OrderID = OD.OrderID
ORDER BY O.OrderID;
```

The output of the query is shown in Figure 7.11:

ORDERID	CUSTOMERID	SALES
O1001	C048	136.94
O1002	C049	150.13
O1003	C017	91.44
O1004	C009	50.44
O1004	C009	161.27
O1005	C010	44.98
O1005	C010	75.96
O1005	C010	213.72
O1005	C010	45.14
O1007	C025	25.62
O1007	C025	267.08
O1007	C025	163.18
O1007	C025	69.03
O1008	C030	161.5
O1008	C030	77.05
O1009	C013	242.12
O1010	C020	214.19
O1010	C020	232.93
O1010	C020	181.3
O1010	C020	23.69
O1013	C008	146.05
O1013	C008	35.62
O1013	C008	72.51
O1013	C008	56.11
O1014	C048	63.61
O1014	C048	28.02
O1015	C043	321.62
O1017	C023	47.33
O1021	C046	28.65
O1022	C046	7.17
O1023	C046	23.88
O1024	C042	175.07
O1024	C042	11.63
O1024	C042	14.33
O1024	C042	89.18
O1025	C045	191.2
O1025	C045	55.07
O1026	C030	37.86
O1026	C030	31.06
O1026	C030	41.65
O1026	C030	245.9
O1027	C030	-
O1028	C044	-
O1029	C023	-
O1030	C023	-
O1031	C023	-
O1032	C010	52.75
O1033	C010	278.2
O1034	C017	-
O1035	C017	-

***Figure 7.11**: FULL OUTER JOIN between the Orders and OrderDetails tables*

NOTE: The query output contains 50 rows. For readability, the results are displayed in three parts, each showing consecutive rows.

Query Notes

- **`FULL OUTER JOIN OrderDetails OD`** combines rows from both tables. It includes:
    - All matching rows where `OrderID` values are equal.
    - Unmatched rows from either table, showing `NULL` for missing data.
- **`ON O.OrderID = OD.OrderID`** defines the join condition between the two tables.
- **`ORDER BY O.OrderID`** sorts the result set in ascending order by `OrderID`.

When a FULL OUTER JOIN is applied, rows are returned from both tables according to the following rules:

- If an `OrderID` exists in both `Orders` and `OrderDetails`, all selected columns—`O.OrderID`, `O.CustomerID`, and `OD.Sales`—display values.
- If an `OrderID` exists only in `Orders`, `O.OrderID` and `O.CustomerID` display values, while `OD.Sales` appear as `NULL`.
- If an `OrderID` exists only in `OrderDetails`, columns from `Orders` (`O.OrderID`, `O.CustomerID`) appear as `NULL`, while `OD.Sales` display a value.

In summary, outer joins—whether left, right, or full—are used to include unmatched rows from one or both tables, ensuring that no important data is excluded from the results.

CROSS JOIN

A **CROSS JOIN** produces a Cartesian product by pairing every row from one table with every row from another. When no `WHERE` clause or join condition is specified, each row in the first table is paired with all rows in the second table.

For example, if Table1 contains 10 rows and Table2 contains 10 rows, the result of a CROSS JOIN will be 10 × 10 = 100 rows.

The following diagram illustrates how a CROSS JOIN returns every possible combination of rows from two tables:

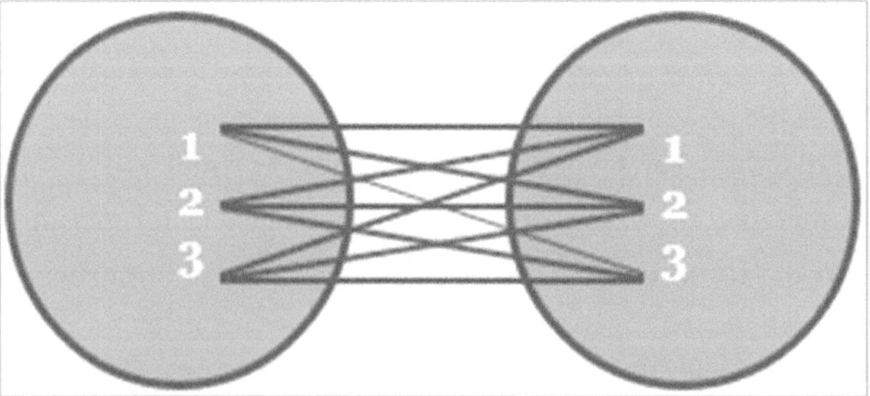

***Figure 7.12**: CROSS JOIN between the two tables*

This type of join is useful for generating all possible combinations between two datasets. However, it should be used cautiously, as the number of resulting rows grows rapidly with larger tables, which can impact performance.

Syntax

```
SELECT e.column1, e.column2, d.column1
FROM table1 e
CROSS JOIN table2 d;
```

Exercise 7: Using CROSS JOIN

Using the `Branches` and `Category` tables, display each `BranchName` with each `CategoryName`, showing all possible combinations (Cartesian product). Sort the results by `BranchName`, and then by `CategoryName`.

Execute the following statement to display each `BranchName` with each `CategoryName`:

```
SELECT B.BranchName, C.Category
FROM Branches B
CROSS JOIN Category C
ORDER BY B.BranchName, C.Category;
```

The output of the query is shown in Figure 7.13:

BRANCHNAME	CATEGORY
Branch 1	Furniture
Branch 1	Furniture
Branch 1	Furniture
Branch 1	Office Supplies
Branch 1	Office Supplies
Branch 1	Office Supplies
Branch 1	Technology
Branch 1	Technology
Branch 1	Technology
Branch 1	Technology
Branch 2	Furniture
Branch 2	Furniture
Branch 2	Furniture
Branch 2	Office Supplies
Branch 2	Office Supplies
Branch 2	Office Supplies
Branch 2	Technology

BRANCHNAME	CATEGORY
Branch 2	Technology
Branch 2	Technology
Branch 2	Technology
Branch 3	Furniture
Branch 3	Furniture
Branch 3	Furniture
Branch 3	Office Supplies
Branch 3	Office Supplies
Branch 3	Office Supplies
Branch 3	Technology
Branch 3	Technology
Branch 3	Technology
Branch 3	Technology
Branch 4	Furniture
Branch 4	Furniture
Branch 4	Furniture
Branch 4	Office Supplies

BRANCHNAME	CATEGORY
Branch 4	Office Supplies
Branch 4	Office Supplies
Branch 4	Technology
Branch 4	Technology
Branch 4	Technology
Branch 4	Technology
Branch 5	Furniture
Branch 5	Furniture
Branch 5	Furniture
Branch 5	Office Supplies
Branch 5	Office Supplies
Branch 5	Office Supplies
Branch 5	Technology
Branch 5	Technology
Branch 5	Technology
Branch 5	Technology

***Figure 7.13**: CROSS JOIN between Branches and Category tables*

NOTE: The preceding output shows 50 rows. For readability, the results are displayed in three columns side by side. In the actual SQL output, these rows would appear in a single continuous list.

Query Notes

- **`CROSS JOIN Category C`** produces a Cartesian product—pairing every branch with every category.
- **`ORDER BY B.BranchName, C.CategoryName`** sorts the results first by branch name and then by category name.
- **`B`** and **`C`** are table aliases assigned to `Branches` and `Category`, respectively, for easier reference.

Row Counts:

- Rows in the `Branches` table: 5
- Rows in the `Category` table: 10
- Rows after the CROSS JOIN (5 × 10): 50

CROSS JOIN is useful for generating all possible combinations between two tables, such as pairing every branch with each product category. However, because the number of rows increases rapidly with table size, they should be used cautiously. Applying filters after the join can help keep the result set manageable.

SELF JOIN

A **SELF JOIN** is a join in which a table is joined to itself. It is used when rows within the same table need to be compared or related—for example, to represent hierarchical relationships, compare records, or identify duplicate entries.

The following diagram illustrates how a SELF JOIN relates rows within the same table:

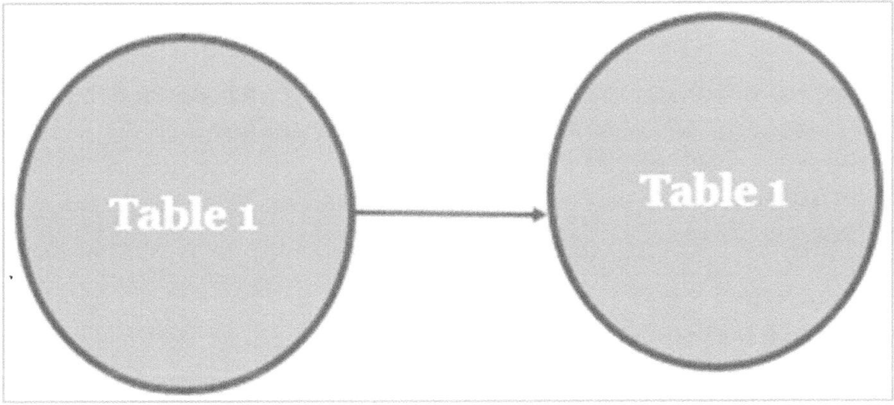

Figure 7.14: *SELF JOIN—a table joining to itself*

Since the same table is referenced more than once in the query, table aliases are required to distinguish between the different instances of the table.

Common Use Cases:

- Displaying employees along with their managers when both are stored in the same table.
- Comparing product prices within the same category.
- Identifying duplicate records based on specific columns.

Syntax

```
SELECT A.column_name, B.column_name
FROM table_name1 A
JOIN table_name1 B
ON A.common_column = B.common_column;
```

Exercise 8: Display SalesPersons and their Managers for a Specific Branch

Using the `SalesPersons` table, retrieve `SalesPersonID`, `SalesPersonName`, and `Position` along with each manager's name and position. Apply a filter so that only salespersons from branch `'B04'` appear in the output.

Execute the following statement to display salespersons and their manager for a specific branch:

```
SELECT SP1.SalesPersonID, SP1.SalesPersonName, SP1.BranchID,
       SP1.Position, SP2.SalesPersonName AS Manager,
       SP2.Position AS MgrPos
FROM SalesPersons SP1
JOIN SalesPersons SP2
ON SP1.ReportsTo = SP2.SalesPersonID
WHERE SP1.BranchID = 'B04'
ORDER BY SP1.SalesPersonName;
```

The output of the query is shown in Figure 7.15:

SALESPERSONID	SALESPERSONNAME	BRANCHID	POSITION	MANAGER	MGRPOS
SP030	Alexander Collins	B04	Sales Associate	Kimberly Ball	Senior Sales
SP026	Bradley Smith	B04	Sales Associate	Kimberly Ball	Senior Sales
SP028	Cynthia Wells	B04	Senior Sales	Tammie Hanson	Regional Manager
SP046	Isaac Turner	B04	Sales Associate	Kimberly Ball	Senior Sales
SP003	Jason Powell	B04	Store Manager	Tammie Hanson	Regional Manager
SP001	Kimberly Ball	B04	Senior Sales	Tammie Hanson	Regional Manager
SP012	Melissa Marshall	B04	Sales Associate	Kimberly Ball	Senior Sales
SP031	Michael Burton	B04	Store Manager	Tammie Hanson	Regional Manager
SP016	Mr. Jeremiah Reeves	B04	Store Manager	Tammie Hanson	Regional Manager
SP029	Pamela Jackson	B04	Senior Sales	Tammie Hanson	Regional Manager
SP015	Paul Larsen	B04	Regional Manager	Patricia Gomez	Director

***Figure 7.15**: SELF JOIN displaying Salespersons along with their Managers*

Query Notes

- `SP1` and `SP2` are aliases for two instances of the `SalesPersons` table, where:
    - `SP1` represents the individual salesperson
    - `SP2` represents their manager
- `ON SP1.ReportsTo = SP2.SalesPersonID` **defines the relationship between each salesperson and their manager.**
- `WHERE SP1.BranchID = 'B04'` **filters the results to include only salespersons from branch `'B04'`.**
- `ORDER BY SP1.SalesPersonName` sorts the results alphabetically by salesperson name.

A self-join is a powerful technique for comparing rows within the same table. It is especially useful for representing hierarchical relationships, such as employees and their managers. Using **table aliases** makes the query easier to read and interpret by clearly distinguishing between the two instances of the same table.

Best Practices for Using Joins

Joins are a fundamental part of SQL, and following best practices ensures that queries remain both accurate and efficient.

These guidelines apply to all join types and help in writing clear, maintainable SQL code:

1. **Use Explicit JOIN Syntax**
    - Prefer the ANSI `JOIN ... ON` style (for example, `INNER JOIN`, `LEFT JOIN`) over the older method of listing tables separated by commas in the `FROM` clause and specifying join conditions in the `WHERE` clause.
    - The explicit join style is easier to read, avoids accidental Cartesian products, and separates join logic from filtering conditions.

Example — Old style (ANSI-89):

```
SELECT C.CustomerName, O.OrderID
FROM Customers C, Orders O
WHERE C.CustomerID = O.CustomerID;
```

Example — Preferred style (ANSI-92):

```
SELECT C.CustomerName, O.OrderID
FROM Customers C
INNER JOIN Orders O
ON C.CustomerID = O.CustomerID;
```

2. **Always Specify the Join Condition**
   - Avoid unintended Cartesian products by ensuring that the `ON` clause correctly defines the relationship between the tables.
   - Verify that the join keys use compatible data types and align with the matching business logic.
3. **Use Table Aliases Wisely**
   - Assign short, meaningful aliases when joining multiple tables.
   - Aliases make queries easier to read and help avoid ambiguity when referencing columns.
4. **Qualify Column Names**
   - When tables share column names (such as `BranchID` or `CustomerID`), always **prefix them** with the table name or alias to prevent confusion and errors.
5. **Filter Early When Possible**
   - Apply `WHERE` conditions early in the query when they significantly reduce the dataset.
   - Early filtering can improve query performance by minimizing the volume of data processed during joins.

6. **Be Careful with Outer Joins**
   - Understand the differences between `LEFT`, `RIGHT`, and `FULL OUTER JOIN` to avoid unexpected `NULL` values.
   - Always review query results containing `NULLs` to ensure that the join is correct.
7. **Use Appropriate Indexing**
   - Index columns used in join conditions (`ON` clauses), especially in large tables.
   - Proper indexing can significantly improve join performance.
8. **Test with Smaller Datasets First**
   - Validate join logic using filtered or sample data before executing the queries on a full production dataset.
   - This helps to ensure correctness and prevents unnecessary resource usage.

Applying these best practices ensures that join queries remain clear, accurate, and efficient. Consistently following these guidelines leads to maintainable SQL code that delivers reliable results across all join types.

Conclusion

This chapter introduced the concept of joins in SQL and explained how they combine related data from multiple tables to produce meaningful results. It covered different join types—INNER JOIN for matching rows, OUTER JOIN for including unmatched rows, CROSS JOIN for generating Cartesian products, and SELF JOIN for comparing rows within the same table.

The chapter also outlined best practices for using joins effectively, emphasizing clarity, accuracy, and performance when building SQL queries.

The next chapter, **Working with Subqueries**, focuses on using queries within other queries to filter, calculate, and restructure results—further enhancing the ability to write powerful and flexible SQL statements.

Practice Questions

Use the training dataset to complete the following practice questions. These exercises reinforce concepts covered in this chapter.

1. Using the `Orders`, `OrderDetails`, and `Products` tables, retrieve `OrderID`, `OrderDate`, `ProductName`, and `CategoryID` for all orders.
2. Using the `Orders` and `SalesPersons` tables, retrieve `OrderID` and `OrderDate` (from `Orders`) and `SalesPersonName` and `Position` (from `SalesPersons`) for all orders.
3. Using the `SalesPersons` and `Branches` tables, retrieve `SalesPersonID`, `SalesPersonName`, and `BranchName` for all salespersons. Return every row from `SalesPersons` and only matching branch rows from `Branches`. Sort the results by `BranchID` in descending order.

   If a salesperson is not assigned to a branch, display `NULL` for `BranchName`.
4. Using the `Products` and `OrderDetails` tables, retrieve `ProductID`, `ProductName`, `OrderID`, and `Quantity` for all products, ensuring products appear even if they have not been ordered.
5. Using the `Customers` and `Orders` tables, retrieve `CustomerID`, `CustomerName`, and `OrderID` so that the results include:
   - Customers who have placed orders
   - Customers who have not placed any orders
   - Orders that do not have a matching customer (if any)

Practice Answers

The answers to the preceding questions are as follows:

Answer 1

```
SELECT O.OrderID, O.OrderDate,
       P.ProductName, P.CategoryID
FROM Orders O
INNER JOIN OrderDetails OD
ON O.OrderID = OD.OrderID
INNER JOIN Products P
ON OD.ProductID = P.ProductID
ORDER BY O.OrderID, P.ProductName;
```

Answer 2

```
SELECT O.OrderID, O.OrderDate,
       S.SalesPersonName, S.Position
FROM Orders O
INNER JOIN SalesPersons S
ON O.SalesPersonID = S.SalesPersonID
ORDER BY O.OrderDate, O.OrderID;
```

Answer 3

```
SELECT S.SalesPersonID, S.SalesPersonName,
       B.BranchName
FROM SalesPersons S
LEFT OUTER JOIN Branches B
ON S.BranchID = B.BranchID
ORDER BY B.BranchID DESC;
```

Answer 4

```
SELECT  P.ProductID, P.ProductName,
        OD.OrderID,OD.Quantity
FROM OrderDetails OD
RIGHT OUTER JOIN Products P
ON OD.ProductID = P.ProductID
ORDER BY P.ProductID;
```

Answer 5

```
SELECT C.CustomerID, C.CustomerName,
       O.OrderID
FROM Customers C
FULL OUTER JOIN Orders O
ON C.CustomerID = O.CustomerID
ORDER BY C.CustomerID, O.OrderID;
```

Chapter 8
Working with Subqueries

Introduction

In many SQL queries, the result of one query is often required to determine the conditions or data for another query. Instead of running multiple separate statements, a subquery allows one query to be embedded inside another, enabling more precise and flexible data retrieval.

A subquery, enclosed in parentheses, can appear in various parts of an SQL statement, such as the `WHERE`, `FROM`, or `SELECT` clause, eliminating the need for temporary tables and keeping SQL code concise for complex requirements.

This chapter will cover the following topics:

- Understanding Subqueries
- Single-Row Subqueries
- Multiple-Row Subqueries
- Multiple-Column Subqueries
- Correlated Subqueries
- Best Practices for Using Subqueries

Understanding Subqueries

A **subquery**, also called a *nested* or *inner query*, is a query placed inside another SQL statement. The result of the subquery is used by the main query, also known as the outer query. Subqueries are always enclosed in parentheses and can appear in various parts of a SQL statement, such as the `SELECT`, `FROM`, or `WHERE` clause.

Subqueries are especially useful for breaking down complex problems into smaller steps. Instead of writing one long query with multiple joins and conditions, a subquery can produce an intermediate result that the outer query uses to generate the final output.

Example:

To find all orders with an amount greater than the average order amount, the logic can be divided into two steps:

1. Calculate the average order amount.
2. Retrieve only those orders that are greater than this average.

The subquery handles the first step, while the outer query handles the second. This approach makes the SQL statement easier to read, maintain, and troubleshoot.

Introduction to Subqueries

A subquery executes first and produces a result set that the outer query then uses to complete its operation. This allows complex problems to be solved in smaller, logical steps. The process works as follows:

1. Oracle executes the subquery first and passes its result to the outer query.
2. The outer query processes the result by applying filters, calculations, or joins as needed.
3. Depending on its type, a subquery may return a single value, multiple values, or multiple columns.

Writing Effective Subqueries

When writing subqueries, follow these guidelines to ensure clarity and correctness:

- Always enclose the subquery in parentheses.
- Use meaningful column or table aliases for readability.
- Ensure that the subquery returns values compatible with the outer query's comparison operator.
- When a subquery appears in the `SELECT` or `FROM` clause, assign it an alias so the outer query can reference it.
- Avoid using `ORDER BY` inside a subquery; apply it in the main query to control the final output order.

Advantages of Using Subqueries

Subqueries provide several benefits when working with complex SQL queries:

- Breaks complex queries into smaller, manageable parts.
- Eliminates the need for temporary tables.
- Improves the readability and maintainability of SQL code.

Subqueries can be categorized into several types, including **single-row**, **multiple-row**, **multiple-column**, and **correlated subqueries**.

The upcoming sections will explore each type in detail with examples.

Single-Row Subqueries

A **single-row subquery** is a subquery that returns exactly **one row containing a single value**. It is typically used with comparison operators such as `=`, `<`, `>`, `<=`, `>=`, and `<>` in the outer query. Because only one value is returned, the comparison is direct and unambiguous.

Single-row subqueries are commonly used to compare a column value against:

- The maximum or minimum value from another table
- The average of a column
- A specific aggregated result from a related dataset

Working with Single-Row Subqueries

The single-row subquery works as follows:

1. The subquery executes first and produces a single value.
2. The outer query then compares its column value to that result using a comparison operator.
3. Single-row subqueries typically contain aggregate functions or conditions that ensure only one row is returned.

NOTE: If a single-row subquery returns more than one row, Oracle raises the following error: `ORA-01427: single-row subquery returns more than one row.`

Exercise 1: Find the Salesperson(s) with the Highest Salary

Using the `SalesPersons` table, write a query to find the salesperson(s) receiving the highest salary.

A subquery is required because this task involves two logical steps:

1. Compute the maximum salary using the `MAX()` function:

```
SELECT MAX(Salary)
FROM SalesPersons;
```

   This query returns the highest salary in the table (for example, 82000 in the current dataset).

2. Retrieve the salesperson(s) whose salary matches that value.

```
SELECT SalesPersonID, SalesPersonName, Salary
FROM SalesPersons
WHERE Salary = <result from Step 1>;
```

A subquery allows both steps to be combined into a single statement, where the inner query calculates the maximum salary and the outer query retrieves the corresponding salesperson(s).

Run the following statement in the SQL Worksheet to execute the combined query:

```
SELECT SalesPersonID, SalesPersonName, Salary
FROM SalesPersons
WHERE Salary = (
  SELECT MAX(Salary)
  FROM SalesPersons
);
```

The output of the query is shown in Figure 8.1:

SALESPERSONID	SALESPERSONNAME	SALARY
SP102	Patricia Gomez	82000

***Figure 8.1**: Salesperson with the highest salary*

Query Notes

- The **inner subquery** (`SELECT MAX(Salary) FROM SalesPersons`) returns the highest salary value.
- The **outer query** retrieves rows from `SalesPersons` where the salary equals the maximum value.
- This ensures that all salespersons earning the highest salary are displayed, including ties.

Check Your Understanding

Task: Remove `MAX()` from the inner query and execute the following statement:

```
SELECT SalesPersonID, SalesPersonName, Salary
FROM SalesPersons
WHERE Salary = (SELECT Salary FROM SalesPersons);
```

Expected Result:

Oracle raises the following error:

`ORA-01427: single-row subquery returns more than one row.`

Reason: Without the `MAX()` function, the subquery returns multiple salary values. The = operator can only compare against a single value. Using `MAX(Salary)` reduces the result into one value, making it valid for a single-row subquery.

Exercise 2: Find Products Starting with 'P' and Priced Above the Average cost

Using the `Products` table, retrieve the `ProductID`, `ProductName`, and `Cost` columns for all products whose names start with `'P'` and whose cost is greater than the average cost of all products beginning with `'P'`.

Execute the following statement in the SQL worksheet to display product details:

```
SELECT ProductID, ProductName, Cost
FROM Products
WHERE Cost > (
  SELECT AVG(Cost)
  FROM Products WHERE ProductName like 'P%'
)
AND ProductName like 'P%';
```

The output of the query is shown in Figure 8.2:

PRODUCTID	PRODUCTNAME	COST
P0006	Paper 6	16.13
P0014	Phones 14	18.59
P0037	Paper 37	12.65

***Figure 8.2**: Products costing more than the average cost of Products starting with 'P'*

Query Notes

- The **subquery** `(SELECT AVG(Cost) FROM Products WHERE ProductName LIKE 'P%')` calculates the average cost for all products whose names begin with `'P'`.

- The **outer query** retrieves only those products whose cost is greater than the average.
- The condition `AND ProductName LIKE 'P%'` appears in both the subquery and the outer query to ensure that the comparison is performed within the **same subset of products**. Without this condition, the query would compare product costs against an average calculated from a different set of rows. Since the subquery returns a single numeric value, this is a single-row subquery.

Subqueries in the HAVING Clause

The `HAVING` clause filters groups after aggregation, and a subquery can be used within it to provide a comparison value for those aggregated results. This allows grouped data (such as category averages) to be compared against a single overall metric.

Exercise 3: Using a Subquery in the HAVING Clause

Using the `Products` table, list the `CategoryID` values for categories whose average cost is greater than the overall average cost of all products. Sort the result by `CategoryID`.

Execute the following statement in the SQL Worksheet to find categories with above-average cost:

```
SELECT CategoryID
FROM Products
GROUP BY CategoryID
HAVING AVG(Cost) > (
  SELECT AVG(Cost)
  FROM Products
)
ORDER BY CategoryID;
```

The output of the query is shown in Figure 8.3:

CATEGORYID
4
6
7
9

***Figure 8.3**: Categories with above-average cost*

Query Notes

- The **outer query** groups products by `CategoryID` and calculates the average cost for each category.
- The **subquery** `(SELECT AVG(Cost) FROM Products)` computes the overall average cost across all products.
- The `HAVING` clause filters categories whose average cost is **greater than** the overall average.
- The `ORDER BY` clause sorts the results by `CategoryID` for clarity.

NOTE: The condition in this query compares group-level aggregates—each category's average cost—to a single benchmark (the overall average). Because this comparison depends on aggregated values, it must be applied **after grouping**. Therefore, the `HAVING` clause is used instead of `WHERE`. The `WHERE` clause filters rows before grouping, while `HAVING` filters groups after aggregation.

Single-row subqueries return exactly one value and are commonly used in comparisons within the `WHERE` or `HAVING` clauses. They work with operators such as `=`, `<>`, `<`, `<=`, `>`, and `>=`. Typical use cases include comparing a column value to an aggregate result—such as `MAX(Salary)` or `AVG(Cost)`—calculated from the same or a related table.

Multiple-Row Subqueries

A **multiple-row subquery** returns more than one row and is used when the outer query needs to compare a value against a **set of values** rather than a single one. These subqueries are typically used with **set and quantified comparison operators** such as `IN`, `ANY` (or `SOME`), and `ALL`.

This approach is useful when filtering for membership in a list, comparing values against a range, or matching results from another table.

Working with Multiple-Row Subqueries

A multiple-row subquery executes first and returns a set of values. The **outer query** then evaluates each row against that set using one of several comparison operators. These operators determine how the results from the subquery are interpreted by the outer query.

The following table summarizes the most common operators, their purpose, and an example of how each is applied in SQL:

***Table 8.1**: Common operators in multi-row Subqueries*

Operator	**Description**	**Example Use**
`IN`	Checks whether a value exists within the returned set	`WHERE BranchID IN (SELECT BranchID FROM SalesPersons)`
`> ANY (or > SOME)`	Returns **TRUE** if the value is greater than at least one item in the set (equivalent to greater than the minimum)	`WHERE Salary > ANY (SELECT Salary FROM SalesPersons)`
> ALL	Returns **TRUE** only if the value is greater than every item in the set (equivalent to greater than the maximum)	`WHERE Salary > ALL (SELECT Salary FROM SalesPersons)`

These operators provide flexible ways to compare a value against multiple results returned by a subquery.

Writing Effective Multiple-Row Subqueries

When designing multiple-row subqueries, ensure they return only the data needed for the comparison and remain efficient and readable. The following guidelines help in writing effective multiple-row subqueries:

- Use `IN`, `ANY/SOME`, or `ALL` to compare a column's value against a set of results.
- Return only the necessary column(s) from the subquery to improve performance.
- Avoid using `ORDER BY` inside the subquery; apply sorting in the outer query instead.
- Apply filters in the `WHERE` clause to limit rows returned by the subquery. Use DISTINCT only when necessary—although the `IN` operator automatically handles duplicate values.

Exercise 4: Find Orders with Quantity ≥ 9

Using the `Orders` and `OrderDetails` tables, write a query to display `OrderID`, `CustomerID`, and `OrderDate` for all orders that include at least one item with a quantity greater than or equal to 9. Sort the result by `OrderID`.

Execute the following statement in the SQL Worksheet to find orders with quantity ≥ 9:

```
SELECT o.OrderID, o.CustomerID, o.OrderDate
FROM Orders o
WHERE o.OrderID IN (
  SELECT od.OrderID
  FROM OrderDetails od
  WHERE od.Quantity >= 9
)
ORDER BY o.OrderID;
```

The output of the query is shown in Figure 8.4:

ORDERID	CUSTOMERID	ORDERDATE
O1005	C010	10-JAN-23
O1007	C025	13-JAN-23
O1009	C013	24-JAN-25
O1013	C008	02-FEB-25
O1015	C043	09-FEB-23
O1025	C045	05-NOV-25

***Figure 8.4**: Orders with Quantity greater than or equal to 9*

Query Notes

- The **outer query** retrieves order details (`OrderID`, `CustomerID`, and `OrderDate`) from the `Orders` table.
- The **subquery** scans `OrderDetails` and returns all `OrderID` values where any item has a quantity ≥ 9.
- The `IN` operator compares each `OrderID` from the outer query to the list returned by the subquery, filtering only those orders that meet the condition.
- Duplicates returned by the subquery (if any) do not affect the final result because `IN` automatically handles duplicates.
- The `ORDER BY` clause in the outer query sorts the results by `OrderID` in ascending order.

NOTE: This query uses a **multiple-row subquery**, where the inner query returns several `OrderID` values. The **`IN`** operator is used to compare against this set of values. Using a single-value operator, such as `=`, would raise the error **`ORA-01427: single-row subquery returns more than one row`**.

Exercise 5: Find Products with Names Starting with 'A' and Priced Above at Least One Product Starting with 'P'

Using the `Products` table, write a query to display `ProductID`, `ProductName`, and `Cost` for products whose names start with `'A'` and whose cost is greater than that of *at least one product* whose name starts with `'P'`.

Execute the following statement in the SQL Worksheet to find products starting with `'A'` and priced above products starting with `'P'`:

```
SELECT ProductID, ProductName, Cost
FROM Products
WHERE ProductName LIKE 'A%'
  AND Cost > ANY (
    SELECT Cost
    FROM Products
    WHERE ProductName LIKE 'P%'
)
ORDER BY Cost DESC, ProductName;
```

The output of the query is shown in Figure 8.5:

PRODUCTID	PRODUCTNAME	COST
P0034	Accessories 34	19.99
P0020	Accessories 20	19.16
P0050	Accessories 50	17.03
P0042	Accessories 42	16.34
P0012	Accessories 12	15.84
P0024	Accessories 24	13.17
P0017	Accessories 17	12.4

Figure 8.5: *Output of multiple-row subquery using > ANY*

Query Notes

- The outer query retrieves all products whose names begin with **'A'**.
- The subquery returns the `Cost` values for all products whose names begin with **'P'**.

- The condition `Cost > ANY (subquery)` evaluates to **TRUE** if a product's cost is greater than *at least one* of the cost values returned by the subquery.
- This makes `> ANY` equivalent to "greater than the minimum" of that list.
- The `ORDER BY` clause sorts the results first by `Cost` in descending order and then alphabetically by `ProductName`.

Multiple-row subqueries compare a value to a set of results using operators such as `IN`, `ANY` (or `SOME`), and `ALL`.

The choice of operator depends on the requirement: `IN` tests membership within a list, `ANY` (or `SOME`) evaluates whether the condition is true for at least one value in the set, and `ALL` requires the condition to be true for every value in the set.

Multiple-Column Subqueries

A **multiple-column subquery** returns two or more columns, and the outer query compares a combination of columns (written in parentheses) to the combinations produced by the subquery.

This approach ensures that related attributes stay paired—for example, matching `CategoryID` with its minimum `Cost`, or `CustomerID` with that customer's latest `OrderDate`—rather than comparing each attribute independently.

Working with Multiple-Column Subqueries

A multiple-column subquery compares combinations of values rather than a single value, and it works as follows:

- The subquery executes first and returns a set of column pairs (or combinations), such as `(col1, col2)`.
- The outer query keeps rows whose corresponding column pairs match any combination returned by the subquery, typically using the `IN` operator.
- The **order** and **data types** of columns must align between the outer query's column list and the subquery's `SELECT` list.

When to Use Multiple-Column Subqueries

A multiple-column subquery is useful when a single column alone cannot uniquely identify the correct rows.

It compares paired (or grouped) values from the outer query to the same paired combinations produced by the subquery, ensuring that related attributes remain properly linked. Common use cases include:

- **Keeping related attributes together**: Select rows that match a specific pair, such as `(CategoryID, MIN(Cost))`, or `(BranchID, MAX(Salary))`.
- **Finding per-entity "latest" or "earliest" rows**: Match `(CustomerID, OrderDate)` to `(CustomerID, MAX(OrderDate))` to find the most recent order for each customer.
- **Identifying group winners**: Return the product(s) that achieve the minimum or maximum value within each group (for example, per category or branch).
- **Preventing mismatches**: Avoid cross-matching errors that occur when filtering on a single attribute (for instance, comparing a maximum date from any customer instead of from the same customer).

Writing Multiple-Column Subqueries

When writing a multiple-column subquery, express the condition as a **parenthesized list of columns** on both sides of the comparison.

The column order and data types must match between the outer query and the subquery. These subqueries are most commonly used with the `IN` operator for equality comparisons.

Syntax

```
WHERE (outer_col1, outer_col2)
      IN (SELECT inner_col1, inner_col2
          FROM table_name);
```

If sorting is required, specify the `ORDER BY` clause in the outer query, not within the subquery.

Exercise 6: Return the Latest Order for Customers with More Than One Order

Using the `Orders` table, write a query to display `CustomerID`, `OrderID`, and `OrderDate` for the most recent order placed by each customer who has placed **more than one order**. Include cases where multiple orders share the same latest date. Sort the results by `CustomerID`, then `OrderDate` (descending), and finally by `OrderID`.

Execute the following statement in the SQL Worksheet to find the latest order per customer:

```
SELECT o.CustomerID, o.OrderID, o.OrderDate
FROM Orders o
WHERE (o.CustomerID, o.OrderDate) IN (
  SELECT CustomerID, MAX(OrderDate)
  FROM Orders
  GROUP BY CustomerID
  HAVING COUNT(*) > 1
)
ORDER BY o.CustomerID, o.OrderDate DESC, o.OrderID;
```

The output of the query is shown in Figure 8.6:

CUSTOMERID	ORDERID	ORDERDATE
C010	O1033	02-AUG-25
C017	O1035	21-DEC-25
C023	O1030	23-OCT-25
C030	O1026	15-JUN-25
C046	O1021	27-MAY-25
C048	O1014	07-FEB-24

***Figure 8.6**: Latest order per Customer*

Query Notes

- The outer query retrieves `CustomerID`, `OrderID`, and `OrderDate` for all orders whose `(CustomerID, OrderDate)` pairs match those returned by the subquery.

- The subquery groups records by `CustomerID` and uses `MAX(OrderDate)` to identify the latest order date for each customer.
- The `HAVING COUNT(*) > 1` condition ensures that only customers with **more than one order** are included.
- The comparison `(O.CustomerID, O.OrderDate) IN (subquery)` matches each customer's order date to their latest order date.
- Customers with multiple orders on the same latest date are automatically included.
- The **`ORDER BY`** clause sorts results by *`CustomerID`*, then *`OrderDate`* (descending), and finally *`OrderID`*.

Exercise 7: Find Cheapest Product(s) in Each Category

Using the `Products` table, write a query to display `CategoryID`, `ProductID`, `ProductName`, and `Cost` for the product(s) with the **lowest cost** within each `Category`. Include cases where multiple products share the same minimum cost. Sort the results by `CategoryID`, `Cost`, and `ProductName`.

Execute the following statement in the SQL Worksheet to find the cheapest product(s) in each category:

```
SELECT p.CategoryID, p.ProductID, p.ProductName, p.Cost
FROM Products p
WHERE (p.CategoryID, p.Cost) IN (
  SELECT CategoryID, MIN(Cost)
  FROM Products
  GROUP BY CategoryID
)
ORDER BY p.CategoryID, p.Cost, p.ProductName;
```

The output of the query is shown in Figure 8.7:

CATEGORYID	PRODUCTID	PRODUCTNAME	COST
1	P0033	Chairs 33	5.06
2	P0046	Tables 46	6.53
3	P0031	Bookcases 31	5.78
4	P0025	Phones 25	9.05
5	P0018	Computers 18	6.23
6	P0017	Accessories 17	12.4
7	P0045	Binders 45	5.27
8	P0032	Paper 32	6.7
9	P0044	Storage 44	6.16

***Figure 8.7**: Cheapest product in each Category*

Query Notes

- The outer query retrieves `CategoryID`, `ProductID`, `ProductName`, and `Cost` for products that match the `CategoryID` and `Cost` combinations returned by the subquery.
- The subquery groups products by `CategoryID` and uses `MIN(Cost)` to calculate the lowest cost within each category.
- The condition `(P.CategoryID, P.Cost) IN (subquery)` ensures that the category and its minimum cost remain correctly paired.
- If multiple products share the same minimum cost within a category, all of them are automatically included in the result.
- The `ORDER BY` clause sorts the final results by `CategoryID`, then `Cost`, and finally `ProductName` for readability.

Multiple-column subqueries compare a combination of columns from the outer query with corresponding column combinations returned by the subquery, maintaining the logical relationship between related attributes.

This technique is particularly useful for identifying per-group results—such as the cheapest product in each category or the latest order for each customer—while ensuring that paired values remain accurately linked.

Correlated Subqueries

A **correlated subquery** is a subquery that references one or more columns from the outer query. Because of this dependency, the subquery is evaluated once for each row processed by the outer query, and its result may vary from row to row.

Correlated subqueries are especially useful for performing **row-by-row comparisons** against group-level aggregates or related data in another table.

Unlike a non-correlated subquery—which executes once and returns a fixed result set—a correlated subquery is **re-evaluated for every row** processed by the outer query. Although this approach can be less efficient on large datasets, Oracle's optimizer often applies internal optimizations to minimize redundant evaluations.

Working of a Correlated Subquery

A correlated subquery functions like a loop within a query, where the outer query drives the process and the inner query runs for each candidate row. Conceptually, the process works as follows:

1. The **outer query** selects one candidate row.
2. The **inner query** executes, using one or more column values from that outer row (for example, `BranchID`, `CategoryID`, or `OrderID`).
3. The **subquery** returns a single value or a Boolean result (often through `EXISTS`, `NOT EXISTS`, or a comparison expression).
4. The **outer query** then evaluates whether the returned result satisfies its condition.
5. This process repeats for every row processed by the outer query (though Oracle may internally optimize execution to avoid full re-evaluation where possible).

Writing Correlated Subqueries

A correlated subquery links the inner and outer queries through one or more common columns. Table aliases and clear linking conditions make this relationship explicit. The inner query must reference at least one column from the outer query to create the correlation.

Syntax

```
SELECT ...
FROM outer_table ot
WHERE ot.col <operator> (
  SELECT single_value
  FROM inner_table it
  WHERE it.key_column = ot.key_column  -- linking condition

);
```

When writing or optimizing correlated subqueries, the following guidelines help ensure clarity, correctness, and good performance:

- The inner query should return **a single value** when used with comparison operators such as =, <, or >.
- Keep **sorting** (`ORDER BY`) in the outer query; the inner query should handle only per-row filtering or calculations.
- Use **consistent aliases** (for example, `S` for `SalesPersons`) to make outer and inner references clear.
- Always include an **explicit linking condition** between the two queries (for example, `it.BranchID = ot.BranchID`).
- Avoid unnecessary sorting in the subquery; handle final presentation order in the outer query.

Exercise 8: Find SalesPersons Whose Salary Is Above Their Branch Average

Using the `SalesPersons` table, write a query to display `SalesPersonID`, `SalesPersonName`, `BranchID`, and `Salary` columns for salespersons whose salary is greater than the average salary of their own branch. Sort the results by `BranchID`, then by `Salary` in descending order, and finally by `SalesPersonName`.

Execute the following statement in the SQL Worksheet to find salespersons whose salaries are above their branch average:

```
SELECT s.SalesPersonID, s.SalesPersonName, s.BranchID, s.Salary
FROM SalesPersons s
WHERE s.Salary > (
      SELECT AVG(Salary)
       FROM SalesPersons sp
       WHERE sp.BranchID = s.BranchID
)
ORDER BY s.BranchID, s.Salary DESC, s.SalesPersonName;
```

The output of the query is shown in Figure 8.8:

SALESPERSONID	SALESPERSONNAME	BRANCHID	SALARY
SP004	Todd Byrd	B01	79759
SP034	Sandra Zimmerman	B01	78776
SP027	Marissa Webster	B01	75926
SP044	Pamela Lopez	B01	67250
SP049	Ashley Jones	B01	67085
SP042	Joseph Coleman	B02	79475
SP008	Trevor Young	B02	72578
SP039	Kellie Lee	B02	62431
SP036	Samuel Rivas	B02	53937
SP048	Julie Alexander	B02	50987
SP019	Randy Shah	B03	78815
SP018	Jason Daniels	B03	69965
SP006	Erica Ramos	B03	69161
SP002	Tammie Hanson	B03	68214
SP022	Allen Rogers	B03	65481
SP038	Daniel Salinas	B03	65317
SP023	Veronica	B03	64513
SP047	Edgar Raymond	B03	64180
SP031	Michael Burton	B04	77852
SP026	Bradley Smith	B04	77069
SP003	Jason Powell	B04	69086
SP012	Melissa Marshall	B04	68231
SP025	Jesse Rogers	B05	67255
SP011	Paul Carrillo	B05	51590

***Figure 8.8**: Salespersons whose salaries are above their branch average*

NOTE: The preceding output shows 24 rows. For display purposes, the result set is presented in two parts. In the actual SQL output, these rows appear as a single continuous list.

Query Explanation

- `SELECT`: Returns `SalesPersonID`, `SalesPersonName`, `BranchID`, and `Salary` for qualifying salespersons.
- `FROM`: Reads rows from the `SalesPersons` table, aliased as **s** for clarity.
- `WHERE`:
  - The condition `s.Salary > (SELECT AVG(Salary) FROM SalesPersons sp WHERE sp.BranchID = s.BranchID)` compares each salesperson's salary with the average salary of their own branch.
  - The subquery is **correlated** because it references `s.BranchID` from the outer query.
  - For every salesperson in the outer query, the inner query recalculates the branch average (`AVG(Salary)`), and the outer row is returned only if the salary exceeds that average.
- `ORDER BY`: Sorts the results first by `BranchID`, then by `Salary` (highest first), and finally by `SalesPersonName`.

Existence Checks Using EXISTS

The `EXISTS` operator is a logical operator used in the `WHERE` clause to test whether a subquery returns **at least one row**. It evaluates to **TRUE** if the subquery produces any row and **FALSE** if it produces none.

Unlike `IN`, which compares individual values returned by a subquery, `EXISTS` simply checks whether **any matching row exists**. The subquery's `SELECT` list is not evaluated for comparison; therefore, it is common to use `SELECT 1` or `SELECT NULL` to emphasize that only the existence of rows matters.

`EXISTS` is most often used with **correlated subqueries**, where the inner query references columns from the outer query. This allows SQL to perform **row-by-row existence checks** across related tables.

Syntax

```
SELECT ...
FROM outer_table o
WHERE EXISTS (
  SELECT 1
  FROM inner_table i
  WHERE i.key = o.key      -- linking condition to the outer row
    AND <additional conditions>
);
```

Key Points:

The following points summarize how the `EXISTS` and `NOT EXISTS` operators behave and when to use them effectively:

- **`EXISTS`** stops evaluating once the first matching row is found; duplicates in the subquery have no effect on the result.
- **`NOT EXISTS`** is the logical inverse; it returns outer rows for which the subquery finds **no matching rows**.
- Sorting and presentation should be handled in the **outer query**, since the `EXISTS` subquery is used only to test for **presence**, not to order or display data.

Exercise 9: Find Products That Have Been Ordered

Using the `Products` and `OrderDetails` table, write a query to display `ProductID` and `ProductName` for all products that appear in at least one order (that is, where a matching row exists in `OrderDetails`). Sort the results by `ProductID` in ascending order.

Execute the following statement in the SQL Worksheet to find products that have been ordered:

```
SELECT p.ProductID, p.ProductName
FROM Products p
WHERE EXISTS (
  SELECT 1
  FROM OrderDetails od
  WHERE od.ProductID = p.ProductID
)
ORDER BY p.ProductID;
```

The output of the query is shown in Figure 8.9:

PRODUCTID	PRODUCTNAME
P0003	Storage 3
P0004	Tables 4
P0005	Tables 5
P0006	Paper 6
P0008	Storage 8
P0009	Bookcases 9
P0010	Bookcases 10
P0013	Tables 13
P0017	Accessories 17
P0021	Storage 21
P0022	Chairs 22
P0024	Accessories 24
P0025	Phones 25
P0026	Bookcases 26
P0027	Binders 27
P0028	Binders 28

PRODUCTID	PRODUCTNAME
P0029	Storage 29
P0030	Tables 30
P0031	Bookcases 31
P0033	Chairs 33
P0036	Binders 36
P0038	Computers 38
P0040	Storage 40
P0041	Bookcases 41
P0042	Accessories 42
P0045	Binders 45
P0046	Tables 46
P0047	Tables 47
P0048	Storage 48
P0049	Chairs 49
P0050	Accessories 50

Figure 8.9: *List of ordered products*

NOTE: The output shows 31 rows. For display purposes, the result set is presented in two columns side by side. In the actual SQL output, these rows appear as a single continuous list.

Query Notes

- `SELECT`: Returns `ProductID` and `ProductName` of each product that meets the existence condition.
- `FROM`: Reads rows from the `Products` table, aliased as `p` for clarity.
- `WHERE EXISTS (...)`:
    - Performs an existence test to determine whether a matching record exists in `OrderDetails` for each product.
    - The subquery (`SELECT 1 FROM OrderDetails od WHERE od.ProductID = p.ProductID`) is **correlated**, as it references `p.ProductID` from the outer query.
    - The inner query returns a row if a match is found, causing `EXISTS` to evaluate to **TRUE**.
    - The value **1** is arbitrary; The `EXISTS` operator checks only whether at least one row is returned, not the actual value selected.
- `ORDER BY`: Sorts the results by `ProductID` in ascending order (default).

NOTE: The **`EXISTS`** operator stops evaluating once the first match is found. Duplicates in `OrderDetails` do not affect the outcome. If no matching order lines exist for a product, the subquery returns no rows, and **`EXISTS`** evaluates to **FALSE**, thereby excluding that product from the result.

Exercise 10: Find the Products That Have Never Been Ordered

Using the `Products` and `OrderDetails` tables, write a query to display `ProductID` and `ProductName` for products that do not appear in any order. Sort the results by `ProductID` in ascending order.

Execute the following statement in the SQL Worksheet to find the products that have never been ordered:

```
SELECT p.ProductID, p.ProductName
FROM Products p
WHERE NOT EXISTS (
  SELECT 1
  FROM OrderDetails od
  WHERE od.ProductID = p.ProductID
)
ORDER BY p.ProductID;
```

The output of the query is shown in Figure 8.10:

PRODUCTID	PRODUCTNAME
P0001	Paper 1
P0002	Chairs 2
P0007	Chairs 7
P0011	Bookcases 11
P0012	Accessories 12
P0014	Phones 14
P0015	Bookcases 15
P0016	Paper 16
P0018	Computers 18
P0019	Storage 19
P0020	Accessories 20
P0023	Tables 23
P0032	Paper 32
P0034	Accessories 34
P0035	Chairs 35
P0037	Paper 37
P0039	Computers 39
P0043	Chairs 43
P0044	Storage 44

Figure 8.10*: List of Products never ordered*

Query Notes

- `SELECT`: Returns `ProductID` and `ProductName` for each product that meets the filtering condition.
- `FROM`: Reads rows from the `Products` table, aliased as `p` for clarity.
- `WHERE NOT EXISTS (...)`:
  - Returns only those products that do not appear in any order line.
  - The subquery (`SELECT 1 FROM OrderDetails od WHERE od.ProductID = p.ProductID`) is **correlated** with the outer query through `p.ProductID`.
  - For each product, the subquery checks for a matching order line. If no match is found, `NOT EXISTS` evaluates to **TRUE**, meaning the product has never been ordered.
  - `ORDER BY`: Sorts the final result by `ProductID` in ascending order (default).

Correlated subqueries evaluate the inner query once for each row of the outer query, using a linking condition that references columns from the outer row. This approach makes them particularly effective for row-by-row comparisons—for example, checking whether a salesperson's salary exceeds the average salary in their branch or verifying whether related data exists in another table.

Best Practices for Using Subqueries

Effective use of subqueries improves accuracy, readability, and performance in SQL queries. The following guidelines summarize recommended practices for writing clear, correct, and efficient subqueries:

- **Match the Subquery Type to the Requirement**

  Choose the subquery type based on the expected result shape:

  - Single-row subquery: Use when a single value is required (for example, overall `MAX(Salary)`).
  - Multiple-row subquery: Use when comparing against a set of values (`IN`, `ANY`/`SOME`, `ALL`).

  - Multiple-column subquery: Use when related attributes must remain paired (for example, `(CategoryID, MIN(Cost))`).
  - Correlated subquery: Use when the inner query depends on the current row of the outer query (for example, comparing a salary to the average salary of the same branch).

- **Use the Right Operator for the Result Shape**

  Select operators that match the subquery's output:

  - `=`, `<`, `>`: The subquery must return exactly one value; otherwise, Oracle raises error *ORA-01427*.
  - `IN`: Tests membership within a set; duplicates values in the subquery do not affect results.
  - `ANY`/`SOME` and `ALL`: Compare a value to multiple results in the subquery.
  - Prefer `EXISTS`/`NOT EXISTS` for presence or absence checks; these are often clearer and more efficient than `IN`/`NOT IN`.

- **Place Subqueries Where They Belong**

  Use subqueries in the clause that matches the intent:

  - `WHERE`: Filter individual rows using scalar or set results.
  - `HAVING`: Filter grouped results after aggregation (for example, `AVG(Cost) > (SELECT AVG(Cost)…)`).
  - `SELECT`: Return a calculated value per row (must return exactly one value per row).
  - `FROM` (inline view): Stage an intermediate result set; always assign an alias.

- **Guarantee Single-Value Subqueries Correctly**

  Ensure subqueries expected to return one value do so reliably:

  - Filter on unique keys.
  - Avoid using `DISTINCT` to "force" a single row; apply precise conditions instead.

- **Keep Related Attributes Together**

  - When comparing combinations of columns, match parenthesized columns on both sides in the same order:

```
WHERE (CategoryID, Cost) IN (
  SELECT CategoryID, MIN(Cost)
FROM Products
GROUP BY CategoryID
);
```

This prevents cross-matching errors and automatically includes ties.

- **Handle NULLs and Empty Results Carefully**
  - Aggregate functions (`AVG`, `MIN`, `MAX`, `SUM`, `COUNT(expr)`) ignore `NULL` values.
  - Comparisons involving `NULL` evaluate to unknown; use `NVL` or `COALESCE` when appropriate.
  - If a subquery returns no rows:
    - `IN` and `ANY/SOME` evaluate to `FALSE`
    - `ALL` evaluates to `TRUE`
  - Avoid `NOT IN` when the subquery columns may contain `NULL` values; use `NOT EXISTS` instead.
- **Keep Ordering in the Outer Query**
  - Use `ORDER BY` in the outer statement to control the final presentation.
  - Avoid `ORDER BY` inside subqueries unless required for advanced top-N logic.
- **Limit Work Early and Index Wisely**
  - Filter early: Add conditions in the subquery to reduce row counts (for example, `WHERE Quantity >= 9`).
  - Return only required columns—omit unused expressions.
  - Ensure indexes exist on linking columns (`BranchID`, `CustomerID`, `OrderID`, `CategoryID`) to speed up correlated subqueries.
- **Choose Between Subquery, Join, or CTE for Clarity**

  Select the structure that best communicates intent:
  - Subquery: Best when a single benchmark or set is required.
  - Join or Inline View: Clearer when intermediate results must be reused (for example, per-position averages).

    - CTE (Common Table Expression): Best for multi-step logic or improving readability of complex queries.
- **Style and Maintainability**
    - Use short, consistent aliases (`o`, `od`, `p`, `s`) for tables.
    - Keep one logical idea per clause; prefer small, named steps (inline views or CTEs) over deeply nested subqueries.
    - Add brief comments when intent is not obvious (for example, `--latest order per customer; ties included`).

Subqueries at a Glance

This summary provides a quick reference for selecting the appropriate subquery pattern— single value or set, single column or multiple columns—and for recalling the typical operators and placement used with each type.

***Table 8.2**: Summary of Subquery types and example patterns*

Subquery Type	**Example Use Case / Syntax**

Single-Row (Scalar)
Returns one value used in a comparison
	Find the highest salary
	`WHERE Salary = (SELECT MAX(Salary)`
	`FROM SalesPersons);`

Multiple-Row (Set)
Compares a value against a list or set
	Find orders with a large line item
	`WHERE OrderID IN (SELECT OrderID`
	`FROM OrderDetails WHERE Quantity >= 9);`

Multiple-Column (Paired)
Compares combinations of columns
	Find the cheapest product(s) per category
	`WHERE (CategoryID, Cost) IN (`
	`SELECT CategoryID, MIN(Cost)`
	`FROM Products GROUP BY CategoryID);`

Subquery Type	Example Use Case / Syntax

Correlated (Per-Row)
Inner query references the outer query
	Find salespersons earning above their branch average
	`WHERE s.Salary > (SELECT AVG(Salary)`
	`FROM SalesPersons WHERE BranchID = s.BranchID);`

EXISTS / NOT EXIST
(Existence Check)
	Find Products that have (or have not) been ordered
	`WHERE EXISTS (SELECT 1`
	`  FROM OrderDetails od`
	`  WHERE od.ProductID = p.ProductID`
	`);`
	-- *OR*
	
	`WHERE NOT EXISTS (SELECT 1`
	`  FROM OrderDetails od`
	`  WHERE od.ProductID = p.ProductID`
	`);`

NOTE: `EXISTS` and `NOT EXISTS` test only for the presence or absence of rows. The value selected in the subquery is irrelevant; `SELECT 1` is commonly used for clarity.

Effective use of subqueries depends on matching the subquery type and clause placement to the logical requirement, and applying consistently to produce the intended result.

Conclusion

Subqueries enable step-by-step logic within a single SQL statement, allowing comparisons against a single value, a set of values, a combination of columns, or even row-specific conditions through correlation and existence checks.

This chapter explored key subquery patterns—including single-row, multiple-row, multiple-column, correlated subqueries, and existence checks using EXISTS and NOT EXISTS—each serving a distinct analytical purpose.

The next chapter, **Mastering Set Operators**, introduces the UNION, UNION ALL, INTERSECT, and MINUS operators, which are used to combine and compare result sets efficiently.

Practice Questions

Use the training dataset to complete the following practice questions. These exercises reinforce concepts covered in this chapter.

1. Using the `Products` table, write a query to display `ProductID`, `ProductName`, and `Cost` for the product(s) with the highest `Cost` in the table. *(Use a Single-Row subquery.)*
2. Using the `Orders` and `Customers` tables, write a query to display `OrderID`, `CustomerID`, and `OrderDate` for orders placed by customers in the 'Consumer' Segment. *(Use a Multiple-Row subquery.)*
3. Using the `Orders` table, write a query to display `CustomerID`, `OrderID`, and `OrderDate` for the earliest order of each customer. Include ties when multiple orders share the earliest date. *(Use a Multiple-Column subquery.)*
4. Using the `Products` table, write a query to display `ProductID`, `ProductName`, `CategoryID`, and `Cost` for products whose cost is greater than the average cost of their own `CategoryID`. *(Use a Correlated subquery.)*
5. Using the `Customers` and `Orders` tables, write a query to display `CustomerID` and `CustomerName` for customers who placed at least one order in 2025. *(Use EXISTS.)*

Practice Answers

The answers to the preceding questions are as follows:

Answer 1

```
SELECT ProductID, ProductName, Cost
FROM Products
WHERE Cost = (SELECT MAX(Cost) FROM Products)
ORDER BY ProductName;
```

Answer 2

```
SELECT o.OrderID, o.CustomerID, o.OrderDate
FROM Orders o
WHERE o.CustomerID IN (
  SELECT c.CustomerID
  FROM Customers c
  WHERE c.Segment = 'Consumer')
ORDER BY o.CustomerID, o.OrderDate;
```

Answer 3

```
SELECT o.CustomerID, o.OrderID, o.OrderDate
FROM Orders o
WHERE (o.CustomerID, o.OrderDate) IN (
  SELECT CustomerID, MIN(OrderDate)
  FROM Orders
  GROUP BY CustomerID
)
ORDER BY o.CustomerID, o.OrderDate, o.OrderID;
```

Answer 4

```
SELECT p.ProductID, p.ProductName, p.CategoryID, p.Cost
FROM Products p
WHERE p.Cost > (
  SELECT AVG(p2.Cost)
  FROM Products p2
  WHERE p2.CategoryID = p.CategoryID
)
ORDER BY p.CategoryID, p.Cost DESC, p.ProductName;
```

Answer 5

```
SELECT c.CustomerID, c.CustomerName
FROM Customers c
WHERE EXISTS (
  SELECT 1
  FROM Orders o
  WHERE o.CustomerID = c.CustomerID
    AND o.OrderDate BETWEEN DATE '2025-01-01' AND DATE '2025-12-31'
)
ORDER BY c.CustomerName;
```

Chapter 9
Mastering Set Operators

Introduction

In SQL, set operators are powerful tools used to combine the results from two or more queries into a single result set. Instead of analyzing data from one query or table at a time, set operators allow query results to be merged, compared, or contrasted—similar to mathematical operations performed on sets.

This capability is particularly useful for identifying common or distinct records, comparing datasets, and consolidating query outputs for analysis and reporting.

Oracle SQL supports several set operators; each is designed to serve a specific purpose.

Mastering these operators helps simplify complex reporting logic and reduces the need for multiple joins or temporary tables.

This chapter will cover the following topics:

- Understanding Set Operators
- UNION Operator
- UNION ALL Operator
- INTERSECT Operator
- MINUS Operator

Understanding Set Operators

Set operators in Oracle SQL are used to combine the results of two or more queries into a single result set. Each query output is treated as a set of rows, and the operator performs a mathematical operation—such as union, intersection, or difference—on those sets.

This concept parallels set theory in mathematics, where sets can be merged, overlapped, or compared to identify common or unique elements.

The primary advantage of using set operators is their ability to simplify complex reporting logic. Instead of manually comparing multiple query results, a single SQL statement can consolidate the required outcome.

This makes set operators particularly useful in analytical and reporting scenarios where data must be unified across time periods, regions, or business entities.

Example:

If one query lists all customers who placed orders in 2024 and another query lists those who placed orders in 2025, the set operator can easily identify:

- All customers from both years
- Customers who placed orders in both years
- Customers who placed orders in one year but not the other

Set operators are most effective when combining result sets that return similar information, such as comparable columns from different tables or queries filtered by different criteria.

Types of Set Operators in Oracle

Oracle SQL provides four main set operators:

- `UNION`: Combines two result sets and removes duplicate rows.
- `UNION ALL`: Combines two result sets and retains duplicate rows.
- `INTERSECT`: Returns only the rows that appear in both result sets.
- `MINUS`: Returns rows from the first result set that do not appear in the second.

Each of these operators will be discussed in detail later in this chapter, along with examples.

Set Operators versus Joins

It is important to distinguish between **set operators** and **joins**, as both combine data but serve different purposes:

- **Joins** operate at the **row level**, combining columns from two or more tables based on a related condition (such as matching keys). They expand the result *horizontally* by bringing together related data from different tables.
- **Set operators** operate at the **result set level**, stacking rows from separate queries. They expand the result *vertically* by merging or comparing complete query outputs.

The following Figure 9.1 compares the behavior of joins and set operators:

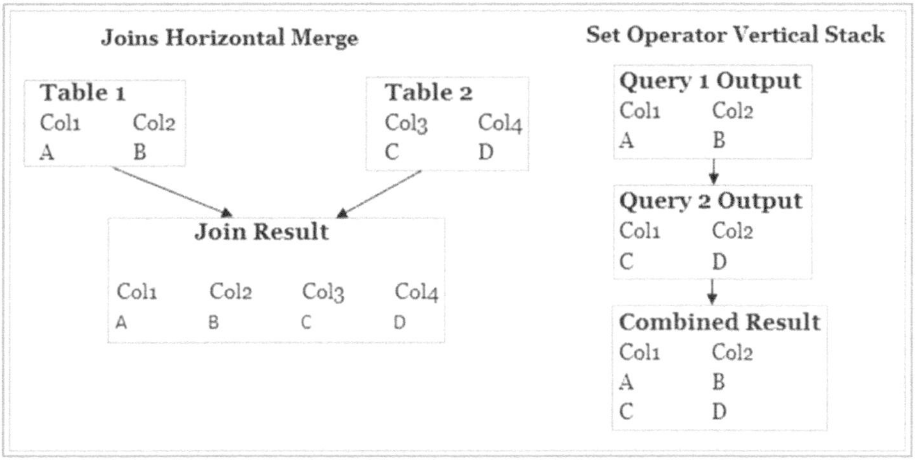

***Figure 9.1**: Comparison between Joins and Set Operators*

The following table highlights the key differences between joins and set operators:

Table 9.1: *Comparison of Join and Set Operators*

Function	**Joins**	**Set Operators**
Purpose	Combine related columns across tables	Combine or compare complete query results
Operation Level	Row-level (based on matching conditions)	Result set-level (works on entire queries)
Result Orientation	Horizontal expansion (adds more columns)	Vertical expansion (adds or filters rows)
Common Usage	Viewing related data together (for example, Orders with Customers)	Finding common, unique, or combined results from queries
Example	Match `Orders.CustomerID` with `Customers.CustomerID`	Combine customer lists from 2024 and 2025 orders

In summary, *joins* are used to view related data from multiple tables, while *set operators* are used to consolidate, compare, or contrast the results of multiple queries.

UNION Operator

The **`UNION`** operator in Oracle SQL is used to combine the results of two or more `SELECT` statements into a single result set. When merging results, `UNION` automatically removes duplicate rows, ensuring that each record appears only once in the output.

This operator is particularly useful when consolidating data from different sources or tables while keeping the result set distinct and clean.

Syntax

```
SELECT column1, column2, ...
FROM table1
UNION
SELECT column1, column2, ...
FROM table2;
```

Key Points about UNION:

When using the `UNION` operator, the following rules apply:

- Each `SELECT` statement must return the **same number of columns**.
- The **data types** of corresponding columns must be compatible.
- **Column names** in the final result set are derived from the **first** **`SELECT`** statement.
- **Duplicate rows** are automatically removed from the combined output.

Exercise 1: List Unique Customer and Year Combinations

Using the `Orders` table, write a query to display all unique combinations of `CustomerID` and `OrderYear` for orders placed in the years 2024 and 2025. Sort the results by `CustomerID`.

Execute the following statement in the SQL Worksheet to list unique `CustomerID` and `OrderYear` combinations:

```
SELECT CustomerID, EXTRACT(YEAR FROM OrderDate) As OrderYear
FROM Orders
WHERE EXTRACT(YEAR FROM OrderDate) = 2024
UNION
SELECT CustomerID, EXTRACT(YEAR FROM OrderDate) As OrderYear
FROM Orders
WHERE EXTRACT(YEAR FROM OrderDate) = 2025
ORDER BY CustomerID;
```

The output of the query is shown in Figure 9.2:

CUSTOMERID	ORDERYEAR
C008	2025
C009	2024
C010	2025
C013	2025
C017	2025
C023	2025
C030	2025
C042	2025
C044	2025
C045	2025
C046	2025
C048	2024
C049	2024

***Figure 9.2**: List unique CustomerID and OrderYear*

Query Explanation

- **`SELECT`** (First query): Retrieves `CustomerID` and extracts the year portion from `OrderDate`, assigning it the alias `OrderYear`.
- **`FROM`**: Specifies that data is being selected from the `Orders` table.
- **`WHERE EXTRACT(YEAR FROM OrderDate) = 2024`**: Filters rows to include only orders placed in 2024.
- **`UNION`**: Combines the results of both queries and automatically removes duplicates.
- **`SELECT`** (Second query): Retrieves the customer ID and order year for orders placed in 2025.
- **`ORDER BY`**: Sorts the combined result by `CustomerID` in ascending order.

NOTE: This query produces a distinct list of `CustomerID` and `OrderYear` combinations for customers who placed orders in either 2024 or 2025. Duplicate combinations are automatically removed by the `UNION` operator, ensuring that each combination appears only once in the output.

UNION ALL Operator

The **`UNION ALL`** operator functions similarly to `UNION`, but it **does not remove duplicate rows**. Instead, it combines the results of multiple queries and includes all rows, even when some appear more than once.

Because Oracle does not perform duplicate elimination, `UNION ALL` is typically more efficient `than` UNION, especially when working with large datasets.

Syntax

```
SELECT column1, column2, ...
FROM table1
UNION ALL
SELECT column1, column2, ...
FROM table2;
```

Key Points about UNION ALL:

When using the `UNION ALL` operator, the following rules apply:

- The same structural rules apply as with `UNION`; both queries must return the same number of columns with compatible data types.
- Unlike `UNION`, duplicate rows are retained in the final output.
- `UNION ALL` is faster and more efficient than `UNION` because Oracle skips the duplicate-checking step.

Exercise 2: List All Customer and Year Combinations

Using the `Orders` table, write a query to display all combinations of `CustomerID` and `OrderYear` for orders placed in the years 2024 and 2025. Include all rows, even if a customer appears multiple times in the same year. Sort the results by `CustomerID`.

Execute the following statement in the SQL Worksheet to list all `CustomerID` and `OrderYear` combinations:

```
SELECT CustomerID, EXTRACT(YEAR FROM OrderDate) As OrderYear
FROM Orders
WHERE EXTRACT(YEAR FROM OrderDate) = 2024
UNION ALL
SELECT CustomerID, EXTRACT(YEAR FROM OrderDate) As OrderYear
FROM Orders
WHERE EXTRACT(YEAR FROM OrderDate) = 2025
ORDER BY CustomerID;
```

The output of the query is shown in Figure 9.3:

CUSTOMERID	ORDERYEAR
C008	2025
C009	2024
C010	2025
C010	2025
C013	2025
C017	2025
C017	2025
C023	2025
C023	2025
C023	2025
C023	2025

CUSTOMERID	ORDERYEAR
C030	2025
C030	2025
C042	2025
C044	2025
C045	2025
C046	2025
C046	2025
C046	2025
C048	2024
C049	2024

***Figure 9.3**: Union ALL to list all CustomerID and OrderYear combinations*

NOTE: The preceding output displays 21 rows. For layout purposes, the result set is presented in two columns side by side. In the actual SQL output, these rows would appear in a single continuous list.

Query Explanation

- **`SELECT`** (First query): Retrieves `CustomerID` and extracts the year portion from `OrderDate`, assigning it to the alias `OrderYear`.
- **`FROM`**: Specifies that the data is being selected from the `Orders` table.

- `WHERE`: Filters rows so that only orders placed in 2024 are included in the first query.
- `UNION ALL`: Combines the results of both queries **without removing duplicates**. Unlike `UNION`, `UNION ALL` includes all rows, even if some are repeated.
- `SELECT` (Second query): Retrieves `CustomerID` and order year for orders placed in 2025.
- `ORDER BY`: Sorts the combined result set by `CustomerID` in ascending order.

NOTE: This query lists all combinations of `CustomerID` and `OrderYear` for orders placed in 2024 and 2025. If a customer has multiple orders in the same year, all corresponding rows are included because `UNION` ALL preserves duplicates.

UNION versus UNION ALL

Both `UNION` and `UNION ALL` combine the results of multiple queries, but they differ in behavior:

- `UNION` removes duplicates and returns only distinct rows
- `UNION ALL` retains all rows, including duplicates, and is generally faster because it does not perform duplicate elimination.

In practice, `UNION` is preferred when unique results are required, whereas `UNION ALL` is ideal when all data must be preserved or when query performance is a higher priority.

INTERSECT Operator

The `INTERSECT` operator returns only those rows that are common to the result sets of two queries. It automatically removes duplicates, ensuring that only distinct rows appearing in both datasets are included in the final result.

This operator is especially useful for identifying records that meet multiple conditions or occur in more than one dataset.

Syntax

```
SELECT column1, column2, ...
FROM table1
[WHERE condition]
INTERSECT
SELECT column1, column2, ...
FROM table2
[WHERE condition];
```

Key Points about INTERSECT:

When using the `INTERSECT` operator, keep the following rules in mind:

- Each query must return the same number of columns with compatible data types.
- Only the rows common to both queries are returned.
- Duplicate rows are automatically removed.
- Column names in the final result set are taken from the first query.

Exercise 3: Find Customers Who Placed Orders in Both Years

Using the `Orders` table, write a query to retrieve the list of `CustomerID` values for customers who placed orders in both 2023 and 2025.

Execute the following statement in the SQL Worksheet to list the Customer IDs who placed orders in both 2023 and 2025:

```
SELECT CustomerID
FROM Orders
WHERE EXTRACT(YEAR FROM OrderDate) = 2025
INTERSECT
SELECT CustomerID
FROM Orders
WHERE EXTRACT(YEAR FROM OrderDate) = 2023;
```

The output of the query is shown in Figure 9.4. Only three customers placed orders in each of these years.

CUSTOMERID
C010
C017
C030

***Figure 9.4**: Customer IDs of those who placed orders in both 2023 and 2025*

Query Explanation

- `SELECT` (First query): Retrieves the `CustomerID` column.
- `FROM`: Specifies that the data is being selected from the `Orders` table.
- `WHERE EXTRACT(YEAR FROM OrderDate) = 2025`: Filters rows for orders placed in 2025.
- `INTERSECT`: Returns only the rows common to both query results—customers who appear in both sets.
- `SELECT` (Second query): Retrieves the `CustomerID` values for customers who placed orders in 2023.

NOTE: This query produces a list of customers who appear in both result sets—that is, customers who placed orders in both 2023 and 2025.

The `INTERSECT` operator is most effective when identifying overlapping data, such as customers, products, or transactions, that satisfy conditions in multiple queries.

It automatically removes duplicate rows and provides a concise way to pinpoint shared results across datasets.

MINUS Operator

The `MINUS` operator returns the rows from the first query that are **not present** in the second query. It effectively performs a subtraction operation between two result sets, displaying only those records that exist in the first dataset and not in the second.

This operator is particularly useful for identifying differences between datasets or locating records that appear in one table but not in another.

Syntax

```
SELECT column_list
FROM table1
MINUS
SELECT column_list
FROM table2;
```

Key Points about MINUS:

When using the `MINUS` operator, keep the following key rules in mind:

- Duplicate rows are automatically removed from the result set, similar to the `UNION` operator.
- Both queries must return the same number of columns with compatible data types.
- Column names in the final result set are derived from the first query.

Exercise 4: Find Customers Who Placed Orders Only in 2025

Using the `Orders` table, write a query to display all `CustomerID` values for customers who placed orders in 2025 but not in 2024 or 2023. Execute the following statement in the SQL Worksheet to list customers who placed orders only in 2025:

```
SELECT CustomerID
FROM Orders
WHERE EXTRACT(YEAR FROM OrderDate) = 2025
MINUS
SELECT CustomerID
FROM Orders
WHERE EXTRACT(YEAR FROM OrderDate) = 2024
MINUS
SELECT CustomerID
FROM Orders
WHERE EXTRACT(YEAR FROM OrderDate) = 2023;
```

The output of the query is shown in Figure 9.5:

CUSTOMERID
C008
C013
C023
C042
C044
C045
C046

Figure 9.5*: Customer IDs of those who placed orders only in 2025*

Query Explanation

- **`SELECT`** (First query): Retrieves the `CustomerID` column.
- **`FROM`**: Specifies the `Orders` table as the data source.
- **`WHERE EXTRACT(YEAR FROM OrderDate) = 2025`**: Filters rows to include customers who placed orders in the year 2025.
- **`MINUS`** (First operation): Subtracts the result of the second query (2024) from the first query (2025). This removes customers who placed orders in both 2025 and 2024.
- **`SELECT`** (Second query): Retrieves the `CustomerID` values for customers who placed orders in the year 2024.
- **`FROM`**: References the same `Orders` table.
- **`WHERE EXTRACT(YEAR FROM OrderDate) = 2024`**: Filters the data for customers who placed orders in 2024.
- **`MINUS`** (Second operation): Applies an additional subtraction by removing the result of the third query (customers who placed orders in 2023) from the already filtered result for 2025–2024. This ensures that customers who ordered in 2023 are also excluded.

- `SELECT` (Third query): Retrieves the `CustomerID` values for orders placed in the year 2023.
- `FROM`: Uses the same `Orders` table.
- `WHERE EXTRACT(YEAR FROM OrderDate) = 2023`: Filters rows to include customers who placed orders in 2023.

NOTE: This query performs two consecutive **`MINUS`** operations, creating a *chained difference* effect—first removing customers who ordered in 2024, and then excluding those who ordered in 2023—to return only the customers who placed orders exclusively in 2025.

The `MINUS` operator identifies differences between result sets by returning rows from the first query that do not appear in any subsequent queries. This makes it useful for finding records that are exclusive to a specific dataset, such as customers, products, or transactions that appear in one time period but are absent in others.

Conclusion

This chapter explored the use of set operators in Oracle SQL to combine and compare result sets from multiple queries. The discussion began with an overview of the concept, followed by detailed explanations of the UNION, UNION ALL, INTERSECT, and MINUS operators. Each operator serves a distinct purpose, such as merging results, identifying common records, or isolating data unique to a specific dataset.

Mastering these operators allows users to write more flexible and efficient queries, particularly when analyzing differences, overlaps, or consolidated results across tables and time periods. These concepts form a key part of advanced data reporting and analysis in Oracle SQL.

The next chapter, **Views and Materialized Views**, focuses on creating virtual tables that simplify data access and enhance query performance. It explains how views can be used to present data securely and efficiently, and how materialized views improve performance by storing precomputed query results for faster retrieval.

Practice Questions

Use the training dataset to complete the following practice questions. These exercises reinforce concepts covered in this chapter.

1. Using the `Orders` table, write a query to retrieve the list of unique customers who placed orders at Branch `B01 or` Branch `B02`. (*Use the `UNION` operator.*)
2. Using the `Orders` table, write a query to retrieve the list of **all** customers who placed orders in 2024 or 2025, including duplicates. (*Use the `UNION ALL` operator.*)
3. Using the `Orders` table, write a query to retrieve the list of customers who placed orders at Branch `B01` and used Same-Day shipping. (*Use the `INTERSECT` operator.*)
4. Using `Products` and `OrderDetails` tables, write a query to find all products in `CategoryID = '1'` that have never been ordered. (*Use the `MINUS` operator.*)
5. Using the `Orders` table, write a query to retrieve the list of customers who have used Same-Day or Priority shipping methods, but have never placed an order at Branch `B03`. (*Combine the set operators.*)

Practice Answers

The answers to the preceding questions are as follows:

Answer 1

```
SELECT CustomerID
FROM Orders
WHERE BranchID = 'B01'
UNION
SELECT CustomerID
FROM Orders
WHERE BranchID = 'B02'
ORDER BY CustomerID;
```

Answer 2

```
SELECT CustomerID
FROM Orders
WHERE EXTRACT(YEAR FROM OrderDate) = 2024
UNION ALL
SELECT CustomerID
FROM Orders
WHERE EXTRACT(YEAR FROM OrderDate) = 2025
ORDER BY CustomerID;
```

Answer 3

```
SELECT CustomerID
FROM Orders
WHERE BranchID = 'B01'
INTERSECT
SELECT CustomerID
FROM Orders
WHERE ShipMode = 'Same-Day';
```

Answer 4

```
SELECT ProductID
FROM Products
WHERE CategoryID = '1'
MINUS
SELECT ProductID
FROM OrderDetails;
```

Answer 5

```
SELECT CustomerID
FROM Orders
WHERE ShipMode = 'Same-Day'
UNION
SELECT CustomerID
FROM Orders
WHERE ShipMode = 'Priority'
MINUS
SELECT CustomerID
FROM Orders
WHERE BranchID = 'B03';
```

Chapter 10

Views and Materialized Views

Introduction

In Oracle, views and materialized views offer efficient ways to simplify access to complex data. A view is a virtual table based on a SQL query. It does not store data physically but retrieves results dynamically from one or more base tables each time it is queried. Views are commonly used to simplify complex queries, enhance data security, and provide a consistent interface to the database.

A materialized View, on the other hand, stores the query results physically in the database. It improves performance for queries involving large datasets, complex joins, or aggregations. Materialized views can be refreshed periodically to stay synchronized with their underlying base tables.

Together, views and materialized views support data abstraction, reusability, and performance optimization in Oracle databases.

This chapter will cover the following topics:

- Introduction to Views
- Creating and Managing Views
- Updating Data through Views
- Introduction to Materialized Views
- Creating and Managing Materialized Views
- Comparing Views and Materialized Views

Introduction to Views

A **view** in Oracle is a *virtual table* derived from the result of a SQL query. Unlike a regular table, a view does not store data physically; instead, it retrieves data dynamically from one or more base tables each time it is queried.

Views simplify data access by encapsulating complex joins, filters, and calculations into a reusable database object. They are commonly used to present specific subsets of data, enforce security rules, and standardize query logic across applications.

When a view is queried, Oracle executes the underlying SQL statement in real time, ensuring that the data displayed by the view remains current and synchronized with the base tables.

For example, in a business environment with tables such as `Orders`, `Customers`, and `SalesPerson`, a view can be created once to combine the required data. This eliminates the need to repeatedly write complex join queries, improving both efficiency and consistency in data retrieval.

Advantages of Views

Views offer several benefits that simplify data management and enhance database security:

- **Simplify complex queries**: Frequently used joins or calculations can be stored in a view, allowing predefined logic to be reused instead of rewriting lengthy SQL statements.
- **Enhance security**: Views can restrict access to specific columns or rows, providing controlled visibility of sensitive data without modifying the base tables.
- **Provide data abstraction**: Applications and users can continue to query the same view even if the underlying table structure changes, reducing dependency on schema design.

Limitations of Views

Despite their advantages, views also have certain limitations that should be considered when designing database solutions:

- **Not always updatable**: Views that include joins, aggregates, or `GROUP BY` clauses typically do not support direct `INSERT`, `UPDATE`, or `DELETE` operations.
- **Performance overhead**: Since data is retrieved dynamically from base tables each time, querying a view may be slower than accessing a physical table.
- **Dependency on base tables**: Structural changes to base tables (such as renamed columns or altered data types) can invalidate dependent views and may require them to be recreated.

Views provide an efficient way to simplify data access, strengthen security, and maintain consistency across SQL queries. Although they do not store data physically, their ability to present complex information in a reusable and controlled manner makes them an essential feature of Oracle database design.

Creating and Managing Views

Views are created using the **`CREATE VIEW`** statement. A view stores a reusable SQL query definition that simplifies complex joins, filters, or frequently used query logic, allowing it to be referenced like a table.

Syntax

```
CREATE [OR REPLACE] VIEW view_name AS
SELECT column1, column2, ...
FROM table_name
WHERE condition;
```

Key points to remember when creating and managing views are as follows:

- `CREATE VIEW` defines a new view in the database.
- `OR REPLACE` updates an existing view without requiring it to be dropped first.

- The query that defines a view can include joins, filters, and aggregate functions.
- Once created, a view can be queried just like a regular table using a `SELECT` statement.

Dropping a View

A view can be dropped when it is no longer needed or when a new version of the same view must be created with a different definition. Dropping a view removes only the stored query definition and does not affect the data in the underlying base tables.

Syntax

```
DROP VIEW view_name;
```

Exercise 1: Creating a View

In a business environment, queries often require joining multiple tables to retrieve related information. Writing the same join repeatedly can be inefficient and error prone. Instead, a view can be created once to combine the required data and then reused whenever needed.

This exercise demonstrates how to create a view named `VW_CUSTOMER_ORDERS` that combines customer information with their corresponding orders.

The steps are used to create a view are as follows:

1. Create a View.

   In the SQL Worksheet, execute the following statement:

   ```
   CREATE OR REPLACE VIEW vw_customer_orders AS
   SELECT o.OrderID, o.OrderDate,
      c.CustomerName, c.Segment, o.SalesPersonID,
      o.ShipMode, o.ShipDate
   FROM Orders o
   JOIN Customers c
   ON o.CustomerID = c.CustomerID;
   ```

Once this statement executes successfully, Oracle displays the message:

```
View created.
```

2. Query the View.

   To verify that the view is working correctly, execute the following statement:

```
SELECT *
FROM vw_customer_orders;
```

Query Explanation

- `CREATE OR REPLACE VIEW`: Defines a new view or replaces an existing one with the same name.
- `SELECT`: Specifies the columns to be retrieved in the view.
- `FROM` / `JOIN`: Combines data from the `Orders` and `Customers` tables using the matching `CustomerID`.

NOTE: This view encapsulates the join logic between `Orders` and `Customers`, allowing analysts to query customer order data easily and consistently without writing repetitive SQL code.

Updating Data through Views

In Oracle, certain views support data manipulation operations such as `INSERT`, `UPDATE`, and `DELETE`. These are known as **updatable views**. Any changes made through such updatable views are automatically reflected in the underlying base tables.

However, not all views allow data modifications. A view generally updatable when it is based on a **single table** and does **not** include any of the following elements:

- Aggregate functions (for example, `SUM`, `AVG`)
- `GROUP BY` or `DISTINCT` clauses
- `JOIN` operations
- Set operators (`UNION`, `MINUS`, `INTERSECT`)

When these elements are present, the view becomes **read-only**, meaning data cannot be inserted, updated, or deleted through it.

Read-Only View

A **read-only view** does not permit data modification operations such as `INSERT`, `UPDATE`, or `DELETE`. This restriction occurs when the view definition introduces ambiguity, for example, when multiple tables, aggregate functions, or grouping operations are involved.

Read-only views are most commonly used for reporting, analysis, and dashboards, where users need visibility into data but should not be allowed to modify the underlying records.

Exercise 2: Updating Data through a View

This exercise demonstrates how data in a base table can be updated through an updatable view. To avoid modifying data, a copy of the `Customers` table is created first, and all updates are performed on that copy.

The steps to update data through a view are as follows:

1. Create a copy of the `Customers` table:

   ```
   CREATE TABLE Customers_Copy AS
   SELECT * FROM Customers;
   ```

2. Create a View to display customers in the Corporate segment:

   ```
   CREATE OR REPLACE VIEW vw_corporate_customers AS
   SELECT CustomerID, CustomerName, Region, Segment
   FROM Customers_Copy
   WHERE Segment = 'Corporate';
   ```

3. Verify the rows in the view:

   ```
   SELECT *
   FROM vw_corporate_customers;
   ```

4. Update data in the base table through the View.

   Update the region of the customer with `CustomerID = 'C005'` from *Pennsylvania* to *Midwest.*

   ```
   UPDATE vw_corporate_customers
   SET Region = 'Midwest'
   WHERE CustomerID = 'C005';
   ```

   Once executed, Oracle updates the corresponding row in the base table `Customers_Copy`.

5. Verify the update in the base table:

   ```
   SELECT CustomerID, CustomerName, Region, Segment
   FROM Customers_Copy
   WHERE CustomerID = 'C005';
   ```

The output confirms that the `Region` value has been updated to `Midwest` in the `Customers_Copy` table.

Query Explanation

- **`CREATE TABLE`**: Creates a copy of the `Customers` table for safe modification.
- **`CREATE OR REPLACE VIEW`**: Defines a single-table view filtered by customers in the `Corporate` segment.
- **`SELECT`**: Retrieves records from the view to validate its content.
- **`UPDATE`**: Modifies the `Region` column through the view.
- **`SELECT (Verification)`**: Confirms that the update propagated to the base table.

Updating data through a view provides a controlled and simplified interface for modifying underlying tables.

Only simple, single-table views support data updates while views involving joins, aggregations, or grouping are read-only and best suited for reporting or analysis.

Introduction to Materialized Views

A **Materialized View** is a *physical copy* of the result set of a query. Unlike a regular view, which retrieves data dynamically each time it is queried, a materialized view stores the query results on disk. This stored data can be refreshed periodically to remain synchronized with the underlying base tables.

Materialized views are primarily used to improve query performance, especially for complex queries involving large tables, aggregations, or joins. Since the results are precomputed and stored, queries against a materialized view execute much faster than re-running the base query each time.

These views are widely used in data warehousing and reporting environments, where real-time data is not required but efficient retrieval of summarized information is critical.

Use Case

A sales manager frequently analyzes total sales by region and category. Instead of running a complex aggregation query each time, a materialized view can store the pre-aggregated results, allowing instant retrieval of summarized sales data.

The following points highlight the main characteristics that distinguish materialized views from regular views in Oracle:

- Physically store query results in the database rather than generating them dynamically.
- Can be refreshed manually or automatically at scheduled intervals to stay synchronized with base tables.
- Improve performance for analytical and reporting queries by minimizing query execution time.
- Require additional storage space, as data is stored on disk rather than computed on demand.

Creating and Managing Materialized Views

Materialized views are created using the `CREATE MATERIALIZED VIEW` statement. When a materialized view is created, Oracle executes the underlying query and stores the results physically in the database. This stored data can later be refreshed—either manually or automatically—to remain synchronized with the base tables.

Syntax

```
CREATE MATERIALIZED VIEW view_name
[BUILD IMMEDIATE | BUILD DEFERRED]
[REFRESH [FAST | COMPLETE | FORCE] ON DEMAND | ON COMMIT]
AS
SELECT columns
FROM table_name
WHERE condition;
```

BUILD and REFRESH Options

When creating a materialized view, Oracle provides several `BUILD` and `REFRESH` options that control how the data is populated and maintained:

- **`BUILD IMMEDIATE`**: Creates the materialized view and populates it with data immediately.
- **`BUILD DEFERRED`**: Creates only the view definition; data is populated later during the first refresh.
- **`REFRESH FAST`**: Updates only changed data since the last refresh. This option requires materialized view logs on the base tables.
- **`REFRESH COMPLETE`**: Rebuilds the entire materialized view by re-executing the base query.
- **`REFRESH FORCE`**: Attempts a FAST refresh first; if not possible, Oracle performs a COMPLETE refresh.
- **`ON DEMAND`**: Refresh occurs only when manually triggered by the user.
- **`ON COMMIT`**: Automatically refreshes the materialized view whenever a transaction on the base table is committed.

Refreshing a Materialized View

As data in base tables changes over time, a materialized view must be *refreshed* to reflect the most recent state of the data. Refreshing can be performed manually (**ON DEMAND**) or automatically (**ON COMMIT**) depending on how the view was defined.

Manual Refresh (ON DEMAND)

In a manual refresh mode, the materialized view is refreshed only when explicitly requested by the user or application. This approach provides greater control over when the refresh occurs and is well suited for scenarios where data changes are infrequent or where refresh operations should be scheduled during off-peak hours.

Manual refreshes are typically performed using the `DBMS_MVIEW.REFRESH` procedure.

Syntax for Manual Refresh

```
EXEC DBMS_MVIEW.REFRESH('materialized_view_name');
```

NOTE: `DBMS_MVIEW.REFRESH` is a built-in Oracle PL/SQL procedure used to refresh one or more materialized views. It is a part of the `DBMS_MVIEW` package, which provides tools for managing and maintaining materialized views.

This command refreshes the stored data in the materialized view to match the current state of the base tables. Depending on how the materialized view was defined, Oracle performs either a **FAST refresh** (updating only changed data) or a **COMPLETE refresh** (rebuilding the entire result set).

Automatic Refresh (On Commit)

A materialized view can be configured to refresh *automatically* whenever a transaction on the base table is committed. This is enabled by specifying the `REFRESH ON COMMIT` clause during creation.

This approach is suitable when:

- The base tables are relatively small or
- The volume of data changes is manageable and near-real-time accuracy is required

However, because the refresh occurs during each commit, `ON COMMIT` refresh introduces additional overhead and can impact transaction performance—especially in systems with frequent updates.

Syntax

```
CREATE MATERIALIZED VIEW view_name
BUILD IMMEDIATE
REFRESH FAST ON COMMIT
AS
SELECT columns
FROM table_name;
```

NOTE: The `ON COMMIT` refresh is commonly used with **FAST** refresh, as it updates only the data that has changed. Although a **COMPLETE** refresh can also be specified, but it may significantly increase commit time and is therefore rarely recommended in high-transaction environments.

Dropping a Materialized View

When a materialized view is no longer needed, it can be removed from the database using the `DROP MATERIALIZED VIEW` statement. This operation deletes both the stored data and the materialized view, but does not affect the underlying base tables.

Syntax

```
DROP MATERIALIZED VIEW view_name;
```

Materialized views are best suited for scenarios where query performance is critical but near-real-time data is acceptable. With appropriate refresh strategies, they significantly reduce query execution time for analytical and reporting workloads while maintaining data consistency.

Exercise 3: Creating and Refreshing a Materialized View

This exercise demonstrates how to create and refresh a materialized view that summarizes total sales by region.

The steps to create and refresh a materialized view are as follows:

1. Create the materialized view.

```
CREATE MATERIALIZED VIEW mv_sales_by_region
BUILD IMMEDIATE
REFRESH COMPLETE ON DEMAND
AS
SELECT c.Region,
    SUM(od.Sales) AS Total_Sales
FROM OrderDetails od
JOIN Orders o
ON od.OrderID = o.OrderID
JOIN Customers c
ON o.CustomerID = c.CustomerID
GROUP BY c.Region;
```

   Once the statement executes successfully, Oracle displays the message:

```
Materialized view created.
```

2. Verify the stored data.

   Execute the following statement to view the contents of the Materialized view:

```
SELECT *
FROM mv_sales_by_region;
```

3. Refresh the materialized view.

   When new data is added or existing data is modified in the base tables, refresh the materialized view to update the stored results:

```
EXEC DBMS_MVIEW.REFRESH('MV_SALES_BY_REGION');
```

   After the refresh completes, the materialized view reflects the most recent data from the underlying tables.

Query Explanation

- **`CREATE MATERIALIZED VIEW`**: Defines and stores the result of a query physically in the database.
- **`BUILD IMMEDIATE`**: Executes the underlying query immediately and loads data into the materialized view.

- `REFRESH COMPLETE ON DEMAND`: Specifies that the materialized view is refreshed manually when required.
- `JOIN and GROUP BY`: Combines and summarizes total sales by region using data from multiple tables.

NOTE: A **COMPLETE** refresh is used here because the materialized view contains aggregations and joins. This approach is suitable for reporting scenarios where refreshes are performed periodically rather than in real time.

This exercise illustrates how materialized views improve performance for aggregated queries by storing precomputed results. Regular refreshes keep the data synchronized with the base tables while delivering faster query execution for reporting and analysis.

Comparing Views and Materialized Views

Both views and materialized views simplify data access by presenting query results as logical tables. However, they differ in how data is stored, maintained, and retrieved.

A view retrieves data dynamically from base tables each time it is queried, ensuring that the results are always current. In contrast, a materialized view stores a physical snapshot of the query results, enabling faster retrieval but requiring periodic refreshes to stay synchronized with the source data.

The following table summarizes the key differences between views and materialized views in Oracle:

Table 10.1: Views versus Materialized Views

Feature	View	Materialized View
Definition	A virtual table that displays data dynamically from one or more base tables.	A physical copy of the query result set stored on disk.
Storage	Does not store data physically; only the query definition is stored.	Stores data physically, consuming additional disk space.
Data Freshness	Always displays the most current data from the base tables.	Displays stored data that requires periodic refresh to stay current.
Performance	Query execution can be slower for complex joins or aggregations, as data is retrieved dynamically.	Faster query performance because results are precomputed and stored.
Use Case	Simplifying queries, restricting access, and providing data abstraction.	Analytical and reporting environments where performance is critical.
Refresh Mechanism	No refresh mechanism; always retrieves live data.	Can be refreshed manually (`ON DEMAND`) or automatically (`ON COMMIT`).
Data Modification	Updatable if based on a single table without aggregates or joins.	Read-only; updates occur through refresh operations, not DML statements.
Storage Requirement	Minimal (stores only query definition).	Requires extra storage for the materialized data.
Dependency on Base Tables	Directly depends on base tables for every query execution.	Depends on base tables only during refresh operations.

Both views and materialized views play a crucial role in Oracle database design. A view is best suited for real-time queries, data abstraction, and enforcing security. A materialized view, on the other hand, is preferred for analytical and reporting scenarios where query performance and precomputed results take precedence over immediate data freshness.

Conclusion

This chapter introduced the concepts of Views and Materialized Views in Oracle, highlighting how they simplify complex queries, enhance data security, and improve performance.

While views provide real-time access to data through virtual tables, materialized views store precomputed results that significantly boost query speed for analytical and reporting tasks. The choice between them depends on the requirement—whether real-time data accuracy or optimized performance is the priority.

The next chapter, **Creating and Managing Tables**, explains how to define tables in Oracle, establish their structure, and insert data, laying the foundation for designing and managing relational databases effectively.

Practice Questions

Use the training dataset to complete the following practice questions. These exercises reinforce concepts covered in this chapter.

1. Create a view that displays order details with customer names.

   Create a view named `VW_ORDER_CUSTOMERS` that joins the `Orders` and `Customers` tables and displays:

   - `OrderID`
   - `OrderDate`
   - `CustomerName`
   - `Region`

2. Create a view for express orders.

   Create a view named `VW_EXPRESS_ORDERS` that displays `OrderID`, `CustomerID`, `OrderDate`, and `ShipMode` for orders shipped using `'Express'` shipping mode.

3. Create a materialized view summarizing total sales by branch.

   Create a materialized view named `MV_SALES_BY_BRANCH` using the `Orders`, `OrderDetails`, and `Branches` tables to display total sales for each branch.

4. Update data through an updatable view.

   Create a copy of the `SalesPersons` table so that original data remains unchanged. Then create a view that displays only salespersons working the *Morning* shift, and update a record using this view.

5. Compare the usage of views and materialized views.
   Which of the following statements is true?

   a) A View stores data physically while a Materialized View does not.

   b) A Materialized View always retrieves the latest data.

   c) A View retrieves data dynamically, while a Materialized View stores the query result physically.

   d) Both are always updatable.

Practice Answers

The answers to the preceding questions are as follows:

Answer 1

```
CREATE OR REPLACE VIEW vw_order_customers AS
SELECT
    o.OrderID, o.OrderDate,
    c.CustomerName, c.Region
FROM Orders o
JOIN Customers c
ON o.CustomerID = c.CustomerID;
--Verify the View
SELECT * FROM vw_order_customers;
```

Answer 2

```
CREATE OR REPLACE VIEW vw_express_orders AS
SELECT OrderID, CustomerID,
       OrderDate, ShipMode
FROM Orders
WHERE ShipMode = 'Express';
```

Answer 3

```
CREATE MATERIALIZED VIEW mv_sales_by_branch
BUILD IMMEDIATE
REFRESH COMPLETE ON DEMAND
AS
SELECT b.BranchName,
       SUM(od.Sales) AS Total_Sales
FROM OrderDetails od
JOIN Orders  o
ON od.OrderID = o.OrderID
JOIN Branches b
ON o.BranchID = b.BranchID
GROUP BY b.BranchName;

-- Refresh the materialized view when base data changes:
EXEC DBMS_MVIEW.REFRESH('MV_SALES_BY_BRANCH');
```

Answer 4

```
-- create a copy of the SalesPersons table
CREATE TABLE SalesPersons_Copy AS
SELECT * FROM SalesPersons;

--Create a view for Morning shift salespersons
CREATE OR REPLACE VIEW vw_morning_salespersons AS
SELECT SalesPersonID,
       SalesPersonName,
      Position,
      Shift,
      BranchID
FROM SalesPersons_Copy
WHERE Shift = 'Morning';

--Query the View
SELECT *
FROM vw_morning_salespersons;
```

```
--Update data though the View
UPDATE vw_morning_salespersons
SET Shift = 'Evening'
WHERE SalesPersonID = 'SP001';

--Verify the change in the base table
SELECT *
FROM SalesPersons_Copy
WHERE SalesPersonID = 'SP001';
```

Answer 5

Correct Answer:

c) A View retrieves data dynamically, while a Materialized View stores the query result physically.

Chapter 11
Creating and Managing Tables

Introduction

A relational database is built on tables that store structured data in rows and columns. Defining tables correctly forms the foundation for all SQL operations, as every query, report, and analysis depends on how data is organized and stored.

Oracle SQL provides powerful tools to create tables, define constraints that enforce business rules, and safely insert, update, or delete data within those tables.

In SQL, operations that create and modify database structures fall under Data Definition Language (DDL), while operations that insert, update, or delete data fall under Data Manipulation Language (DML). Together, these categories represent the essential building blocks for designing, managing, and maintaining relational databases.

This chapter will cover the following topics:

- Introduction to DDL and DML Statements
- Table Structure and Data Types
- Creating Tables
- Defining Constraints
- Inserting Data into Tables
- Updating Data in Tables
- Deleting Data from Tables
- Managing Tables

NOTE: In this chapter, the exercises create new tables directly in the database. When using the Oracle FreeSQL environment, open the SQL Worksheet to enter and execute the statements. When using SQL Developer, connect to the database and execute the same commands. The tables will be created in the currently connected schema.

Introduction to DDL and DML Statements

Structured Query Language (SQL) is organized into categories based on the type of operations performed on a database. Among these, the Data Definition Language (DDL) and Data Manipulation Language (DML) form the core foundation of database development and usage.

DDL (Data Definition Language)

DDL statements define and manage the structure of database objects. They are used to create new objects, modify existing ones, or remove them entirely.

For example:

- `CREATE TABLE`: Defines a new table.
- `ALTER TABLE`: Modifies an existing table.
- `DROP TABLE`: Permanently removes a table.

DDL statements operate at the schema level and implicitly perform a commit after execution. As a result, their changes are permanent and cannot be rolled back.

DML (Data Manipulation Language)

DML statements operate on the actual data stored within database objects. They allow rows to be added, modified, or deleted.

For example:

- `INSERT`: Adds new rows of data.
- `UPDATE`: Modifies existing rows.
- `DELETE`: Removes rows from a table.

Unlike DDL, DML operations are transactional. This means changes can be committed to make them permanent or rolled back to undo them, providing flexibility and control when managing data.

In essence, DDL defines the database structure, while DML populates and maintains that structure. For example, a `Customer` table may be created using a DDL statement, and records can then be inserted into it using DML statements. Both are indispensable—without DDL, there is no structure; without DML, there is no data.

The following table summarizes the key differences between DDL and DML statements in Oracle SQL:

***Table 11.1**: Comparison of DDL and DML Statements*

Function	**DDL (Data Definition Language)**	**DML (Data Manipulation Language)**
Purpose	Defines and manages database objects	Inserts, updates, and deletes data within objects
Examples	`CREATE`, `ALTER`, `DROP`, `TRUNCATE`, `RENAME`	`INSERT`, `UPDATE`, `DELETE`, `MERGE`
Scope	Schema-level (database structure)	Row-level (table contents)
Transaction Behavior	Auto-commit; changes become permanent immediately	Requires explicit `COMMIT` or `ROLLBACK`
Rollback Possible?	No	Yes
Typical Usage	Creating tables or adding constraints	Adding or modifying rows of data

Together, DDL and DML form the foundation of relational database operations. DDL establishes the structure of the database, while DML brings that structure to life by inserting and managing data.

Table Structure and Data Types

A table organizes data into rows and columns. Each row represents a record, and each column represents a field that stores a specific type of information.

The structure of a table determines how data is stored, retrieved, and related to other tables in the database.

In Oracle SQL, a table consists of the following elements:

- **Table name**: Must begin with a letter and can include letters, numbers, and underscores. Oracle SQL reserved keywords should not be used as table names.
- **Column definitions**: Each column has a name and a data type that defines the kind of values it can store, such as text, numbers, or dates.
- **Constraints**: Rules that enforce data integrity and maintain validity. Constraints can apply to individual columns or to the entire table—for example, ensuring uniqueness, disallowing null values, or enforcing relationships between tables.

Types of Constraints in Oracle

The following table summarizes the main types of constraints available in Oracle, their purpose, and where they can be applied:

***Table 11.2**: Types of constraints in Oracle*

Type	Purpose	Example	Applies To
`PRIMARY KEY`	Ensures that each row is uniquely identified in the table.	`CustomerID NUMBER PRIMARY KEY`	Column or Table
`FOREIGN KEY`	Establishes a relationship between tables by referencing a primary key in another table.	`BranchID REFERENCES Branches (BranchID)`	Column or Table
`NOT NULL`	Prevents a column from containing null values.	`FirstName VARCHAR2(50) NOT NULL`	Column

Type	Purpose	Example	Applies To
`UNIQUE`	Ensures that all values in a column are distinct.	`Email UNIQUE`	Column or Table
`CHECK`	Validates that values meet a specific condition.	`Salary CHECK (Salary > 0)`	Column or Table
`DEFAULT`	Assigns a default value when none is specified.	`Status VARCHAR2(10) DEFAULT 'Active'`	Column

By defining constraints at the time of table creation, Oracle ensures that only valid, accurate, and consistent data is stored.

Common Oracle Data Types

Oracle offers a diverse range of data types to accommodate different types of information. Some of the most commonly used include:

- **`VARCHAR2(size)`**: Stores variable-length character strings (for example, names, addresses).
- **`CHAR(size)`**: Stores fixed-length character strings.
- **`NUMBER(p,s)`**: Stores numeric data, where *p* represents precision (total digits), and *s* represents scale (number of digits after the decimal point).
- **`DATE`**: Stores date and time values.

For example, a column defined as `VARCHAR2(50)` can store up to 50 characters, while `NUMBER(10,2)` can store numbers with up to 10 digits, including 2 digits after the decimal point. Selecting the correct data type for each column is essential for optimizing storage, maintaining data accuracy, and ensuring efficient query performance.

Creating Tables

Tables are created using the `CREATE TABLE` statement. This command defines the table name, columns, data types, and any constraints required to maintain data integrity.

When a table is first created, it is an empty structure containing no rows. Data can later be inserted using DML statements such as `INSERT`. After creation, a table can be modified with the `ALTER TABLE` statement to add, drop, or modify columns and constraints as needed.

Syntax

```
CREATE TABLE table_name (
    column_name1 data_type constraint,
    column_name2 data_type constraint,
    ...
);
```

Key Points about Creating Tables:

When creating tables in Oracle SQL, keep the following points in mind:

- The `CREATE TABLE` statement defines the table structure within the database schema.
- Each column must have a valid data type, and optional constraints can be applied to enforce rules.
- Tables are created empty; data must be inserted separately using DML statements.
- The `ALTER TABLE` statement is used to make structural changes after creation.

Exercise 1: Creating a Branch_BDS Table

This exercise demonstrates how to create a table named `Branch_BDS` to store branch details of an organization.

***Table 11.3**: Structure of the `Branch_BDS` table*

Column Name	**Data Type**	**Constraint**	**Purpose**
`BranchID`	`VARCHAR2(10)`	`PRIMARY KEY`	Unique identifier for each branch
`BranchName`	`VARCHAR2(50)`	`NOT NULL, UNIQUE`	Name of the branch
`City`	`VARCHAR2(30)`	`NOT NULL`	City where the branch is located

NOTE: Before writing the `CREATE TABLE` statement, it is a good practice to design the table's structure first—either on paper or using a data modeling tool. Planning column names, data types, and constraints in advance helps reduce errors and ensure consistency.

The steps to create the `Branch_BDS` table are as follows:

1. Create the table.

   In the SQL Worksheet, execute the following statement:

   ```
   CREATE TABLE Branch_BDS (
       BranchID     VARCHAR2(10),
       BranchName   VARCHAR2(50),
       City         VARCHAR2(30)
   );
   ```

   Once the statement executes successfully, Oracle displays the message:

   ```
   Table created.
   ```

2. Verify the table creation.

   ```
   SELECT *
   FROM Branch_BDS;
   ```

   The output will display:

   ```
   no data found.
   ```

This indicates that the `Branch_BDS` table has been successfully created but currently contains no rows.

Defining Constraints

Constraints are rules applied to tables and columns to maintain accuracy, integrity, and consistency of the data. As discussed in the section *Table Structure and Data Types*, constraints can be defined at either the **column level** (affecting a single column) or the **table level** (affecting multiple columns).

Constraints can be defined during table creation or added later using the `ALTER TABLE` statement. When constraints are added after a table already exists, the `ALTER TABLE` command modifies the table structure without requiring it to be recreated.

The ALTER TABLE Command

After a table has been created, its structure can still be changed using the `ALTER TABLE` command. This statement allows structural changes without requiring the table to be dropped and recreated.

Common modifications include:

- Adding or dropping columns
- Modifying column data types
- Renaming columns
- Adding or dropping constraints

Syntax

```
ALTER TABLE table_name
[ADD column_name data_type constraint]
[MODIFY column_name data_type constraint]
[DROP COLUMN column_name]
[ADD CONSTRAINT constraint_name constraint_type (column_name)]
[DROP CONSTRAINT constraint_name];
```

Key Points about ALTER TABLE:

When modifying a table's structure, keep the following points in mind:

- `ALTER TABLE` is a DDL command; changes are permanent once executed because it triggers an automatic commit.

- When adding a constraint, use meaningful names such as `pk_branchid` or `uq_branchname` to make the database easier to manage.
- Constraints can be defined at the column level (single column) or table level (multiple columns).

Defining and naming constraints clearly helps maintain database integrity and readability. Consistent naming conventions also simplifies maintenance and debugging when working with large schemas.

Exercise 2: Adding Constraints Using the ALTER TABLE Command

This exercise demonstrates how to use the `ALTER TABLE` command to add constraints that ensure data integrity in the `Branch_BDS` table created earlier.

Add the following constraints to the `Branch_BDS` table:

- Add a `PRIMARY KEY` constraint to the `BranchID` column.
- Add a `NOT NULL` constraint to the `BranchName` column.
- Add a `UNIQUE` constraint to the `BranchName` column.
- Add a `NOT NULL` constraint to the `City` column.

The steps to add constraints to the `Branch_BDS` table using `ALTER TABLE` are as follows:

1. Add the `PRIMARY KEY` constraint.

   ```
   ALTER TABLE Branch_BDS
     ADD CONSTRAINT pk_branchid_bds PRIMARY KEY (BranchID);
   ```

   Once executed, Oracle displays the message:

   `Table altered.`

   This confirms that the `PRIMARY KEY` constraint has been successfully added to the `BranchID` column.

2. Add a `NOT NULL` constraint to `BranchName`:

```
ALTER TABLE Branch_BDS
MODIFY BranchName VARCHAR2(50)
CONSTRAINT nn_branchname_bds NOT NULL;
```

   Oracle displays the message:

```
Table altered.
```

   This confirms that the `NOT NULL` constraint has been added to the `BranchName` column.

3. Add the `UNIQUE` constraint to `BranchName`:

```
ALTER TABLE Branch_BDS
ADD CONSTRAINT uq_branchname_bds UNIQUE (BranchName);
```

   Oracle displays:

```
Table altered.
```

   This confirms that the `UNIQUE` constraint has been added, ensuring no two branches share the same name.

4. Add a `NOT NULL` constraint to `City`:

```
ALTER TABLE Branch_BDS
MODIFY City VARCHAR2(30)
CONSTRAINT nn_city_bds NOT NULL;
```

   Oracle displays the message:

```
Table altered.
```

   This confirms that the `NOT NULL` constraint has been added to the `City` column.

Query Explanation

- **`ALTER TABLE`**: Modifies an existing table structure without recreating it.
- **`ADD CONSTRAINT`**: Creates a new constraint on the specified column(s).
- **`MODIFY`**: Changes the definition of an existing column to apply constraints.
- **Constraint names**: Follow a consistent pattern such as pk_, nn_, or uq_ for clarity and easy identification.

This exercise demonstrates how the `ALTER TABLE` command enhances an existing table by adding constraints that enforce data integrity and reliability.

Verifying Constraints Using Data Dictionary Views

Oracle maintains a set of data dictionary views that store metadata about database objects. These views allow developers to query information about tables, columns, indexes, and constraints to verify their definitions and status.

When working with constraints, the following two views are most commonly used:

1. **USER_CONSTRAINTS**
   This view provides information about all constraints owned by the current user. The key columns in this view include:
   - CONSTRAINT_NAME: Specifies the name of the constraint.
   - CONSTRAINT_TYPE: Indicates the type of constraint, coded as:
     - P: Primary key
     - R: Foreign key
     - U: Unique
     - C: Check constraint (includes NOT NULL constraints)
   - STATUS: Indicates whether the constraint is `ENABLED` or `DISABLED`.
2. **USER_CONS_COLUMNS**
   This view lists the columns associated with each constraint and links them to their respective tables. The key columns in this view include:
   - CONSTRAINT_NAME: Links to the corresponding constraint in the USER_CONSTRAINTS view.
   - TABLE_NAME: Specifies the name of the table where the constraint is defined.
   - COLUMN_NAME: Identifies the column(s) to which the constraint applies.

These data dictionary views are read-only and are particularly useful when verifying constraints after creating or altering a table. They help confirm that constraints are correctly defined, properly named, and currently enabled within the schema.

Exercise 3: Verifying Constraints on the Branch_BDS Table

Display the list of constraints applied to the `Branch_BDS` table along with the columns they apply.

Execute the following statement in the SQL Worksheet to verify constraints on the `Branch_BDS` table:

```
SELECT uc.constraint_name,
       uc.constraint_type,
       ucc.column_name
FROM user_constraints uc
JOIN user_cons_columns ucc
ON uc.constraint_name = ucc.constraint_name
WHERE uc.table_name = 'BRANCH_BDS';
```

The output of the query is shown in Figure 11.1:

CONSTRAINT_NAME	CONSTRAINT_TYPE	COLUMN_NAME
PK_BRANCHID_BDS	P	BRANCHID
NN_BRANCHNAME_BDS	C	BRANCHNAME
UQ_BRANCHNAME_BDS	U	BRANCHNAME
NN_CITY_BDS	C	CITY

***Figure 11.1**: Listing constraints on a table*

Interpreting the Results

- `P` (**Primary Key**): Indicates that `BranchID` uniquely identifies each row in the table.
- `U` (**Unique**): Indicates that `BranchName` must contain distinct values and cannot be duplicated.
- `C` (**Check / Not Null**): Represents check constraints that validate data or enforce non-null values (for example, `BranchName` and `City`).
- `R` (**Referential Integrity**): Represents a foreign key constraint referencing another table (not present in this example).

NOTE: In the USER_CONSTRAINTS view, both `CHECK` and `NOT NULL` constraints are represented by the code **C**. They are not distinguished separately. To identify columns defined specifically as `NOT NULL`, use the `DESC` command on the table.

These results confirm that all constraints on the `Branch_BDS` table have been successfully created and are currently enabled.

By querying the data dictionary views, it becomes easier to verify that the table structure aligns with the intended design and integrity rules.

Exercise 4: Creating the SalesPerson_BDS Table

The next step in building the database is to create a table for salespersons. Each salesperson works in a branch, so the `BranchID` column in this table will reference the `BranchID` from the `Branch_BDS` table.

In this exercise, most constraints will be defined directly within the `CREATE TABLE` statement. The foreign key constraint will be added later using the `ALTER TABLE` command.

***Table 11.4**: Structure of the `SalesPerson_BDS` table*

Column Name	Data Type	Constraint	Purpose
`SPID`	VARCHAR2(10)	`PRIMARY KEY`	Unique identifier for each salesperson
`SPName`	VARCHAR2(50)	`NOT NULL`	Full name of the salesperson
`Location`	VARCHAR2(30)	Optional	Location where the salesperson operates
`Position`	VARCHAR2(30)	`NOT NULL`	Job title or position
`ReportsTo`	VARCHAR2(10)	Optional	Identifies the manager or supervisor
`HireDate`	Date	`NOT NULL`	Date the salesperson was hired
`Salary`	NUMBER(10,2)	`CHECK (Salary > 0)`	Base salary for the salesperson
`BranchID`	VARCHAR2(10)	Foreign Key referencing `Branch_BDS (BranchID)`	Branch to which the salesperson is assigned

NOTE: If working in **Oracle FreeSQL or SQL Developer**, verify that the **`Branch_BDS`** table exists before creating this table. Since `SalesPerson_BDS` will include a foreign key reference to `Branch_BDS`, Oracle will return an error if the referenced table is missing.
To check for its existence, execute: `DESC Branch_BDS;`
If it does not exist, re-run the `CREATE TABLE` and `ALTER TABLE` statements from *Exercises 1* and *2* before proceeding.

The steps to create the `SalesPerson_BDS` table are as follows:

1. In the SQL Worksheet, execute the following `CREATE` statement:

```
CREATE TABLE SalesPerson_BDS (
   SPID        VARCHAR2(10)  CONSTRAINT pk_sp_bds PRIMARY KEY,
   SPName      VARCHAR2(50)  CONSTRAINT nn_spname_bds NOT NULL,
   Location    VARCHAR2(30),
   Position    VARCHAR2(30)  CONSTRAINT nn_position_bds NOT NULL,
   ReportsTo   VARCHAR2(10),
   HireDate    DATE          CONSTRAINT nn_hiredate_bds NOT NULL,
Salary    NUMBER(10,2)  CONSTRAINT ck_salary_bds CHECK (Salary > 0),
    BranchID   VARCHAR2(10)
);
```

Once executed successfully, Oracle displays the message:

```
Table created.
```

2. Verify the table creation.

```
SELECT *
FROM SalesPerson_BDS;
```

The output will display:

```
no data found.
```

This indicates that the `SalesPerson_BDS` table has been successfully created but currently contains no data.

The constraints defined in the `CREATE TABLE` statement are as follows:

- **`PRIMARY KEY`**: Defined on `SPID` to uniquely identify each salesperson.
- **`NOT NULL`**: Applied to `SPName`, `Position`, and `HireDate` to ensure required fields are always populated.
- **`CHECK`**: Ensures that salary must always be greater than zero.
- **`BranchID`**: Included as a column without a foreign key constraint at this stage—the relationship to `Branch_BDS (BranchID)` will be added in the next exercise using `ALTER TABLE`.

Defining constraints at the time of table creation helps enforce data integrity rules from the beginning and ensures that only valid, consistent data is entered into the database.

Understanding Foreign Key Constraint

A **Foreign Key** constraint establishes a relationship between two tables by ensuring that the value in one column (the child table) matches an existing value in another column (the parent table).

This enforces referential integrity, meaning that records in the child table cannot reference non-existent rows in the parent table.

For example, in the SalesPerson_BDS table, the BranchID column is defined as a foreign key referencing Branch_BDS (BranchID). This guarantees that every salesperson is assigned to a valid branch already defined in the Branch_BDS table.

ON DELETE CASCADE

The ON DELETE CASCADE option extends the behavior of a foreign key by defining what happens when a related record in the parent table is deleted.

When this option is enabled, deleting a row from the parent table automatically removes all corresponding rows from the child table.

For example, if a branch is deleted from Branch_BDS, all salespersons assigned to that branch will also be automatically deleted from the SalesPerson_BDS table.

NOTE: The **ON DELETE CASCADE** option should be used carefully, as it can result in multiple related rows being removed automatically from other tables. It should be applied only when such cascading deletions are intended and necessary for maintaining data consistency.

Exercise 5: Adding a Foreign Key Constraint to SalesPerson_BDS

The SalesPerson_BDS table includes a BranchID column that identifies the branch where each salesperson works.

To enforce this relationship, a foreign key constraint must be added so that only valid BranchID values from the Branch_BDS table can be used.

In this exercise, the ON DELETE CASCADE option will also be included so that if a branch is deleted from Branch_BDS, all salespersons assigned to that branch are automatically removed from the SalesPerson_BDS table.

For this operation to succeed, both Branch_BDS and SalesPerson_BDS tables must exist in the database.

Execute the `ALTER TABLE` statement to add the foreign key constraint with `ON DELETE CASCADE`:

```
ALTER TABLE SalesPerson_BDS
ADD CONSTRAINT fk_branchid
FOREIGN KEY (BranchID)
REFERENCES Branch_BDS (BranchID)
ON DELETE CASCADE;
```

Once executed, Oracle displays the message:

```
Table altered.
```

This confirms that the foreign key constraint has been successfully added.

The constraints created using the `ALTER TABLE` statement are as follows:

- **`fk_branchid`** is the name of the foreign key constraint.
- **`FOREIGN KEY (BranchID)`** specifies the column in the child table (`SalesPerson_BDS`).
- **`REFERENCES Branch_BDS (BranchID)`** identifies the parent table (`Branch_BDS`) and referenced column.
- **`ON DELETE CASCADE`** ensures that when a row in the parent table is deleted, all related rows in the child table are automatically removed.

The `ALTER TABLE` statement enforces referential integrity by allowing only valid `BranchID` values from `Branch_BDS` to be inserted into `SalesPerson_BDS`.

With `ON DELETE CASCADE`, deleting a branch will also remove all related salespersons automatically.

Caution:

Use the `ON DELETE CASCADE` option carefully. While it helps maintain referential integrity, it can also delete multiple related rows in the child table when a parent row is removed.

Creating Tables Using CTAS

Another way to create tables in Oracle is by using the **`CREATE TABLE AS SELECT`** (**CTAS**) statement. This method creates a new table directly from the result of a `SELECT` query.

The CTAS approach is especially useful for:

- Making quick backups of existing tables.
- Creating test tables with real or sample data.
- Copying specific columns or filtered rows from a larger table.
- Building reporting or temporary tables from query results.

Key Points about CTAS:

Before using the CTAS method, it is important to understand how Oracle handles the structure and data of the new table when the statement is executed:

- The new table inherits the column names and data types from the `SELECT` query.
- Constraints such as `PRIMARY KEY`, `FOREIGN KEY`, `UNIQUE`, or `CHECK` are not copied and must be added separately if required.
- By default, both the structure and data are copied. To create a table structure without copying data, include a condition such as `WHERE 1 = 0` in the query.

Exercise 6: Creating a Table Using CTAS

Create a new table named `SalesPerson_Copy` that contains all rows and columns from the `SalesPerson_BDS` table.

The steps to create a table using CTAS are as follows:

1. Create the table.

```
CREATE TABLE SalesPerson_Copy AS
SELECT *
FROM SalesPerson_BDS;
```

Once executed successfully, Oracle displays the message:

```
Table created.
```

This confirms that the SalesPerson_Copy table has been created successfully.

2. Verify the table creation.

```
SELECT *
FROM SalesPerson_Copy;
```

The output will display:

```
no data found.
```

This message appears if the SalesPerson_BDS table does not currently contain any data. If data existed in SalesPerson_BDS, those rows will also have been copied into the new table.

Inserting Data into Tables

After creating tables and defining constraints, the next step is to populate them with data. In Oracle SQL, this is accomplished using the INSERT statement, which belongs to the Data Manipulation Language (DML) category.

While Data Definition Language (DDL) statements such as CREATE TABLE define the structure of a database, DML statements like INSERT bring that structure to life by adding rows of data.

The INSERT statement can be used in several ways—by inserting values into all columns, inserting into selected columns, or copying data from another table using a SELECT statement. During this process, Oracle automatically enforces any constraints defined earlier, ensuring that only valid data can be inserted.

Syntax

```
INSERT INTO table_name (column1, column2, column3, ...)
VALUES (value1, value2, value3, ...);
```

Query Explanation

- `table_name`: Specifies the table where the row will be inserted.
- `column1, column2, …`: Lists the columns that will receive values (optional if inserting into all columns in defined order).
- `VALUES (…)`: Contains the data to be inserted. The order of values must match the order of the listed columns.

Different Ways to Insert Data

Data can be inserted into a table in several ways, depending on the requirement. The most commonly used variations are:

- **Single-Row Insert**: Inserts one row at a time by providing values for the columns.
- **Multi-Row Insert**: Inserts multiple rows by executing several `INSERT` statements in a script.
- **Insert into Selected Columns**: Inserts values into specific columns, leaving others as `NULL` or using their defined default values.
- **Insert Query Results into a Table**: Uses a `SELECT` query to insert data from another table.

Each of these variations will be demonstrated through examples and exercises in the following sections.

Best Practices for Inserting Data

When inserting data into tables, keep the following guidelines in mind:

- **Match Columns and Values Carefully**:
  Always specify column names in the `INSERT` statement to ensure values are inserted into the intended columns, even if the table structure changes later.
- **Respect Constraints**:
  Inserted values must comply with constraints such as `PRIMARY KEY`, `FOREIGN KEY`, `NOT NULL`, `UNIQUE`, and `CHECK`. Violating these rules results in an Oracle error.

- **Use Appropriate Data Types**:
  Values must match the defined data type of each column (for example, numbers for numeric columns and dates for `DATE` columns). Use functions like `TO_DATE` when inserting date values.
- **Handle NULL values Carefully**:
  Columns that allow `NULL` can be left blank, but attempting to insert a `NULL` value into a column defined as `NOT NULL` will cause an error.
- **Insert Dates Explicitly**:
  Use the `TO_DATE` function with a format mask (for example, `'DD-MON-YYYY'`) to prevent errors caused by date format inconsistencies.
- **Check Foreign Key Dependencies:**
  Ensure that referenced values exist in the parent table before inserting data into a child table. For example, `BranchID` must already exist in `Branch_BDS` before inserting into `SalesPerson_BDS`.
- **Insert Multiple Rows Efficiently:**
  For large volumes of data , use `INSERT INTO … SELECT` instead of executing multiple individual `INSERT` statements to improve performance.
- **Commit or Rollback changes**:
  The `INSERT` statement is a DML operation, so changes are not permanent until a `COMMIT` statement is issued. Use `ROLLBACK` to undo uncommitted changes if necessary.

Managing Transactions (COMMIT and ROLLBACK)

In Oracle, inserting rows into a table is a Data Manipulation Language (DML) operation. DML operations such as `INSERT`, `UPDATE`, and `DELETE` do not permanently modify the database until the changes are explicitly committed.

Key commands are as follows:

- **COMMIT**: Makes all changes permanent in the database and visible to other users.
- **ROLLBACK**: Undoes all changes since the last commit, restoring the data to its previous state.

- **DDL Statements**: Commands such as `CREATE TABLE`, `ALTER TABLE`, and `DROP TABLE` include an implicit commit. Their changes become permanent immediately and cannot be rolled back.

After completing `INSERT`, `UPDATE`, or `DELETE` operations, a `COMMIT` statement should be issued to permanently save the changes.

If an `INSERT`, `UPDATE`, or `DELETE` operation is performed incorrectly, a `ROLLBACK` can be used before committing to undo the changes and restore the database to its prior state.

Exercise 7: Inserting Multiple Rows into the Branch_BDS Table

The `Branch_BDS` table currently has no data. Insert five rows into the table, one row at a time, using the `INSERT` statement.

NOTE: Before inserting rows into a table, ensure that the `Branch_BDS` and `SalesPerson_BDS` tables exist in the database. If these tables do not exist, re-run the `CREATE TABLE` and `ALTER TABLE` statements from *Exercises 1* to *5* before performing the `INSERT` operations.

The following data must be inserted into the `Branch_BDS` table:

Table 11.5*: Sample data for the `Branch_BDS` table*

BranchID	BranchName	City
B1	East Side	New York
B2	West End	Chicago
B3	Central Hub	Dallas
B4	North Point	Boston
B5	South Square	San Diego

The steps to insert rows into the `Branch_BDS` table are as follows:

1. Insert the rows.
   In the SQL Worksheet, execute the following statements one at a time:

   ```
   INSERT INTO Branch_BDS VALUES ('B1', 'East Side', 'New York');
   INSERT INTO Branch_BDS VALUES ('B2', 'West End', 'Chicago');
   INSERT INTO Branch_BDS VALUES ('B3', 'Central Hub', 'Dallas');
   INSERT INTO Branch_BDS VALUES ('B4', 'North Point', 'Boston');
   INSERT INTO Branch_BDS VALUES ('B5', 'South Square', 'San Diego');
   COMMIT;
   ```

   After execution, Oracle displays messages, such as:

   ```
   1 row inserted.
   ```

   This confirms that all five rows have been successfully added to the `Branch_BDS` table.

2. Verify the inserted rows.

   ```
   SELECT *
   FROM Branch_BDS;
   ```

   The output of the query is displayed in Figure 11.2:

BRANCHID	BRANCHNAME	CITY
B1	East Side	New York
B2	West End	Chicago
B3	Central Hub	Dallas
B4	North Point	Boston
B5	South Square	San Diego

***Figure 11.2**: Data in the `Branch_BDS` table*

The figure confirms that all rows have been successfully inserted into the `Branch_BDS` table. Each branch record is now available for use in subsequent exercises involving foreign key relationships with the `SalesPerson_BDS` table.

Exercise 8: Inserting Multiple Rows into the SalesPerson_BDS Table

The `SalesPerson_BDS` table has been created with constraints such as `PRIMARY KEY`, `NOT NULL`, and a `FOREIGN KEY` referencing the `Branch_BDS` table.

Insert five rows using the `INSERT` statement. Each salesperson must be assigned to a valid `BranchID` from the `Branch_BDS` table.

The following data must be inserted into the `SalesPerson_BDS` table:

***Table 11.6**: Sample data for the `SalesPerson_BDS` table*

SPID	SPName	Location	Position	ReportsTo	HireDate	Salary	BranchID
S101	John Smith	New York	Manager	Null	01-JAN-25	6000	B1
S102	Mary Jones	Chicago	SalesRep	S101	15-FEB-25	4500	B2
S103	David Clark	Dallas	Analyst	S101	10-MAR-25	5000	B3
S104	Susan White	Boston	SalesRep	S101	05-APR-25	4700	B4
S105	Robert King	San Diego	Manager	Null	20-MAY-25	6500	B5

The steps to insert rows into the `SalesPerson_BDS` table are as follows:

1. Insert the rows.
   In the SQL Worksheet, execute the following statements one by one (or as a block):

```
INSERT INTO SalesPerson_BDS
VALUES ('S101', 'John Smith', 'New York', 'Manager', NULL,
        TO_DATE('01-JAN-2025','DD-MON-YYYY'), 6000, 'B1');

INSERT INTO SalesPerson_BDS
VALUES ('S102', 'Mary Jones', 'Chicago', 'SalesRep', 'S101',
        TO_DATE('15-FEB-2025','DD-MON-YYYY'), 4500, 'B2');
```

```
INSERT INTO SalesPerson_BDS
VALUES ('S103', 'David Clark', 'Dallas', 'Analyst', 'S101',
        TO_DATE('10-MAR-2025','DD-MON-YYYY'), 5000, 'B3');

INSERT INTO SalesPerson_BDS
VALUES ('S104', 'Susan White', 'Boston', 'SalesRep', 'S101',
        TO_DATE('05-APR-2025','DD-MON-YYYY'), 4700, 'B4');

INSERT INTO SalesPerson_BDS
VALUES ('S105', 'Robert King', 'San Diego', 'Manager', NULL,
        TO_DATE('20-MAY-2025','DD-MON-YYYY'), 6500, 'B5');
COMMIT;
```

NOTE: The `TO_DATE` function ensures date strings are interpreted correctly regardless of session date settings. Using a format mask such as `TO_DATE('20-MAY-2025','DD-MON-YYYY')` stores the value consistently.

2. Verify the inserted rows.

```
SELECT *
FROM SalesPerson_BDS;
```

The output of the query is shown in Figure 11.3:

SPID	SPNAME	LOCATION	POSITION	REPORTSTO	HIREDATE	SALARY	BRANCHID
S101	John Smith	New York	Manager	-	01-JAN-25	6000	B1
S102	Mary Jones	Chicago	SalesRep	S101	15-FEB-25	4500	B2
S103	David Clark	Dallas	Analyst	S101	10-MAR-25	5000	B3
S104	Susan White	Boston	SalesRep	S101	05-APR-25	4700	B4
S105	Robert King	San Diego	Manager	-	20-MAY-25	6500	B5

***Figure 11.3**: Data in the SalesPerson_BDS table*

NOTE: Because `BranchID` in **`SalesPerson_BDS`** is defined as a foreign key referencing `Branch_BDS(BranchID)`, inserting a row with a non-existent `BranchID` results in an error similar to:
`ORA-02291: integrity constraint (FK_BRANCHID) violated - parent key not found`
This occurs because the foreign key constraint enforces referential integrity, ensuring every salesperson is linked to an existing branch.

Inserting Values into Selected Columns

It is not always necessary to insert values into **all columns** of a table. The `INSERT` statement allows data to be inserted only into specific columns, while the remaining columns are set to `NULL` (unless they are defined as `NOT NULL` or assigned a `DEFAULT` value).

Syntax

```
INSERT INTO table_name (column1, column2, ...)
VALUES (value1, value2, ...);
```

Key Points:

- Only the specified columns will receive values during insertion.
- Columns not listed are set to `NULL`, unless a `NOT NULL` constraint or `DEFAULT` value applies.
- The order of values in the `VALUES` clause must exactly match the order of the listed columns.

Exercise 9: Inserting into Selected Columns of the SalesPerson_BDS Table

The `SalesPerson_BDS` table allows inserting data into selected columns, while the remaining columns are set to `NULL` if no values are provided.

In this exercise, new rows will be inserted into selected columns using the `INSERT` statement.

The following data needs to be inserted into the `SalesPerson_BDS` table (partial columns):

***Table 11.7**: Sample data for Partial Column Insert into `SalesPerson_BDS`*

SPID	SPName	Position	HireDate	Salary	BranchID
S101	John Smith	Manager	01-JAN-25	6000	B1
S102	Mary Jones	SalesRep	15-FEB-25	4500	B2

Execute the following INSERT statements in the SQL Worksheet to insert data into selected columns:

```
INSERT INTO SalesPerson_BDS (SPID, SPName, Position, HireDate)
VALUES ('S202', 'Kevin Brown', 'Manager', TO_DATE('10-JUN-2025','DD-MON-YYYY'));


INSERT INTO SalesPerson_BDS (SPID, SPName, Position, HireDate)
VALUES ('S203', 'Sarah Davis', 'SalesRep', TO_DATE('15-JUN-2025','DD-MON-YYYY'));

INSERT INTO SalesPerson_BDS (SPID, SPName, Position, HireDate)
VALUES ('S204', 'Michael Scott', 'Analyst', TO_DATE('20-JUN-2025','DD-MON-YYYY'));

COMMIT;
```

After execution, Oracle displays messages such as:

```
1 row inserted.
```

This confirms that all three rows have been successfully added to the SalesPerson_BDS table.

Inserting Query Results into a Table

Oracle allows data to be inserted into a table using the results of a SELECT query. This technique is commonly used to copy rows from one table into another or to insert filtered and transformed data based on query results.

When inserting into all columns of a table, the number, order, and data types of columns returned by the SELECT statement must exactly match the structure of the target table.

Syntax

```
-- Insert into all columns
INSERT INTO target_table
SELECT *
FROM   source_table
WHERE  <condition> ;
```

```
-- Insert into specific columns
INSERT INTO target_table (column1, column2, ...)
SELECT column1, column2, ...
FROM   source_table
WHERE  <condition> ;
```

This method is particularly useful for:

- Copying data between tables with identical or compatible structures.
- Inserting filtered rows from a larger dataset.
- Creating summary or derived tables from existing data.
- Populating test or temporary tables with sample records.

Exercise 10: Inserting Query Results into a Table

In this exercise, a copy of the `SalesPerson_BDS` table will be created without data. Rows will then be inserted into the new table using the results of a `SELECT` query.

This demonstrates how to duplicate table structures and selectively copy data based on specified conditions.

The steps to create a copy of the table and insert query results are as follows:

1. Create a new table (Structure Only).

   Create a new table named `SalesPersonBDS_Copy` that has the same structure as `SalesPerson_BDS` but contains no data:

   ```
   CREATE TABLE SalesPersonBDS_Copy AS
   SELECT *
   FROM SalesPerson_BDS
   WHERE 1 = 0;
   ```

   The condition `WHERE 1 = 0` ensures that only the structure of the table is copied, not the data.

2. Insert rows using a `SELECT` query.

   Insert rows from the `SalesPerson_BDS` table into `SalesPersonBDS_Copy` where `Position` is `'SalesRep'`:

```
INSERT INTO SalesPersonBDS_Copy
SELECT *
FROM   SalesPerson_BDS
WHERE  Position = 'SalesRep';

COMMIT;
```

This statement copies only those rows from `SalesPerson_BDS` where the `Position` is `'SalesRep'`.

Using `INSERT INTO ... SELECT` is an efficient way to copy filtered data between tables. It avoids manual re-entry and ensures structural consistency between the source and target tables.

Updating Data in Tables

After inserting rows into a table, it is often necessary to modify existing values. This is accomplished using the `UPDATE` statement, which is part of the Data Manipulation Language (DML) in Oracle SQL.

The `UPDATE` statement allows data to be modified in several ways:

- Modify a single column in one or more rows.
- Update multiple columns in the same row simultaneously.
- Update all rows in a table (if no `WHERE` clause is specified).

Because an `UPDATE` statement changes existing data, using a `WHERE` clause is critical to control which rows are affected.

Omitting the `WHERE` clause updates all rows in the table and may result in unintended changes.

NOTE: The `UPDATE` statement is a DML operation. A `COMMIT` is required to make the changes permanent in the database. If an update is performed in incorrectly, a `ROLLBACK` statement can be used before committing to undo the changes.

Syntax

```
UPDATE table_name
SET column1 = value1,
    column2 = value2, ...
WHERE condition;
```

Syntax Explanation

- `table_name`: Specifies the table containing the data to be updated.
- `SET` clause: Specifies the column(s) to be updated and their new values.
- `WHERE` clause: Identifies which rows to update; if omitted, all rows are updated.

Updating data is one of the most frequently used DML operations and should be performed carefully to maintain data integrity and accuracy.

Exercise 11: Updating Data in the SalesPerson_BDS Table

In this exercise, specific values in the `SalesPerson_BDS` table will be updated using the `UPDATE` statement.

In this exercise, the following updates will be performed:

- Change the salary of the salesperson with `SPID = 'S102'` to *6200*.
- Change the position of the salesperson with `SPID = 'S103'` from *Analyst* to *Manager*.

Before updating the table, execute the following statement to view the current data in the table:

```
SELECT *
FROM SalesPerson_BDS;
```

The current salary of `SPID = 'S102'` is `4500`, and the position of `SPID = 'S103'` is `Analyst`. These values will be updated in the next steps.

The steps to update the data in the `SalesPerson_BDS` table are as follows:

1. Update the salary.
   In the SQL Worksheet, execute the following statement:

```
UPDATE SalesPerson_BDS
SET Salary = 6200
WHERE SPID = 'S102';
COMMIT;
```

After execution, Oracle displays the message:

```
1 row(s) updated.
```

This confirms that the salary has been successfully modified.

2. Update the position.

```
UPDATE SalesPerson_BDS
SET Position = 'Manager'
WHERE SPID = 'S103';
COMMIT;
```

After execution, Oracle displays the message:

```
1 row(s) updated.
```

This confirms that the position has been successfully changed.

3. Verify the updated data.

```
SELECT *
FROM SalesPerson_BDS;
```

This output will display the updated salary for `S102` and the new position for `S103`.

The `UPDATE` statement modifies existing rows in a table. Always include a `WHERE` clause to target specific rows. As a DML operation, changes must be explicitly committed to make them permanent or rolled back to undo them if necessary.

Deleting Data from Tables

The `DELETE` statement is used to remove existing rows from a table. It is a Data Manipulation Language (DML) operation and requires a `COMMIT` to make the changes permanent in the database.

If the `WHERE` clause is omitted, all rows in the table will be deleted. Therefore, it must be used carefully to avoid unintended data loss.

Syntax

```
DELETE FROM table_name
WHERE condition;
```

Syntax Explanation

- `table_name`: Specifies the table from which rows will be deleted.
- `WHERE condition`: Specifies which rows to remove. If omitted, all rows in the table are deleted.

As with other DML operations, changes made by a `DELETE` statement are not permanent until a `COMMIT` is issued.

If a deletion is made in error, a `ROLLBACK` can be used before committing to restore the data to its previous state.

Exercise 12: Deleting Data from the SalesPerson_BDS Table

In this exercise, a specific record will be deleted from the `SalesPerson_BDS` table using the `DELETE` statement.

The goal is to remove the row for the salesperson with `SPID = 'S103'`.

The steps to delete data from `SalesPerson_BDS` table are as follows:

1. Delete the row.
   In the SQL Worksheet, execute the following statement:

   ```
   DELETE FROM SalesPerson_BDS
   WHERE SPID = 'S103';
   ```

   Once executed, Oracle displays the message:

   ```
   1 row(s) deleted).
   ```

   This confirms that the record for `SPID = 'S103'` has been successfully removed.

2. Verify deletion.

   ```
   SELECT *
   FROM SalesPerson_BDS;
   ```

The record for `SPID = 'S103'` will no longer appear in the results.

The `DELETE` statement removes existing rows from a table. Always include a `WHERE` clause to target specific rows—omitting it will delete all rows in the table. As a DML operation, changes must be committed to make them permanent, or rolled back if not yet committed.

Managing Tables

Once tables are created and populated with data, it may become necessary to modify or remove them. Oracle provides Data Definition Language (DDL) commands such as `ALTER TABLE`, `DROP TABLE`, and `TRUNCATE` to manage the structure of tables.

These operations are permanent because DDL statements perform an implicit commit upon execution.

Common commands for managing tables include:

- `DROP TABLE`: Removes a table and all its data permanently.
- `TRUNCATE TABLE`: Deletes all rows in a table quickly while retaining the structure.
- `RENAME`: Changes the name of an existing table.
- `ALTER TABLE… ADD`: Adds new columns to a table.
- `ALTER TABLE… MODIFY`: Changes a column's data type, size, or nullability.
- `ALTER TABLE… DROP COLUMN`: Removes a column from a table.
- `DISABLE/ENABLE CONSTRAINT`: Temporarily disables constraints (such as foreign keys) during bulk operations and re-enables them afterward.

Dropping Tables

A table that is no longer required can be permanently removed using the `DROP TABLE` statement.

When a table is dropped, both its structure and data are deleted. Because DDL statements perform an implicit commit, this operation cannot be rolled back.

Syntax

```
DROP TABLE table_name;
```

Use the `DROP TABLE` command with caution. Once executed, the table and its data are permanently removed from the database unless a backup exists.

Exercise 13: Dropping a Table

This exercise demonstrates how the `DROP TABLE` command permanently removes a table from the database.

A copy of the `SalesPerson_BDS` table is first created and then dropped.

The steps to drop a table are as follows:

1. Create a copy of the table.
   In the SQL Worksheet, execute the following statement:

   ```
   CREATE TABLE SalesPerson_Delete AS
   SELECT * FROM SalesPerson_BDS;
   ```

   This statement creates a new table, `SalesPerson_Delete`, containing all the data from the `SalesPerson_BDS` table.
2. Verify that the table exists.

   ```
   SELECT *
   FROM SalesPerson_Delete;
   ```

   The query should display all the copied rows, confirming that the table has been created successfully.
3. Drop the table.
   Execute the following statement to remove the table permanently:

   ```
   DROP TABLE SalesPerson_Delete;
   ```

   Once executed, Oracle displays the message:

   ```
   Table dropped.
   ```
4. Verify that the table has been removed.

   Attempt to query the table again:

```
SELECT *
FROM SalesPerson_Delete;
```

Oracle will return the following error message:

```
ORA-00942: table or view does not exist
```

This error confirms that the `SalesPerson_Delete` table has been permanently removed from the database.

The `DROP TABLE` statement permanently removes both the table structure and its data. Because DDL operations in Oracle perform an implicit `COMMIT`, this action cannot be rolled back.

Truncating Tables

The `TRUNCATE` command removes all rows from a table while preserving its structure, allowing new data to be inserted later.

Unlike `DELETE`, which can be rolled back before a `COMMIT`, `TRUNCATE` is a Data Definition Language (DDL) operation and cannot be rolled back.

It is also faster than `DELETE` because it does not generate undo information for each deleted row.

Syntax

```
TRUNCATE TABLE table_name;
```

Exercise 14: Truncating a Table

This exercise will demonstrate the `TRUNCATE TABLE` command by creating a copy of the `Branch_BDS` table with data and then truncating it.

The steps to truncate a table are as follows:

1. Create a copy of the table.
   In the SQL Worksheet, execute the following statement:

   ```
   CREATE TABLE BranchBDS_Trun AS
   SELECT *
   FROM Branch_BDS;
   ```

This statement creates a new table named BranchBDS_Trun containing all the data from Branch_BDS.

2. Verify that the table exists.

```
SELECT *
FROM BranchBDS_Trun;
```

The output should display all rows copied from Branch_BDS, confirming that the table was created successfully.

3. Truncate the table.

```
TRUNCATE TABLE BranchBDS_Trun;
```

Once executed, Oracle displays the message:

```
Table truncated.
```

4. Verify that the data has been removed.

Run the following query again:

```
SELECT *
FROM BranchBDS_Trun;
```

The output will display:

```
no data found.
```

This confirms that all rows have been removed while the table structure remains intact for future inserts.

Renaming Tables

Tables can be renamed in Oracle when a clearer or more descriptive name is required—such as during archiving, versioning, or schema reorganization—without recreating the object.

Renaming affects only the object name; the data, constraints, indexes, and privileges remain intact. However, dependent objects that reference the table by its old name may need to be updated or recompiled.

Syntax

```
ALTER TABLE old_table_name
RENAME TO new_table_name;
```

Alternative Syntax

```
RENAME old_table_name TO new_table_name;
```

Key points in Renaming Tables:

- Renaming a table does not affect its data, structure, or constraints—only the name changes.
- Dependent views, triggers, or stored procedures that reference the old table name may become invalid and must be updated or recompiled.
- Foreign key relationships remain valid because Oracle tracks them internally using object identifiers rather than table names.
- Any SQL queries, scripts, or application code that reference the old table name must be manually updated to use the new name.

Renaming is a quick and safe way to improve database clarity or manage version control without impacting existing data integrity.

Exercise 15: Renaming a Table

This exercise demonstrates how to rename a table using the `ALTER TABLE` command.

A new table named `BranchBDS_Archive` will be created as a copy of `Branch_BDS` and then renamed to `BranchBDS_bk`.

The steps to rename a table are as follows:

1. Create a copy of the table.
   In the SQL Worksheet, execute the following statement:

   ```
   CREATE TABLE BranchBDS_Archive AS
   SELECT *
   FROM Branch_BDS;
   ```

This statement creates a table named `BranchBDS_Archive` containing all the data from `Branch_BDS`.

2. Verify that the table exists.

```
SELECT *
FROM BranchBDS_Archive;
```

The query should display all rows copied from `Branch_BDS`, confirming that the table exists.

3. Rename the table.

```
ALTER TABLE BranchBDS_Archive
RENAME TO BranchBDS_bk;
```

The command renames `BranchBDS_Archive` to `BranchBDS_bk`.

4. Verify the renaming, execute:

```
SELECT *
FROM BranchBDS_bk;
```

The query confirms that the table has been successfully renamed, with all data and structure preserved.

Renaming a table affects only its name; all data, constraints, and relationships remain unchanged. Any dependent SQL queries, views, or stored procedures referencing the old name must be updated manually.

Adding New Columns

At times, additional information needs to be stored in an existing table. Oracle supports this using the `ALTER TABLE ... ADD` command, which allows one or more new columns to be added to a table.

Each new column must have a name and a data type and may optionally include constraints.

Syntax

```
ALTER TABLE table_name
ADD (column_name data_type [constraint], ...);
```

Syntax Explanation

- `column_name`: Specifies the name of the new column.
- `data_type`: Specifies the type of values the column will store (for example, `VARCHAR2`, `NUMBER`, `DATE`).
- `[constraint]`: Refers to the optional constraints, such as `NOT NULL` or `DEFAULT`.

Exercise 16: Adding a Column to an Existing Table

In this exercise, a new column named `Commission` will be added to the `SalesPerson_BDS` table. The column will be of type `NUMBER(5,2)`, and will include a `DEFAULT` value of `0`.

The steps to add a new column to an existing table are as follows:

1. Add the new column.

   In the SQL Worksheet, execute the following statement:

   ```
   ALTER TABLE SalesPerson_BDS
   ADD (Commission NUMBER(5,2) DEFAULT 0);
   ```

2. Verify that the column was added.

   ```
   DESC SalesPerson_BDS
   ```

The output will now include the `Commission` column with a default value of `0`, confirming that it has been successfully added. Future insert operations may include a commission value explicitly or omit it. If the **`Commission`** column is omitted during insertion, Oracle automatically applies the default value of **`0`**.

Modifying Columns

Oracle allows modifications to existing columns using the `ALTER TABLE … MODIFY` command. This operation is useful when increasing a column's size, changing its data type, or updating its constraint.

Syntax

```
ALTER TABLE table_name
MODIFY (column_name new_data_type [constraint], ...);
```

Syntax Explanation

- `column_name`: Specifies the column to be modified.
- `new_data_type`: Specifies the new data type or size of the column.
- `[constraint]`: Refers to optional constraints, such as `NOT NULL` or `DEFAULT`.

These operations make it possible to adapt a table's structure as business requirements evolve, without recreating the table or losing existing data.

Exercise 17: Modifying a Column in a Table

In this exercise, the `Location` column in the `SalesPerson_BDS` table will be modified to increase its size from `30` to `50` characters.

The steps to modify the size of a column are as follows:

1. Verify the current size of the column.

   In the SQL Worksheet, execute the following statement:

   ```
   DESC SalesPerson_BDS;
   ```

   The output will show that the `Location` column is currently defined as `VARCHAR2(30)`.

2. Modify the column size.

   ```
   ALTER TABLE SalesPerson_BDS
   MODIFY (Location VARCHAR2(50));
   ```

Once executed, Oracle displays the message:

```
Table altered.
```

3. Verify the modification.

```
DESC SalesPerson_BDS;
```

The `Location` column now appears as `VARCHAR2(50)`, confirming that its size has been successfully modified.

A column's size can be modified only if the new size is greater than or equal to the length of the existing data. Increasing the size allows the column to store longer text values without affecting current records.

Dropping Columns

If a column is no longer required, it can be permanently removed from a table using the `ALTER TABLE … DROP COLUMN` command. Once a column is dropped, all data stored in it is lost. Because this is a Data Definition Language (DDL) operation, it performs an implicit `COMMIT` and cannot be rolled back.

Syntax

To Drop a Single Column:

```
ALTER TABLE table_name
DROP COLUMN column_name;
```

To Drop Multiple Columns:

```
ALTER TABLE table_name
DROP (column_name1, column_name2, ...);
```

Syntax Explanation

- `column_name`: Specifies the name of the column to be removed from the table.

Exercise 18: Dropping a Column

In this exercise, the `Commission` column added earlier to the `SalesPerson_BDS` table will be removed using the `ALTER TABLE ... DROP COLUMN` command.

The steps to Drop a Column are as follows:

1. Verify that the column exists.

   ```
   SELECT *
   FROM SalesPerson_BDS;
   ```

   The result set should display the `Commission` column.
2. Drop the `Commission` column.

   ```
   ALTER TABLE SalesPerson_BDS
   DROP COLUMN Commission;
   ```

   Once executed, Oracle displays the message:

   ```
   Table altered.
   ```

3. Verify the change.
   Run the following query again to confirm that the column has been removed:

   ```
   SELECT *
   FROM SalesPerson_BDS;
   ```

   The `Commission` column will no longer appear in the output.

Dropping a column permanently removes both the column and all the data stored in it. The remaining structure and data in the table are unaffected. Because this is a DDL operation, the action cannot be rolled back. Use this command with caution.

Enabling and Disabling Constraints

Constraints maintain data integrity, but there are situations where they may need to be temporarily disabled—for example, during bulk data loading.

Disabling constraints can improve performance and prevent constraint violations while data is being staged.

Once the load is complete, the constraints can be re-enabled to restore full data validation and enforce referential integrity.

Oracle provides the `ALTER TABLE ... ENABLE | DISABLE CONSTRAINT` command to manage this process.

Syntax

```
-- Disable a Constraint
ALTER TABLE table_name
DISABLE CONSTRAINT constraint_name;

-- Enable a Constraint
ALTER TABLE table_name
ENABLE CONSTRAINT constraint_name;
```

Syntax Explanation

- `constraint_name`: Specifies the name assigned to the constraint, either by Oracle (system-generated) or defined by the user during creation.

Exercise 19: Disabling a Constraint

In this exercise, the `FK_BRANCHID` foreign key constraint on the `SalesPerson_BDS` table will be disabled.

The steps to disable a constraint are as follows:

1. Disable the foreign key constraint.

   In the SQL Worksheet, execute the following statement:

   ```
   ALTER TABLE SalesPerson_BDS
   DISABLE CONSTRAINT FK_BRANCHID;
   ```

   Once executed, Oracle displays the message:

   ```
   Table altered.
   ```

2. Verify that the constraint has been disabled.

   Execute the following statement to check the status of constraints on the table:

```
SELECT constraint_name, constraint_type, status
FROM   user_constraints
WHERE  table_name = 'SALESPERSON_BDS';
```

   The output of the above statement is shown in Figure 11.4:

CONSTRAINT_NAME	CONSTRAINT_TYPE	STATUS
NN_SPNAME_BDS	C	ENABLED
NN_POSITION_BDS	C	ENABLED
NN_HIREDATE_BDS	C	ENABLED
CK_SALARY_BDS	C	ENABLED
PK_SP_BDS	P	ENABLED
FK_BRANCHID	R	DISABLED

Figure 11.4*: Constraint status*

The `STATUS` column of `FK_BRANCHID` indicates that it is disabled.

Disabling a constraint temporarily suspends its enforcement, allowing data to be loaded or modified without validation. However, constraints should always be re-enabled after data changes to maintain referential integrity.

Conclusion

This chapter explored the core principles of managing data structures in Oracle SQL, including creating tables with appropriate data types and constraints, and as well as performing essential data operations such as inserting, updating, and deleting records.

It also examined techniques for modifying existing tables —altering columns, renaming objects, enabling or disabling constraints, and truncating or dropping data when necessary.

Together, these concepts form the foundation for designing, building, and maintaining relational tables in Oracle SQL.

With a solid understanding of both Data Definition Language (DDL) and Data Manipulation Language (DML) operations, database structures can be created with confidence and managed with precision. These skills provide the practical capability to design robust schemas, enforce data integrity, and maintain reliable database systems. This concludes the foundational journey through Oracle SQL, equipping readers with the essential knowledge required to design, manage, and optimize relational data effectively.

Practice Questions

Complete the following practice questions to reinforce the concepts covered in this chapter:

1. Create a table named `Dept_BDS` with the following columns:
    - `DeptID` – VARCHAR2(10) Primary Key
    - `DeptName` – VARCHAR2(50) **NOT NULL**
    - `Location` – VARCHAR2(30)
2. Insert three rows into `Dept_BDS`, then execute a `COMMIT` statement.
3. Update the `Location` value of the HR department (`DeptID = 'D102'`) to `'Boston'`.
4. Delete the IT department (`DeptID = 'D103'`) and verify that the row has been removed.
5. Add a new column, `HeadCount` of type `NUMBER(5)`, to `Dept_BDS`, and then drop it.

Practice Answers

The answers to the preceding questions are as follows:

Answer 1

```
CREATE TABLE Dept_BDS (
    DeptID     VARCHAR2(10) CONSTRAINT pk_deptid_bds PRIMARY KEY,
    DeptName   VARCHAR2(50) CONSTRAINT nn_deptname_bds NOT NULL,
    Location   VARCHAR2(30)
);
```

Answer 2

```
INSERT INTO Dept_BDS VALUES ('D101', 'Finance', 'New York');
INSERT INTO Dept_BDS VALUES ('D102', 'HR', 'Chicago');
INSERT INTO Dept_BDS VALUES ('D103', 'IT', 'Dallas');
COMMIT;
```

Answer 3

```
UPDATE Dept_BDS
SET Location = 'Boston'
WHERE DeptID = 'D102';

COMMIT;
```

Answer 4

```
DELETE FROM Dept_BDS
WHERE DeptID = 'D103';
COMMIT;
```

Answer 5

```
-- View existing data
SELECT * FROM Dept_BDS;


-- Add column
ALTER TABLE Dept_BDS
ADD (HeadCount NUMBER(5));

-- Drop column
ALTER TABLE Dept_BDS
DROP COLUMN HeadCount;
```

INDEX

A

ALTER TABLE command12, 29, 275-295, 301-330

B

BETWEEN operator18, 19, 79-85, 112, 129, 232

C

CASE expression 9, 22, 124-136
COMMIT command 5-14, 262-277, 300-329
Constraints 284-329
CHECK........................7, 279, 290-300
FOREIGN KEY 7, 8, 279-303
NOT NULL ..7, 18, 44, 76-78, 279-329
PRIMARY KEY 7, 8, 278-329
UNIQUE 7, 279-300
Create Table As Select (CTAS)30, 296, 297
CREATE TABLE statement4, 29, 36, 258-329

D

Data Definition Language (DDL) 4-6, 14-29, 274-328
Data Manipulation Language (DML)5-14, 29, 268-328
DELETE statement.............5-14, 255-329
DESC command16, 42-56, 136-160, 194, 210-232, 290-324
DISTINCT clause8, 16, 38-98, 131-146, 207, 226, 258
DROP TABLE command 275, 301-317

F

Functions
AVG 9, 23, 87, 140-162, 202-257
COUNT 9, 23, 87, 140-162, 213-227
MAX..............9, 23, 140-162, 200-231
MIN 9, 23, 140-162, 212-231
NVL 9, 22, 124-227
SUBSTR 19, 89-136
SUM 9, 23, 87, 140-162, 227-272
TO_DATE 21, 22, 110-119, 300-308

G

GROUP BY clause9, 22, 23, 45, 87, 133-162, 203-272

H

HAVING clause9, 26, 45, 87, 139-162, 203-226

I

IN operator9, 18, 79-83, 126, 173, 206-231

INSERT statement....... 5-19, 36, 255-329

J

Joins...............9, 24-45, 163-196, 257-288

i

INNER JOIN..................9, 24, 163-194

LEFT JOIN.................................9, 189

RIGHT JOIN......................................9

L

LIKE operator........9, 18, 72-85, 203, 210

M

Materialized views.......................262-272

O

ORDER BY clause.8, 16, 38-87, 129-252

R

RENAME command...........276, 315-321

ROLLBACK command 5-14, 277, 300-314

S

SELECT statement.........5-19, 24, 37-329

Set operators

INTERSECT................10, 27, 230-258

MINUS.........................10, 27, 230-258

UNION...........................9, 27, 230-258

UNION ALL..................9, 27, 230-252

T

Transaction Control Language (TCL) 5-14

TRUNCATE TABLE command.315, 318

U

UPDATE statement............5-19, 255-329

V

Views 255-272

W

WHERE clause........8-16, 38-87, 104-329

Made in United States
Cleveland, OH
02 November 2026

47473304R00172